To all those who helped in
making this publication
possible.

CONTENTS

ACKNOWLEDGEMENTS

It is simply not possible to mention everyone who assisted in the writing (and researching) of this book. Many who did, work for the security forces both North and South, or operate within the various sets of paramilitary organisations. To name them would not only place their lives at risk, it would be a serious breach of that bond of confidentiality and trust built up between them and I over a long number of years.

However, a number of people who assisted and who do not fall into that category deserve a special mention. Foremost amongst them is my special assistant, Annette, who typed the manuscript and provided invaluable appraisal of the work in its many and varied stages. To her I owe a debt of gratitude. The staff of the Berkeley Library in Trinity College Dublin and the nearby National Library deserve a special mention for their patience and kindness. The Fine Gael politician Austin Curry deserves a mention for his friendship and encouragement, particularly in relation to the chapters on the Murder Triangle. The former Labour leader Ruairi Quinn for his invaluable advice vis-a-vis the Hamilton-Barron Enquiry and the affable and amiable Justice Hamilton himself for his friendship and many phone calls before his untimely death. Colin Wallace and Fred Holroyd deserve a mention for their help over the years. Mike Dutfield, the Channel 4 producer who was tragically killed in a freak road accident, I miss greatly. To John Mulcahy and Paddy Prendeville at the *Phoenix* I say thanks for the publicity. Eric Luke the photographer was most helpful and Barry Penrose of the *Sunday Times* helped with library material. And last but not least my wife Tess and son Christian Anthony, whose unstinting love and support during the many trials and tribulations encountered during the writing and publishing of this book, deserve a very special thank you.

INTRODUCTION

For twenty-eight years the 1974 Dublin and Monaghan bombings have remained the biggest single scandal of the Northern Ireland Troubles. Thirty-three innocent men, women and children perished and almost 300 others were injured in four car-bombings in the centre of Dublin city and Monaghan town during Friday evening rush hour on 17 May 1974. Decapitated bodies were plucked from the streets, arms and legs were recovered from shop windows and supermarket rooftops and the entrails of infant babies were scraped from the floors of public-house cellars. And yet not a single individual has been made to pay for these ghastly crimes.

This is a scandal of seismic proportions. A fumbling Garda investigation back then uncovered the plot and the names of the perpetrators but little effort was made to bring them to justice.

In 1993 an ITV television documentary uncovered the extent of the scandal and what amounted to a cover-up by the security authorities north and south of the border. Since then the relatives of those killed, and some of those injured, have formed a coherent and powerful pressure group, which is seeking to uncover the truth as to why no one has been made amenable.

Many people in high places know, and have known for years, that everything is not right. The whiff of something rotten fills the air and until its source is fully exposed and dealt with it will continue to contaminate the authorities North and South and possibly others too. And adding insolence to injury the British authorities, from whose territory the bombs originated and against whose security forces the finger of suspicion has long been pointing, have steadfastly refused to even acknowledge that such an atrocity occurred. Even the British mainland media appears inscrutably deaf when the scandal raises its head.

In late 1999 the Dublin government, after months of prevarication, finally announced the setting up of a preliminary inquiry, albeit a private one, under the chairmanship of the retiring Chief Justice, Liam Hamilton, and later Justice Henry Barron. Let's wish it well and hope that the cloud that has for so long hung over a very dark episode in recent Irish history will once and for all be dispelled.

But the process of discovery will be a long and tortuous one and if the truth doesn't out and justice isn't dispensed, then the fight must go on.

The Dublin and Monaghan bombings remain unique in the ferocity of their *modus operandi*. No warnings were given, nor, unlike the Omagh massacre in more recent times, even attempted. The unleashing of such savagery on urban streets crowded with ordinary humble civilians was legitimised in the name of 'God and Ulster'.

But with the trademarks of the paramilitaries missing - or almost missing - from everyday life in Northern Ireland for almost ten years now, and the bad old days of car bombs, kidnappings and bullets in the back of the neck consigned to history, let's not forget those who helplessly cry out to us for justice.

This book traces the story of the Dublin and Monaghan bombings: the conspiracy, the planning, the execution and the personnel involved. It also looks at the bungled Garda investigation, which appeared more concerned with retaining good relations with the RUC than with finding the truth and punishing those responsible.

The book also looks at the area of Northern Ireland that for a period of almost seven years in the 1970s became infamously known as the Murder Triangle. This is (or was) a triangle of territory stretching from Banbridge in south County Down to Aughnacloy in south Tyrone and Pomeroy in mid-Tyrone, where a catalogue of random murders - some put the figure as high as 100 - was carried out mainly by the loyalist Ulster Volunteer Force (UVF) between 1972 and 1979. Today most of these murders remain unsolved and the majority of the perpetrators remain unpunished. The campaign was masterminded and led by the notorious loyalist killer Robin Jackson (the Jackal) and his unit, which played a key role in the Dublin and Monaghan bombings. Other members of Jackson's unit included Harris Boyle and the Sommerville brothers, John and Wesley, whose names first came to public attention following the massacre at the Miami Showband ambush north of Newry in July 1975. The book traces the genesis of this notorious killer squad, which operated with virtual impunity under the noses of the police and army.

And last, but by no means least, the book looks at collusion - that sinister world of law-breaking where the so-called law-enforcers become the law-breakers under the guise of defeating terrorism. Where dark and nefarious elements within the various branches of the security forces believe the law does not apply to them.

Note: As most of this book was written prior to the publication of the Patten Report, the police in Northern Ireland are referred to throughout as the RUC.

CHAPTER I

BLOOD AND SLAUGHTER

Friday, 17 May 1974 was a mild showery day in Dublin. The city was thronged with Friday shoppers, many of who had travelled in from the suburbs to do their weekend shopping. Large suburban shopping centres like The Square in Tallaght had not yet reached Dublin and many suburban dwellers travelled to the city centre on Fridays and Saturdays to shop in such fashionable streets as Henry Street, Grafton Street, Moore Street and Talbot Street. As hundreds of shoppers, as well as factory and office staff, made their way through the labyrinth of city centre streets towards the city's three main train stations - Dublin's bus crews were on strike depriving thousands of commuters of transport - three massive no-warning car-bombs exploded in the city centre killing twenty-six people and injuring up to 300 others. The blasts occurred within three minutes of each other during evening rush hour in Parnell Street, Talbot Street and South Leinster Street at approximately 5.30 p.m. Ninety minutes later a fourth bomb exploded in Monaghan town on the border with Northern Ireland, killing seven more.

All four bombs were packed into cars stolen earlier in the day in Belfast and Portadown. At the time no organisation admitted responsibility but no one was in any doubt that loyalist extremists from Northern Ireland were involved. (A month later a previously unheard-of group, the Young Militants, said it planted the bombs, but no such organisation ever existed).

Taken together, the two attacks constitute the worst atrocity perpetrated anywhere in Ireland or Britain - including the Omagh massacre - since the conflict began thirty-three years ago. To this day no one has been charged with the outrage and, despite continuing campaigning by the victims' relatives that those responsible be arrested and put on trial, the Northern authorities from where the bombs originated are refusing to cooperate. Over half of those involved are now dead (mostly killed in loyalist feuds, although some have died of natural causes). Those still living are either hiding abroad or in bad health.

The bombings took place during a period of great turmoil in Northern Ireland in which the economy was being paralysed by a 'workers strike' organised by a previously unheard-of organisation - the Ulster Workers Council (UWC). This was in essence a congeries of loyalist paramilitaries, extremist loyalist politicians and a smattering of loyalist trade union muscle men from the Harland and Wolff shipyard. The strike was called to oppose the Sunningdale Agreement, an accord which had been negotiated six months earlier between the constitutional parties of both communities under the auspices of the British and Irish governments in which nationalists, for the first time since partition, would have a say in the running of their own affairs through a new Northern Ireland Executive. The agreement also provided for a Council of Ireland, involving the Dublin government. But unlike the Good Friday Agreement the paramilitaries were not invited to participate, and the initiative was short-lived.

The Catholic community, much less the Dublin government, was not trusted by hardline unionists represented by the likes of Ian Paisley and the former Home Affairs Minister William Craig. Sections of the right wing of the British establishment represented by the back benches of the Tory Party, many serving and retired members of the armed forces and the security service MI5, supported those unionists who claimed sharing power with Catholics would undermine the union and lead eventually to a united Ireland.

On 14 May, nineteen weeks into the life of the new power-sharing executive, the UWC announced the start of the strike. For two weeks the economy was brought to a virtual standstill with electricity blackouts, factory stoppages, road blockades and fuel shortages. The bombings in Dublin and Monaghan which occurred three days into the strike were seen as an escalation of the strike and were believed by many to have been a spontaneous attack on the South which had been hurriedly organised over the previous number of days. Nothing could be further from the truth. The decision to bomb the South had been taken a number of months earlier (long before the strike) and was in direct response to the setting up of the Executive and the role given to the Dublin government through the proposed Council of Ireland. The aim of both the strike and the bombings was two-fold: to destroy the Sunningdale Agreement and force the Dublin government into cracking down on the activities of the IRA.

Within minutes of the Dublin explosions a Major Accident Plan, sometimes called the Red Alert Plan (formulated eighteen months earlier following the 1972/73 bombings to deal with such a catastrophe), swung into action. The plan involved a coordinated - and synchronised - response by the Gardai, the Army, Dublin Fire Brigade, the hospital authorities, the Irish Medical Association, the Irish Red Cross, St John Ambulance Brigade, the Knights of Malta, and the Civil Defence.

Dublin's main hospitals, the Mater, Temple Street, the Richmond, the Rotunda, Jervis Street, St James's, Dr Stephen's, the Eye and Ear, Vincent's, Mercer's, the Meath, Sir Patrick Dun's and Baggot Street were all put on emergency standby to deal with the dead and injured in Dublin's biggest blitz for over fifty years. Off-duty staff in all of the services were either summoned, or reported voluntarily, to their posts.

As news of the bombings reached the hospitals, special alarm bells were sounded and within sixty seconds the first ambulances were on the city streets. Dublin Fire Brigade and the Stillorgan Ambulance Service arrived at the scenes of the blasts within minutes. Makeshift emergency medical centres were set up in several centres around the city and Gardai, in some instances, commandeered buses and coaches and used them as ambulances to ferry the dead and injured to hospital. The basement dancehall of Moran's hotel, situated within yards of the Talbot Street blast, was turned into an emergency casualty centre where scores of injured men, women and children, many with limbs missing and covered in blood, were brought from the street by hotel staff and members of the public. Two Indian student doctors, visiting Ireland and staying in the hotel, were summoned from their rooms to the basement to render what medical aid they could. The casualties were later transferred to one or other of the city's hospitals.

Within ten minutes of the blasts over twenty ambulances under the direction of Dublin Fire Brigade headquarters, whose role in the Accident Plan was to coordinate the use of ambulance and rescue services, including all voluntary organisations trained to act in such emergencies, were chewing their way through the chaos and confusion to reach the gruesome scenes of the disaster. Special emergency operating theatres were set up in a number of hospitals, and the Richmond in North Brunswick Street - the best equipped in the country at the time to deal with such emergencies - was forced to close its doors except to those with 'special business'. Security measures were introduced at the main entrance to deal with the chaos, as a stream of taxis and private cars converged on the hospital carrying blood plasma for use in the theatre.

There were harrowing scenes in some hospitals as news of the bombings spread and relatives arrived to enquire anxiously about husbands, wives, sons or daughters who had failed to arrive home. Even as the injured were being treated, reception staff at some of the hospitals were forced to summon extra help to control the crowds. Some broke down uncontrollably when informed of a relative's admission, while others became irascible when informed they could not visit the injured until after treatment. In some cases relatives became hysterical and had to be sedated when informed that a loved one had died.

At the hospitals nearest the bomb scenes, off-duty nurses, members of volunteer corps and even members of the public who came to donate blood assembled to help in whatever way they could and in the end, with the help of Gardai, queues were formed to control the crowds. At Jervis Street, the hospital nearest the Talbot Street explosion and where most of the dead and seriously injured were taken, the enormity of the carnage could be seen in stark reality. The first two casualties to arrive were brought there in a fishmonger's van within minutes of the explosion. Frank Kilfeather, a reporter with *The Irish Times*, was present at the hospital as the casualties were brought in. He described the harrowing scenes:

Ambulances, their sirens wailing, converged on the hospital from all directions. The one-way street system was abolished minutes after the explosions. Gardai cordoned off a large number of streets to leave every route to the hospital free. The dead - there must have been about 10 there when I arrived - were brought to a special section of the hospital. The injured were quickly examined by doctors and given labels to work out a system of priority. The most poignant scenes, however, were to be seen in the rooms where friends and relations awaited news on the injured... or to know if a relative was dead. Nurses moved quickly around among the shocked, weeping and white-faced people asking for information which might be of help in identifying the dead, or to see if there was a relation of an injured person present. There were elderly people looking for sons and daughters - husbands looking for wives, wives seeking their husbands, friends looking for friends. Dr. Anthony Walsh told relatives: 'We are sorting out the information as fast as we can. As soon as we have positive information we will give it to you'. The doctors and nurses carried out their work with a discipline, kindness and understanding which merits recording. In the waiting rooms, nurses made sure that the relatives received tea and something to eat. They went among the people checking to see if any were suffering from shock. Quite a few were, and they were quickly taken care of.

By 6.30 p.m. fourteen bodies, from Talbot Street and Parnell Street, had been brought to Jervis Street and were laid out in the 'special room' in the hospital. The cries of the injured being treated in the casualty wards, as doctors and nurses worked tirelessly to clean and dress the wounds of the many bloodied and shattered limbs, could be heard throughout the building.

At Temple Street Hospital almost two dozen children - many of them mere toddlers, shocked and crying and separated from their parents - were admitted within the first hour. A twelve-year-old boy, who was hit on the head by a flying object walked to Temple Street by himself. A four-year-old boy, Justin McHugh, whose parents had moved to Dublin from Belfast to escape the Troubles and who developed a speech impediment due to the fear of explosions, sustained an arm injury when struck by flying debris and was rushed to Temple Street where doctors immediately stitched the wound. His mother, who was with her son at the time, became hysterical following the explosion and had to receive first aid to bring her to.

Three children aged eleven, nine and seven, from the Malahide Road on Dublin's northside, were shopping with their mother in Talbot Street when struck by flying debris. Mrs Maeve Taylor, whose daughter Lisa was due to make her First Communion the following day, took her children on a last-minute shopping trip before the big day. Lisa received twelve stitches to a head wound and had to have her hair shaved off, while the other two children were treated for facial injuries. Their mother, who escaped injury herself, carried her three children, streaming with blood, to a nearby pharmacy shop where the owner drove all four in his car to Temple Street. A woman injured in Parnell Street walked and stumbled to the nearby Rotunda hospital with a piece of the bomb-car embedded in her back and collapsed in the hallway as she entered. Such was the confusion and panic in the street that nobody noticed the distressed woman or offered to help.

At the bomb-sites themselves the scenes of carnage were the worst ever witnessed in Dublin city centre since the slaughter in O'Connell Street during the fighting of Easter Week. Of the twenty-six people killed in Dublin, nineteen were women - due mainly to the fact that more women than men work in offices (many office staff leaving their place of work were caught in the blasts) and more women than men do the family shopping. Women, therefore, are more likely to be found in city centre streets during evening rush hour, particularly at weekends.

In Talbot Street, where nine people were killed and almost 100 injured, the body of a decapitated woman lay on the pavement. Another woman lay dead nearby with a piece of a car engine embedded in her body. A man lay dying with an iron bar through his abdomen, while a woman choking on her own blood was tended to by a Belfast anaesthetist, Dr John Cooper, who happened to be passing through Talbot Street at the time and missed death or injury by inches. Dr Cooper told an *Irish Independent* reporter afterwards that he did not have his medical bag with him and could not 'do much' for the injured woman. He did not know if she died. Dr Cooper then described what he saw:

> Some had lost limbs. Others had broken limbs and the only thing we could do was patch them up with rough splints from broken timbers picked up from the streets. We tied the splints with pieces of torn clothing. A woman held a seven months' old baby covered in blood in her arms but I was able to assure her the baby was uninjured. The blood had spurted from the wounds of her uncle who was gashed about the face and bleeding heavily. It appeared to me that several of those who had lost limbs were unlikely to survive. Two priests moved among the injured and the dead giving what spiritual and practical aid they could.

In his book, *The Point of No Return*, the distinguished British journalist Robert Fisk, who worked as a *Times* reporter in Belfast at the time, described the scene in Talbot Street.

> Hundreds of people, deprived of transport during a bus strike, were walking to Connolly station for their trains home when the bomb exploded. Five of the people who died instantly were women but the ambulance men and civic guards who ran into the street could not distinguish the living from the dead. Dozens of people lay on the pavements and in the road and in the front of broken shops, dead, dying or screaming with pain and shock. One newspaper photographer was sick when he saw a gutter literally running with blood. A few feet away was a human leg and next to it a head.

A nineteen-year-old married woman, Colette Doherty, who was in an advanced state of pregnancy and who was wheeling her two-year-old daughter in a pram close to where the bomb exploded in Talbot Street, was killed instantly. The unborn child was also killed but miraculously - and no one can explain how - the little girl survived (with scratches to her face and head) and was later found huddled in her pram crying amongst the Talbot Street debris by four teenage girls who carried her in their arms to Temple Street Hospital. Today, Wendy Doherty, the 'little toddler' from Talbot Street, is a healthy, bubbly 29-year-old with a six-year-old son of her own.

For those injured (or at least seriously) life would never be the same again and all because of a chance presence in the vicinity of one of the blasts. Sixteen-year-old Bernadette O'Hanlon from Artane, on Dublin's northside, was struck by flying glass and flung to the floor as she tended customers in O'Neill's shoe shop in Talbot Street (yards from where the blast occurred), where she worked as an assistant. She sustained serious injuries to her eye, head and hip and, despite numerous operations, lost the sight in her right eye. John O'Neill, the forty-year-old owner of the shop - which was severely damaged in the blast - was struck by a chunk of metal from the bomb-car and received sixty stitches to his stomach. He later rebuilt his shattered shop and returned to work. Not so lucky were 55-year-old Mary McKenna, who lived over the shop and was killed instantly, or 66-year-old Brigid Hand, who lost both legs and was fitted with artificial limbs.

Vincent Browne, a youthful 30-year-old reporter with the *Irish Independent* at the time, gave a poignant and moving description of what he saw when he reached Talbot Street.

> The sickening distinctive smell of gelignite was discernible once we entered Nth Earl Street. We saw blackened objects in a store front move slightly - it took a few numbed moments to appreciate that these were human beings. Three or four bodies were strewn along the pavement across from Guiney's store. A human

torso protruded from a shop window. In one store front there were two bodies - a man and a woman, both alive - but only just. The man was covered in blood but still conscious. We went over to him and he asked quietly, 'am I going to die?'. A piece of metal was stuck in his neck and another piece in his side. We lifted him, with the help of two others and took him into Moran's hotel. On the way, he complained slightly about a pain in the left leg and cried, 'my two little boys, my two little boys'. We took him into a large room in the basement, where a number of people with slight injuries and shock were being 'treated'. There was pandemonium, when the more distraught women saw his condition. We laid him on the floor and went back outside. We returned to the shop window, where the injured woman lay. Her face was severely burnt and a metal object protruded from her neck. Her legs were very badly lacerated, one of them seemed to fall off. While attending her, the Gardai, through a loud hailer, advised everybody to get out of the street as they believed that another car bomb was planted nearby and was about to go off. We disguised our fear by attending an old woman lying on the pavement, suffering badly from shock and from a cut in her head. There wasn't much we could do for her and we returned to the woman in the window. With the help of two other onlookers we lifted her from the wreckage and brought her down to the corner where we laid her on the roadway to await an ambulance. She was unconscious and had really no hope of survival. On these trips back and forth we gingerly stepped over dead bodies, which seemed mutilated almost beyond recognition.

A passing motorist, Sean Geraghty, spent several hours ferrying the dead and injured from Talbot Street to Jervis Street hospital in his private car. It was a gesture of enormous generosity by a man in deep shock himself from what he had witnessed. A year later he told Frank McDonald, a reporter with the *Irish Press* at the time, that he was determined that evening not to allow the 'terrible carnage' to deter him from his work of mercy. But the shocking experience later took its toll on the kindly passerby. McDonald wrote: 'He [Geraghty] became nervous and jittery and was out of work for several weeks afterwards. His condition became so serious that he could not sleep and couldn't listen to the radio news lest he heard a report of another bombing.'

Eighteen-year-old Teresa Farrell from Cabra, on Dublin's northside, was leaving Guiney's drapery store in Talbot Street (where she worked) with five of her work colleagues when the bomb went off. As they walked towards the exit to enter the street the glass door in front was blown in on top of them. Teresa received an arm injury and remembers 'someone' telling her to go to Moran's Hotel to await medical help. As she picked her way through the carnage she saw the body of a young woman dead on the footpath. The hotel was like a 'slaughterhouse', she told the *Irish Press*. She saw a young boy who she thought was dead lying on the floor and a man with his stomach 'opened up' being carried in.

Twenty-year-old Marie Butler from Cappoquin in County Waterford was due to start a nursing career in Sir Patrick Dun's Hospital in Lower Canal Street in Dublin and was working temporarily in Clery's in O'Connell Street. She was rushing down Talbot Street to catch a train at Connolly Station to spend the weekend with her family when a chunk of the engine of the bomb-car embedded in her spine and she bled to death.

Nineteen-year-old Siobhán Roice from Wexford worked in the tax office in O'Connell Street and was also rushing to catch the train home. As she hurried through North Earl Street towards Talbot Street she bumped into friends who attempted to persuade her to go shopping in nearby Boyers drapery store. She declined, saying she wished to 'keep walking' as she was anxious to get home. Seconds later she was dead.

Also on her way to catch a train was 22-year-old Anne Marren from Streamestown in County Sligo. She worked for the Department of Posts and Telegraphs and was on her way to spend the weekend with her family when she was also killed in Talbot Street.

In the Talbot Bar close to the bomb scene a number of customers were injured, some seriously, when a plate-glass window crashed in on top of them. A man standing near a window in Moran's Hotel was thrown off his feet and 'hurled back into the room' when the window came crashing in. He was covered in blood and received stitches to his face.

Another intrepid reporter with the *Irish Independent*, Frank Khan, who was on the scene within minutes, described seeing the dead

> ...scattered around the street, some covered in blankets. One young girl had evening newspapers over her. An elderly woman sat in the middle of the junction, attended by a young man. She was covered in blood. The bomb-car was lying on the path in front of Guiney's store. At least six other cars were badly damaged and a lorry owned by a mineral water firm was thrown across the road. Part of the bomb-car was blown over the top of the buildings and ended up at the junction of Deverall Place and Gardiner Street about 100 yards away.

Nineteen-year-old Kevin O'Driscoll of Kilbarrack in north Dublin was blown off his feet outside the Talbot Lounge where he was talking to two friends. As he raised himself up from the ground he saw one of his friends 'trying to crawl away through the debris'. When he eventually came to he was 'completely deaf' and could not remember what had happened.

Breda Turner was twenty and also worked in the tax office. From Thurles in Tipperary, she was engaged to be married and was due to sit the tax inspector's exams. She lived in Phibsboro on Dublin's northside and, unlike the other young women killed in Talbot Street, was not on her way home but was bringing clothes to the cleaners when she was killed in the blast. Concepta Dempsey from Drogheda and her friend Teresa Byrne worked together in Guiney's store in Talbot Street. They heard the Parnell Street explosion and rushed to the window to investigate. Thirty seconds later the bomb exploded outside the door and knocked them both to the floor. Concepta, a single woman in her sixties was nearest the window and took the full force of the blast. She died two weeks later in hospital. Teresa sustained an eye injury when struck by flying glass but was not seriously hurt.

The Parnell Street bomb, the largest of the three, was the first to explode and killed twelve people and injured over 100. It severely damaged the Welcome Inn Bar - outside of which the bomb-car was directly parked - on the corner of Marlborough Street, one of Dublin's oldest pubs, which was owned by Michael Fitzpatrick, a brother to the former Fianna Fáil TD and Junior Minister in Jack Lynch's government, Tom Fitzpatrick. Staff and customers inside the pub were hurled to the floor by the force of the blast and a number of customers sustained minor injuries. A number of surrounding buildings on both sides of the street were also badly damaged, including the seven-storey Posts and Telegraphs office block around the corner in Marlborough Street, which had most of its windows blown in. The then Minister for Posts and Telegraphs, Dr Conor Cruise O'Brien, who was in the building when the bomb went off, rushed to the scene to survey the carnage. Part of the ground floor of the building was later used as a makeshift casualty centre to where the dead and injured were brought before being transferred to one or other of the city hospitals.

The explosion killed an entire family of four, who were caught directly between the exploding bomb and the front wall of the Welcome Inn. John O'Brien, a 23-year-old Dublin man, and his 22-year-old wife Anna, who lived in a tenement block in nearby Gardiner Street, were taking their two baby daughters, Jacqueline, seventeen months, and Ann Marie, seven months, for a stroll through the city centre when disaster struck. The babies were being wheeled in a buggy by their mother as she and John headed towards O'Connell Street. Anna's father, Paddy Doyle, one of the founders of the campaign group The Dublin and Monaghan Relatives, who died in 1997, believed his family may have been on their way for a stroll in St Stephen's Green. 'I knew they visited the "Green" from time to time,' he told me a short time before he died, 'but if they were going there that evening, why go through O'Connell Street, which was something of a roundabout. But then maybe they wanted the kids to see O'Connell Street on a busy Friday afternoon and they decided to go that way.' John O'Brien, a shift worker at the Palm Grove ice-cream factory, had the afternoon off and decided to take his family for a walk. Anna, who married John less than three years earlier, gave up her job to look after her two young children.

Michael Curley, an elderly neighbour, who lived in a flat over the family, said he saw them leave the building. Later, when he noticed they had not taken in the evening paper, he became concerned for their safety. Following removal of the four bodies to the city morgue, staff there became concerned that no one had turned up to enquire about the babies. It was only when Anna's sister Marie arrived to identify the bodies that the mystery was cleared up. The babies belonged to the adults - the entire family had been wiped out. The manager of the Welcome Inn bar, Dominic O'Shea, saw the family pass the door of the pub seconds before the blast. A short time later the mutilated body of one of the babies was found in the bar cellar, where it had been blasted through the footpath grating, which was used to lower barrels and crates of beer from delivery lorries to the pub. A packet of biscuits the older girl was eating was found on the footpath. Mr O'Shea told *The Irish Times* how fortunate he and his staff and customers were not to have suffered higher casualties.

> There were about two or three dozen people in the bar at the time. Usually there would be 50 or 60, but because of the bus strike many had to go home early. The bomb went off outside and threw a shock wave into the bar and we were knocked off our feet. They were all minor injuries in the bar. Just before the bomb went off I saw a lady with a pram going by the door. Afterwards the child was found in the cellar of the bar. We were all very fortunate with the amount of material that was flying

around. I was sure we would have had higher casualties.'

Seventeen-year-old Vincent Geraghty, a barman at the pub, was making sandwiches for a customer when he was blown off his feet. Later he discovered the body of the baby in the basement and directed an ambulance crew to the spot. Paddy Philips, a voluntary worker with St John Ambulance Brigade, was at home in nearby Summerhill when he heard the blast. Abandoning his tea he dashed from his house and was one of the first paramedics on the scene. The first body he encountered had his head severed from his body. Another casualty lost an eye. One of the first policemen on the scene was Garda Kenny from Fitzgibbon Street station (on Dublin's northside), who was directing traffic at the Parnell Monument in Parnell Street, at the northern end of O'Connell Street, when the bomb exploded. He spoke to the *Irish Press* a short time later. 'There was a blast. I knew it was a bomb. I rushed down and saw a man lying beside a car. I don't know if he was dead.'

Andrew Hamilton, a reporter with *The Irish Times*, captured in stark reality the devastation in Parnell Street.

> Parnell Street, with small shops and working-class folk, had pathetic heart-breaking reminders. The bodies and the maimed had been rushed off in ambulances by 5.45 p.m. but the terrible smell of death could not be erased so easily. There, littering the roadway with the debris of smashed cars and the broken glass, were the personal paraphernalia of the dead and injured, shoes, scarves, coats, shopping bags, even a bag of chips. Women were crying because they heard that one of their children or a relative had been taken away to hospital. Some were demented with grief and I heard one woman say in a sobbing voice: 'He'll never be back'. In the confused and chaotic situation it was not easy to be a comforter. Little pools of blood splattered the roadway and the upholstery of one wrecked car was badly stained.

One of two foreign nationals killed in the bombings was the owner of the Venezian Café situated four doors west of the Welcome Inn bar. Antonio Magillo, an Italian national, was standing at his car within yards of the bomb when it exploded, killing him instantly. Seconds before the blast, Mary Murphy, the then owner of Crowley's shop, saw Mr Magillo standing in the street. When she 'ran into the street' following the explosion he was 'blown to bits' on the footpath, she told reporters at the scene.

Edward O'Neill and his wife Rita, from nearby Dominick Street, took their two sons, Edward Junior, seven, and Billy, five, to a barber's shop in Parnell Street to have their hair cut. Mr O'Neill was killed, his wife and sons injured and the barber's shop destroyed. Patrick Fay, a 47-year-old married man from Artane on Dublin's northside, stopped to buy petrol at the Westbrook Garage two doors from the Welcome Inn. He was killed instantly.

Una Condon, a widow who lived and ran a hairdressing salon from her home in Parnell Street, was injured and had both her home and business destroyed by the blast. She had lived in the street for twenty years but was forced to take refuge with the Little Sisters of the Assumption in Camden Street as a result. Within a year, however, she rebuilt her home and reopened her business. Mrs Condon's neighbour, Christine Sex, also a widow, had her butcher shop destroyed and then looted by vandals, who stole £170 from the till within minutes of the blast. She herself sustained facial injuries when the window was blown in. Her son Paddy, who was in the shop at the time, sustained a serious eye injury when he was 'blown into the air' by the force of the blast.

A Catholic priest, Father John Kileen, attached to Berkley Street Church - four streets away - was in his office when he heard the blasts. He jumped in his car and dashed to the scene in Parnell Street and immediately began anointing the dead and dying. 'I anointed seven adults and one little girl', he told reporters. 'They were all in a bad way and seemed to be dying.' The bodies of two of the victims were blown into the Westbrook Garage and the foot of a third was later found on the roof. Buildings on both sides of Parnell Street were damaged, and across the street in Ryan's pub customers were 'knocked off their feet' by the force of the blast. Patrick Duffy, who ran a newsagency and fancy goods shop directly opposite the Welcome Inn said he saw a 'blinding flash' and a second later heard the bang. 'I thought the shop was coming down around me,' he told the assembled media afterwards. 'It was terrible. People were running everywhere in panic. I saw an injured man running with a baby in his arms and I couldn't say if the baby was dead or alive.'

In South Leinster Street the bomb, which was planted alongside the perimeter wall of Trinity College and 200 yards from Dáil Éireann, severely damaged the wall that divides Trinity's College Park from the public street. Forbes McFall, who later made his name as a reporter with RTE's *Today Tonight* programme, was jogging in College Park when the bomb exploded. In an article in *The Irish Times* the following day he described the scene:

> I was in College Park, a stones-throw from the car, when it exploded. It was just after 5.30 on the pavilion clock, a couple of students were playing cricket, a few were on the running track and there was the sound of a party going on somewhere. The blast threw everyone flat to the ground. Then there was a quiet. When we looked up a thick pall of flame and smoke was rising from the roadway. But there wasn't a sound. Nobody moved in case there would be another blast. A black filth was falling from the air. Half-thinking, I got up and joined a crowd of students who were rushing into the street to see what had happened. The road was littered with glass, shop fronts obliterated and every window in sight shattered. The car was blazing fiercely and lots of people were milling about and just staring at it. Two gardai were doing little to hold people back from the scene. It was confusion. Cars were still trying to get through the junction. People were shouting, young girls were crying, people were standing dazed with vacant

bleeding faces. Then there was a high pitched siren sound, somebody shouted 'get back' and people scattered in all directions. I was pushed into the doorway of a pub where some men were still drinking. When the panic subsided I edged closer to the burning car. A charred decapitated body was lying on the pavement. Only the sight of two brown platform boots suggested that she was a young girl. I walked across the road and had to sidestep a dead man lying half-covered in a shop doorway. A little huddle of people in a laneway were trying to help a man whose foot had been blown off. A woman's hat and one black glove were lying in the roadway. Everyone continued to stand and stare until the police finally cordoned off the area, some 20 minutes after the explosion occurred. The ambulances and the fire brigade were even slower to arrive on the scene and the man with the blown-off limb had to be taken to hospital in the back of a nearby estate car.

The bomb, the smaller of the three, killed five people and injured over fifty. As it was Friday the Dáil had adjourned for the weekend, the majority of TDs having returned to their constituencies, but the explosion was heard by staff in Leinster House, including the then Taoiseach Liam Cosgrave, who was sitting in his office at the time. One of the first to visit the scene was the Fine Gael TD for Longford-Westmeath, Gerry L'Estrange (now deceased), who rushed from his office in Leinster House to help 'load the dead and injured' into ambulances. He told assembled reporters at the scene that the bombing was 'obviously linked to Sunningdale' and was a warning to 'this government' to 'keep hands off Northern Ireland'. 'But the men of violence will not intimidate this government to abandon any of its policies,' he said. Among the buildings damaged were Chubb Alarms, Neenan's Travel Agents, the Cherry Tree Restaurant, Stanley's Book Shop, Bowmakers office block and the biochemical laboratory in Trinity College. Staff and customers in most of the buildings told of being 'blown off chairs', 'hit by flying glass' and 'blinded by a massive blue flash'.

One of the youngest casualties of the Leinster Street bomb was 21-year-old Anna Massey from Pearse Villas in Sallynoggin in south county Dublin, who was killed instantly as she walked past the bomb-car on her way to Pearse Street train station. A twin and one of seven daughters of Frank and Annie Massey, she worked as a clerk in Lisneys Estate Agents in St Stephen's Green. She was due to be married eight weeks later and had left work twenty minutes early to catch a train to Glasthule where her fiance was waiting at the station 'with his new car' to collect her. From there the couple were due to travel to meet the local priest to make final arrangements for their wedding in July. In an interview with the *Irish Independent* in 1988 her mother Annie Massey talked about what it was like on hearing the ghastly news and being brought in a police car to identify the body.

> The police were great to us. They came in from Cabinteely station at 10 minutes past 10 that night and took us to Pearse Street station. They couldn't tell us anything because they didn't know. I remember they showed us a bag and asked if it was Anna's; it was. I was so glad. I thought if they had Anna's bag she must be alright. Then they brought us to the Richmond and the Matron gave us tea. I just kept saying: 'Where's Anna?'. The Matron told us she was down in the city morgue. When we went down she was lying there with a sheet over her. There were a lot of bodies around on the floor but they had done a post mortem on Anna so she was on a table at least. They pulled back the sheet and I saw her face. There were marks on it where the glass had hit her.

CHAPTER 2

AFTERMATH OF A BLOODBATH

Within hours of the bombings the two main loyalist paramilitary groups, the UVF and the UDA, issued statements in Belfast denying involvement. Ken Gibson, a brigade staff member of the UVF leadership on the Shankill Road and an official spokesman for the organization, said in a statement that 'this organisation had no part in any bombings and is adhering to its truce called last November'. (In late 1973 the UVF had declared a ceasefire as a quid-pro-quo for the British government's lifting of its ban on the organisation. However, the ceasefire was short-lived and the government reinstated the ban.) The statement went on:

> We want to make it quite clear that we are appalled by these explosions. It is indiscriminate and definitely against our policy. At the present time the U.V.F. have made a firm declaration that we will not engage in any physical activities including bombings or shootings. We at the moment are engaged in the political field of Northern Ireland and we believe that the political solution to Northern Ireland can only be found democratically by the people of Northern Ireland within Northern Ireland. Therefore we are not concerned with the policy of Eire or indeed the dictates of Westminster politicians.

The bombings were, of course, carried out by the UVF, and Gibson, a leading activist in the organisation and close friend of its former leader, Gusty Spence - by this time in prison - was well aware of it. Whether or not he was personally involved in the bombings, or the car hijackings that morning, I have not been able to establish. But as a leading strategist in the UVF's reincarnation after 1966, and throughout the early years of the Troubles, there is little doubt that Gibson was fully aware of the plan to bomb Dublin, not only in 1974 but in 1972 and 1973 as well.

Why the UVF chose to lie through its teeth about such a ghastly deed with such appalling consequences will probably never be known. One theory is that it feared swift and brutal retaliation on its members by republicans. Another is that its handlers in the security forces advised that confusion was the best form of attack. By denying responsibility, the Gardai (and the public) would automatically blame the UDA, who had organised the UWC strike but who were not (officially) involved in the bombings.

Around the same time as the UVF issued its denial, UDA headquarters in East Belfast issued a statement also denying involvement. The statement said 'We categorically deny any involvement in these bombings and regret that anyone should have been killed or injured by bombs wherever they go off.'

In a statement issued in the early hours of Saturday morning the Irish Republican Publicity Bureau on behalf of the Provisional IRA said:

> The Irish Republican Army utterly condemns the vile murder and bombing in Dublin and Monaghan yesterday evening. Needless to say, no branch of the Republican Movement was involved. The events of this afternoon highlight the farcical security situation in this part of the country which is orientated towards assisting these S.A.S. type operations. These S.A.S. units have been apprehended several times near the Border and have been given escorts back to their bases. The Republican Movement extends sympathy to the families and relatives of the bomb victims.

The statement was signed by P. O'Neill, Rúnaí, Irish Republican Publicity Bureau.

Around the same time Official Sinn Féin, through its spokesman Tony Heffernan, condemned the bombings. He said:

Sinn Féin has consistently condemned the civilian bombing campaign in the North. It has destroyed every progressive political move. It has divided and confused workers. It has unleashed uncontrollable sectarian hatred and above all, it has led to the death and injury of so many civilians. The bombs in Dublin and Monaghan may well be a response to bombs in Belfast or indeed they may be British inspired, as they were in December, 1972. Irrespective of whoever was responsible, there can be no justification for adding to the death toll of innocent workers and their children. We are quite sure that the Protestant workers of Belfast are as horrified at today's events as were their Southern co-workers on Bloody Friday, 1972.

Within minutes of the bombings the Gardai launched the biggest manhunt ever conducted in a criminal investigation in the history of the State. A joint Army-Garda security committee, set up eighteen months earlier as part of the Major Accident Plan, met in emergency session in Dublin to coordinate the security response. A forest of Garda checkpoints, backed up by heavily armed detectives and armed soldiers, was thrown up to cover an area over 1,500 square miles between Dublin city and the border to check motorists travelling from the Dublin area. All border crossings - including main roads, secondary roads and unapproved roads - stretching over a distance of almost thirty miles, between Dundalk and Monaghan town, were sealed. Following the Monaghan explosion, however, which occurred ninety minutes after Dublin, a number of Gardai were withdrawn to allow them to travel to the scene to help in the rescue. Planes leaving Dublin airport were checked, and trains travelling from Dublin to Belfast were checked at Connolly Station and again at Dundalk close to the border.

At 6.30 p.m. the government, led by the Taoiseach Liam Cosgrave, met in emergency session at government buildings to discuss the implications of the bombings vis-a-vis the security of the State and its citizens and to draw up plans to deal with the political fallout which was certain to follow. A short time later the Taoiseach, through a Ministerial Order under the Broadcasting Act, pre-empted air time on national television to address a shocked and frightened nation. This is what he said:

The government and I wish to express our profound sympathy to the relatives of the victims of today's outrages and to those who have been injured and maimed. To the evil men who have perpetrated these deeds we express our revulsion and condemnation, which every decent person in this State feels at their unforgivable acts. The government are, as yet, unaware of the identities of those responsible for these crimes but everyone who has preached violence or practised violence or condoned violence must bear a share of responsibility for the outrages. It is in moments of great tragedy like today's that we seriously appreciate the dedicated and unselfish service of members of the Garda, army, ambulance, medical services, doctors, nurses and those engaged in rescue and humanitarian work. To all who have given and, as I am still speaking, are still giving, including hundreds of ordinary men and women who responded so readily and magnificently to donate their blood, I offer, on behalf of the whole community, our sincerest thanks. While our society is menaced by men who perpetrate cowardly acts of violence, the Garda and Army will give the citizens all the protection they can. Their ability to protect you will, however, depend to a large extent on your vigilance and co-operation. I would, therefore, request you to report immediately to the Gardai any suspicious or unusual movements, object or motor vehicle. Occupants of buildings should take care to search and keep a watch upon their premises. What has happened today will help to underline the criminality and utter futility of violent acts as a means of furthering political ends. It will also help to bring home to us here in this part of our island what the people in Northern Ireland have been suffering for five long years. Today's evil deeds will only serve to strengthen the resolve of those, North and South, who have been working for peace.

A short time later the then Minister for Justice, Patrick Cooney, held a news conference at government buildings at which he said the Gardai had an open mind on the inspiration of the attack. They did not know its source, nor did they exclude any group large or small. Although there were warnings that incendiary devices might have been used in the Limerick area that week, there was no indication that a bombing onslaught was imminent in Dublin or Monaghan. 'There was no hint of anything like this being planned,' Cooney said. He expected the security forces to provide him with suggestions for stricter car controls in city areas but it would not be an answer to the problem to seal particular areas of the city. 'If we were to close off parts of the city, the people who used car bombs, not being fussy about where they placed them, might put them outside the cordon. The ones in Dublin had been placed at random,' Mr Cooney said.

Within an hour of the Minister's statement and shortly after the paramilitaries issued their disclaimers, the Gardai issued a statement saying the RUC had established that two of the bomb-cars had been hijacked in loyalist areas of Belfast early that morning. Shortly afterwards, a further Garda statement announced the introduction of near blanket restriction on parking in and around the city centre and said the restrictions would remain in force until further notice. The statement said:

> Parking will be prohibited at all times in the following streets: O'Connell St; North Earl Street; Talbot Street; Lr. Abbey Street; between O'Connell Street and Marlborough Street; Parnell Street; Thomas's Lane; Cathedral Street; Earl Place; Wicklow Street; Exchequer Street; Grafton Street; Church Lane; Andrew Street; Duke Street; Anne Street; Dame Court and Suffolk Street

All normal parking prohibitions at single and double yellow lines, bus stops and clearways, will apply in the central city area at Capel Street, Parnell Street, Gardiner Street, Memorial Road, Westland Row, Upper Merrion Street, St. Stephen's Green, East and South, Cuffe Street, Wexford Street, Aungier Street, South Gt. Georges Street, Dame Street and Parliament Street back to Capel Street. The public are requested to co-operate with the Gardai and to refrain from parking in the central city area until further notice.

Throughout Friday night the Garda Commissioner Patrick Malone briefed Mr Cooney on an hourly basis on developments in the Garda investigation. Mr Cooney in turn briefed the Taoiseach. By Saturday morning the pace of events was quickening. The Cabinet reconvened at government buildings to review overnight progress in the Garda investigation. The mood of the meeting was tense and serious, with a determination amongst Ministers to meet the challenge head on. The integrity and stability of the State would be protected whatever the cost, Ministers assured each other. Cooney addressed the meeting and confirmed to colleagues that the Gardai had indeed established the source of two of the bomb-cars. But the situation remained confused. Ministers were not quite sure what was happening or who or what organisation was behind the bombings or if a further onslaught was on its way. The total absence of forewarning by the RUC to the Gardai - something which had been the hallmark of co-operation between the two forces over the previous five years - coupled with the denials of involvement by all the main paramilitary groupings, had momentarily panicked the government into thinking that something more sinister might be happening. There was, after all, intelligence in Garda files in Store Street station implicating members of the British Army in the 1972/73 bombings. Shortly after the meeting broke up the Department of Foreign Affairs issued a statement saying a request had been made to the United Nations for the return of the '340 officers and men' serving with the UN peace-keeping force in the Middle-East, to help with the security emergency at home. The statement said:

> The Secretary General of the U.N., Dr. Kurt Waldheim, has today conveyed to the Government through the Irish Permanent Representative at the U.N., Mr. Eamonn Kennedy, his deep sympathy at yesterday's bomb outrages in Ireland and his fullest understanding for the security reasons which have caused the troop withdrawal. At the same time he expressed great praise for the magnificent contribution of the Irish contingent to the maintenance of the peace and his regret that they are being withdrawn while at the same time appreciating the circumstances which have made this necessary. About 300 men will leave Tel Aviv on Wednesday and the rest will follow later.

On Wednesday, five days after the bombings, a special Requiem Mass, attended by dignitaries of Church and State, was concelebrated in the Pro-Cathedral in Dublin to honour all those killed in the four attacks. Chief celebrant at the Mass, which was attended by the then President of Ireland, Erskine Childers, the former President, Eamonn de Valera, the Taoiseach and members of the government, was the Archbishop of Dublin, Dr Dermot Ryan. Before the altar were six coffins of victims of the Talbot Street and Parnell Street bombings who lived in Saint Mary's city centre parish, which included the two streets. Two of the six coffins were white miniature caskets containing the infant remains of baby sisters Jacqueline and Ann Marie O'Brien, killed in Parnell Street, flanked by the coffins of their parents John and Anna O'Brien. Also there were the coffins of Mary McKenna, who lived and was killed in Talbot Street, and John Dargle from Portland Row off Parnell Square, killed in Parnell Street. A day earlier Requiem Mass was concelebrated for the Italian victim of the Parnell Street bomb, Antonio Magillo, attended by his young widow, the Italian ambassador to Ireland and the Italian

Defence Minister, Senor Andretti. His body was then flown home to Italy for burial.

As news of the bombings was flashed across the world throughout Friday evening, frantic relatives of people living in Dublin, both at home and abroad, inundated the city's telephone service with calls seeking to ensure that no members of their families were amongst the dead or injured. Thousands of calls poured into the city exchange throughout the evening and into the small hours of Saturday morning from all over Ireland, the UK, Europe and as far afield as the US, Canada and Australia. Because Ireland did not have a modern telephone exchange at the time, callers from outside Ireland and the UK could not dial direct and had to be connected manually by staff at the Dublin exchange. Sixty women telephonists on work to rule for a week at the Dundalk exchange in County Louth returned to normal duties immediately, due to the emergency created by the bombings.

Reaction to the bombings at home and throughout the world was predictable. In Belfast the Chief Minister in the Northern Ireland power-sharing executive, Brian Faulkner, in a message to the Taoiseach, said it was with the 'deepest distress' that he and his colleagues in the Executive learned of the 'atrocious outrages' in Dublin. However, the deep-seated hostility towards the South held by certain sections of the unionist community was articulated by John Laird, a prominent member of the Official Unionist Party at the time, and Sammy Smyth, one of the organisers of the UWC strike. Laird said there was a certain irony in the 'blast killings'. 'The people who are suffering [in Dublin] are people who have quietly condoned a terrorist campaign against the people of this country and sought to gain political ends through violence and indeed have succeeded in making political gains from violence.' Smyth, a verbose, middle-aged bigot who was one of the founders of the UDA and who once said that a full-scale civil war between Catholics and Protestants was the only way to solve Ulster's problems, delivered himself of a chilling comment on the bombings: 'I am very happy about the bombings in Dublin.

There is a war with the Free State and now we are laughing at them.'

The Secretary of State for Northern Ireland, Merlyn Rees, condemned the attacks and the British Prime Minister Harold Wilson sent a message of sympathy to the Taoiseach. Mr Rees said, 'I can only express my complete horror and utter condemnation of the bombings. It is a reflection of what has been happening here in Northern Ireland and I must deplore bombings wherever they occur.'

In Europe the bombings were seen as only one more awful sign of the violence that had torn Ireland apart, North and South, over the previous five years. In France the leading national newspaper, *Le Monde*, described the bombings as 'an unprecedented massacre' and posed the question: 'Is this the Protestant backlash?' Another French newspaper, *Le Soir*, in reporting the bombings said: 'No one claims responsibility for this murderous attack in Southern Ireland. The Catholic IRA and the Protestant UDA deny any participation in these acts of terrorism.' In Brussels the 1000-strong Irish community, shocked and numbed at the scale of the bombings, gathered round radio and television sets as news of the rising death toll reached the city. In several well-known Irish meeting places weekend revelry gave way to sombre and doleful silence as people waited for clarification of the death and injury toll. The *Irish Independent* reporter in Brussels, Frank Byrne, described how one young woman sobbed and screamed: 'Oh my God, my sister works in Talbot Street - she would have been just going for her bus.'

In Rome Pope Paul, condemning the bombings that week together with an upsurge in violence in the Middle East, said 'delinquency has become a monstrous and collective art'.

Back in Dublin the largest of the two Coalition government parties of the time, Fine Gael, which was led by the Taoiseach Liam Cosgrave, cancelled its Árd Fheis (annual conference), which was due to be held in Dublin that weekend. The decision was taken, according to a party statement, because of the tragic circumstances of the bombings, the possible danger to a large number of delegates and the security problems that would be posed. The Seventh World Congress on the Prevention of Occupational Accidents and Diseases, which was also due to be held in the Burlington Hotel in Dublin that weekend (one of the largest conferences ever held in Ireland up to then), received a large number of cancellations from around the world as a result of the bombings.

Meanwhile, as the Garda hunt for the bombers got under way, a hotline of communication was opened up between Garda headquarters in the Phoenix Park in Dublin and RUC headquarters in Knock in East Belfast. Working from the registration numbers of the cars, which had been hurriedly gleaned from the wreckage at the bomb-scenes, senior garda officers in C3, the Crime and Intelligence branch of the force, had, by 9 p.m. established the origin of two of the bomb-cars. They had not yet established the origin of the Talbot Street or Monaghan bomb-cars, mainly (it is thought) because they were both stolen, rather than hijacked, and, because a much greater number of cars were stolen than hijacked each day in Northern Ireland, the RUC had taken longer to identify the stolen bomb-cars.

The people in charge of C3 in the Phoenix Park depot were Ed Garvey, who was a Deputy Commissioner and who later became a highly controversial Commissioner, and his deputy, Chief Superintendent Larry Wren, who also later became Commissioner. In the Republic the Garda Síochána is a single unitary force of (at today's numbers) over 11,000 men and women, headed by a Garda Commissioner with two Deputy Commissioners and a varying number - from six in 1974 to nine today - of Assistant Commissioners. In the UK, including Northern Ireland, the police are divided into a number of independent constabularies each one headed by a Chief Constable. In Ireland the country is divided into twenty-three divisions with a Chief Superintendent in charge of each division. Specialised sections, such as the Special Branch or the Technical Bureau, are also headed by a Chief Superintendent, who is not necessarily head of a division. The force is answerable to and financed by the Department of Justice, and ultimately the Minister for Justice.

In 1974 the Dublin Metropolitan Area, because of its increasing size, was divided into four divisions (today there are six) - North Central and North (north of the river Liffey) and South Central and South (south of the river). The headquarters of the Gardai is situated in Dublin's Phoenix Park, where the Commissioner and his two deputies are based. In 1974 the headquarters of the Dublin Metropolitan Area was housed in Dublin Castle; today it is in Harcourt Square. Many Gardai regard this section of the force as the engine room of the Garda Siochána. It houses the headquarters of the Special Branch (or Special Detective Unit, SDU, as it is known), which has over 500 members, and the Serious Crime Squad (or Central Detective Unit, CDU), which also has up to 500 members. It also houses other specialised units such as the Emergency Response Unit (ERU), the drugs squad and the fraud squad. The Special Branch handles political crime such as subversion and terrorism, while the Serious Crime Squad handles ordinary crime such as bank robberies and all other forms of serious crime, including murder.

The Dublin bombings occurred in two separate Garda divisions of the Dublin Metropolitan Area - North Central, with its divisional headquarters in Store Street, which covered Talbot Street and Parnell Street, and South Central, with its divisional headquarters in Pearse Street, which covered South Leinster Street. Because of a shortage of office space, the Chief Superintendents in charge of both divisions were based in Dublin Castle at the time.

Because of the magnitude of the bombings, the investigation on the ground was handled by three specialised sections of the force. These were the Special Branch, headed by Detective Chief Superintendent John Fleming, who handled the political dimension to the bombings; the Serious Crime Squad, headed by Detective Chief Superintendent John Joy, who handled the criminal side of the investigation; and the Technical Bureau, headed by Detective Chief Superintendent Tony McMahon which up to a point took the lead role in the investigation.

The Technical Bureau, as the name suggests, is that section of the Garda Siochána that handles the technical end of major investigations, particularly where murder is involved. It includes mapping, fingerprinting, photography and ballistics. Until the mid-1980s the Bureau also had under its control a detective unit called the Murder Squad, which was a specialised unit of around a dozen officers whose chief function was to investigate murders throughout the State. Following the disaster of the Kerry Babies case in the early 1980s, the Murder Squad was disbanded by the Garda Commissioner. In 1974 the Technical Bureau was housed in an antiquated seventeenth-century building in St John's Road, Kingsbridge (which had been used as a hospital for treating victims of the Battle of the Boyne in 1690), two miles west of Dublin city centre. (Today, it is based in Garda Headquarters in the Phoenix Park). At the time it was grossly under-manned, under-financed and hopelessly lacking the technical expertise required to deal with a major catastrophe such as the Dublin and Monaghan bombings. It did not have a forensic science laboratory of its own and staff there depended on the State Laboratory in Merrion Street next to government buildings, which belonged to the Department of Finance. Forensic science is the discipline dealing with analysis carried out on residua left at the scene of a crime such as blood, hair, skin tissue, saliva, semen and, as in the case of the Dublin-Monaghan bombings, bomb smears such as nitrate, ammonium, nitroglycerine, etc. Even the State Laboratory in 1974 was in its infancy and in no way possessed the skills or scientific capacity to deal with a major bombing disaster. As a result much of the more complicated analysis throughout the late 1960s and early 1970s was carried out, on behalf of the Gardai, by the Northern Ireland authorities, at the Industrial and Forensic Science Laboratory in Belfast.

Despite its shortcomings, the Technical Bureau was thrust into the forefront and played a central role in the bombing investigation, with Chief Superintendent Tony McMahon a key figure in the day-to-day running of it. McMahon's deputy was Detective Superintendent Dan Murphy, who was also head of the Murder Squad and whose role, and that of his officers, in the bombing investigation was to concentrate on gathering intelligence on the perpetrators, in the hope of building enough evidence to bring charges against them.

However, the overall investigation into the Dublin end of the bombings was led, on a day-to-day basis, by the Assistant Commissioner for the Dublin Metropolitan Area (DMA). Responsibility for Monaghan fell to the Chief Superintendent for the Cavan-Monaghan division at the time, John Paul McMahon.

Because explosive substances were used in the attacks, the Irish Army's Explosives Ordnance Disposal (EOD) was called out by the Gardai to examine the scenes and determine if the bombs planted had fully exploded or if there might be further unexploded bombs in the areas. The army's two leading explosives experts at the time were Commdt Paddy Trears and Colonel Denis Boyle. Both men carried out a detailed search of the three Dublin bomb scenes within an hour of the explosions and throughout the course of the evening destroyed up to a dozen suspect vehicles found with Northern or English registration plates in various parts of the city. However, the painstaking task of sifting through the debris and gathering together all, or as much as possible, of the fragments of the wreckage of all four bomb-cars fell to the ballistics section of the Technical Bureau. These fragments were then delivered to the Technical Bureau headquarters for screening, and from there the relevant fragments were sent to the State Laboratory for chemical analysis. It was the task of the laboratory to forensically examine the material for explosives residue, or any other evidence that might lead Gardai to the bombers. The great difficulty in all of this, of course, is that during bomb attacks much of the evidence is blown away in the explosion and the greater the explosion the less evidence remains for forensic analysis.

On Friday night the Gardai held their first 'police conference' on the bombings. This is a private meeting of police officers who gather to discuss tactics and plan strategy and assess the evidence, if any, available so far in a criminal investigation. Because of the magnitude of the task ahead, the conference was a particularly large one, with officers from almost every section of the force present. The meeting was held in the DMA headquarters in Dublin Castle, and was chaired by the Commissioner, Patrick Malone. Also present was Deputy Commissioner Ed Garvey and Chief Superintendents Tony McMahon, John Fleming, John Joy, John Sheehan (Chief Superintendent in charge of the North Central division) and Eamonn Doherty (Chief Superintendent in charge of the South Central division). Over the following three to four weeks a similar type conference was held each morning in the same building at 11 a.m.

Within hours of the bombings the Gardai issued a confidential telephone number on the RTE television news inviting any member of the public who had seen anything suspicious throughout Friday (or indeed the previous days) to get in touch. They issued the make, model, colour and registration number of each bomb-car, which they had already established from the wreckage of the bomb scenes. They had only yet established the origin of two of the cars, but they were confident, at that stage, that all four had come from Northern Ireland and that the three Dublin cars had probably travelled - more or less - the same route. The public response was overwhelming. Dozens of people from all over Dublin city and county and between Dublin and the border rang in to say they had seen the bombers or the bomb-cars at some stage throughout Friday. Some had seen the cars being parked, others had seen them being driven towards the city, while others had seen the drivers acting suspiciously, driving the wrong way up one-way streets, or showing impatience while trying to park.

Within twenty-four hours of the explosions, the Gardai had sufficient information to piece together a clear picture of the entire bombing operation. They had by this time also established the origin of the two remaining bomb-cars - on further information from the RUC. They had established the routes all four cars had travelled from the border to Dublin city centre and to Monaghan town, and where the bombs had been loaded on to all four bomb-cars and how long all four cars had been in their respective parking positions before the bombs exploded. They also had a clear description of the drivers of three of the cars - Parnell Street, South Leinster Street and Monaghan but in the end were only ever able to identify (by name) the Parnell Street and Monaghan bombers. In the case of Talbot Street the Gardai were given a vague description of the bomber and his passenger - seen by a witness at some distance - but the information led to nothing and to this day the Gardai do not know for certain who planted the Talbot Street bomb. They had a clear and very detailed picture of the South Leinster Street bomber but again were unable to identify him from photographs and again to this day do not know for sure who he is.

Following the deluge of information from the public, a team of detectives - described as the creme de la creme of the force - was drafted in to interview witnesses and follow up on intelligence reports from the RUC as well as information supplied by loyalist informers. Throughout the 1970s the Gardai had a number of well-placed loyalist informers who provided them with intelligence on loyalists, particularly in relation to cross-border attacks. These were mainly in the mid-Ulster area, particularly around Portadown, and were mostly cultivated after the 1974 bombings, which is probably one of the reasons why the Gardai did not receive prior knowledge of the bombings.

The specialist team of detectives was drawn, not just from the Murder Squad, but from many sections of the force, and placed under the direction of Detective Superintendent Dan Murphy. Throughout the following three months (while the investigation remained at a high level of intensity) and indeed until his retirement from the force, Murphy was to become the most important policeman on the investigation. Amongst other experienced detectives assigned to Murphy's squad were Detective Sergeant Colm Browne, a native of County Wicklow but who served most of his career with the Special Branch on the border. Browne, a Protestant, was known as a 'super investigator' who could 'break' suspects under interrogation and 'make them talk'. He had a close working relationship with the RUC and travelled north to meet his Special Branch counterparts on a regular basis. He had a thorough knowledge of loyalist paramilitaries and could speak with a northern accent if circumstances required. In the years since the bombings Brown is credited with being responsible for 'breaking' three loyalists who were arrested in County Leitrim on their way to murder a local IRA man, Francie McGirl, in retaliation for the role he played in the murder of Lord Louie Mountbatten in Sligo in August 1979. He was also a key figure in the investigation into the murder of Captain Nairac outside Dundalk in 1977. As a result of his numerous successes during his early career as a detective, Browne was given a 'special role' within the force and had authority to by-pass his immediate superiors and report to C3 in Garda headquarters during his time in the Special Branch. As a heavyweight he was thrown in at the deep end on the bombing investigation and much depended on his skills as an investigator to deliver the bombers.

Others in Murphy's investigation team were Detective Sergeant Michael Canavan, who had served much of his career with the Serious Crime Squad in Dublin, Detectives Thomas Dunne and Christy Godkin, who were both regarded as able young investigators. On the technical side with a specialised knowledge of ballistic science were Detective Inspector Tom O'Connor, Detective Sergeant Eamonn O'Fiachan and Detective Gardai Michael Niland, Colm Dardis, Pat Ennis and Ted Jones. All six bureau detectives were considered able and intelligent men who carried out the task set them with diligence and enthusiasm. However, the facilities and conditions under which they were forced to work were nothing short of a disgrace and have contributed in no small way to the controversy and boil which have surrounded the failure of the bombings investigation over the past twenty-eight years.

In the days following the bombings, over two dozen plastic dustbins of debris were collected from the streets and taken to the Technical Bureau in Kingsbridge. On Monday, 20 May, three days after the bombings and after the process of sifting the relevant wreckage parts from the waste debris had begun, three samples of material from the Parnell Street explosion were delivered to Dr James Donovan, a senior forensic analyst at the State Laboratory in Merrion Street, Dublin, by Detective Garda Ted Jones for forensic analysis. Three days later, on Thursday 23 May, Dr Donovan sent a report of his analysis back to the Technical Bureau. This is what it said:

> On 20th May 1974, I received from Detective Garda Timothy Jones, at the State Laboratory, samples connected with the explosion. I analysed the samples and obtained the following results:
> 1. Polythene bag containing foam rubber.
>   Five pieces of the foam rubber contained ammonium and sodium nitrate and two of these five contained nitroglycerin.
> 2. Burned and charred white leatherette - piece
>   This had trace quantities of sodium nitrate.
> 3. Scrapings from car used to contain bomb
>   These scrapings contained ammonium and sodium nitrate and nitroglycerin. Microscopic examination showed the presence of two blackened prills of ammonium nitrate.
> Hydrocarbon oils or nitrobenzene were not detected. The results suggest the use of gelignite/dynamite as the explosive substance.

On the same day that Dr Donovan issued his report, he received four further samples from Parnell Street, some of them extra quantities of what he had already analysed, some of them new, again delivered by Garda Jones. Five days later, on Tuesday, May 28, Dr Donovan sent a report of his second test back to the Bureau. This is what it said:

> On 23rd May 1974, I received from Detective Garda Timothy Jones, at the State Laboratory, samples connected with the explosion. I analysed the samples and obtained the following results.
> 1. Pieces of foam rubber

Some pieces gave a positive reaction for chemicals normally found in gelignite.

2. Pieces of jute carpeting

These were too dirty to give any type of reliable results.

3. Pieces of tyre

Very faint traces of ammonium nitrate and sodium nitrate were found on some of these. A smear of heavy hydrocarbon oil such as gas oil or car engine oil was found on the thread side of one of the pieces. It is not possible to make any definite conclusions as a result of the analysis.

4. Scrapings from car used to contain bomb

These contained sodium carbonate, nitrate and ammonium. These chemicals are normally found in high explosives.

On the day Dr Donovan returned his second report something quite unexpected happened. Six containers of a variety of different samples from the scenes of all four explosions were delivered by Garda Ted Jones to Dr R.A. Hall, forensic analyst at the Department of Industrial and Forensic Science, Newtownbreda Road, Belfast, for forensic analysis. Dr Donovan was not informed of this sudden turn of events and did not become aware of it until 1999. Whilst it was known at the time that bomb samples from the loyalist campaign in the Republic of 1972/73 had been sent to Belfast, it was believed by Dr Donovan, and indeed by a number of Gardai, that once the first samples from 1974 were sent to the Irish State Laboratory, then all of them would be sent there.

Seven days after receiving the samples Dr. Hall sent a report of his findings to the Gardai in Dublin. This is what it said:

Statement (Report) of R.A. HALL, Member of Staff, Department of Industrial and Forensic Science, 180 Newtownbreda Road, Belfast, in connection with the bomb explosions at Talbot Street, Dublin, Monaghan

Town; Parnell Street, Dublin and South Leinster Street, Dublin, on the 17th May, 1974.

On 28.5.1974 items were received from Detective Garda Jones for examination. These were marked as follows:

2586/74	Talbot Street	1 item
2587/74	Monaghan Town	3 items
2588/74	Parnell Street	1 item
2589/74	South Leinster Street	1 item

These items have been examined and the following points noted.

2586/74 - the item in this case consisted of a number of twisted and torn fragments of sheet metal, some painted metallic grey and some with red primer. Also included was part of a door lock and a suspension unit. Examination for nitroglycerine ethylene glycel dinitrate, nitre arematics, ammonium, nitrate, nitrite, chlorate, chlorite, chloride and sugar all proved negative. The presence of oily deposits on the fragments made the examination for fuel oil invalid.

2587/74 - Item 1 consisted of a number of twisted and torn fragments of sheet steel, some with black paint on red under coat, and a green painted headlamp rim. A similar examination to that above was carried out with similar results. Item 2 consisted of several fragments of foam rubber. No explosive residues were detected on examination. Item 3 consisted of seven fragments of twisted and torn aluminium and part of a clock cog wheel. All were damaged consistent with them having been closely associated with an explosion. No explosive residues were detected on examination.

2588/74 - This item consisted of a number of twisted and torn fragments of sheet steel, some painted metallic green on blue undercoat and several fragments of foam rubber. Examination of the sheet steel revealed no explosive residues. The only significant feature in the foam rubber was the presence of small quantities of nitrite.

2589/74 - This item consisted of a number of twisted and torn fragments of sheet steel painted metallic blue. Examination revealed the presence of a discrete area on which sodium, ammonium, nitrate, and nitrate ions, were detected and the presence of sugar strongly indicated but not confirmed. No other explosive residues were detected.

Few bombs use commercial explosive as their main charge. It is widely used, however, in relatively small amounts to prime or booster much larger charges of improvised explosives. It is in the area of improvised explosives that the main differences between the groups occur. The two main IRA improvised explosives are:

   a. A mixture of sodium chlorate and nitrobenzene

   b. A mixture of ammonium nitrate and fuel oil.

Regulations controlling sodium chlorate and nitrobenzene are apparently making these materials more and more difficult to obtain with the result that this mixture is being used as a main charge more infrequently and becoming used primarily as a booster. Regulations controlling ammonium nitrate fertilisers have had a similar effect in these instances and obviously large scale processes are being used for the recovery of ammonium nitrate from 'legal' fertilisers for use in ANFO explosives. Both these explosives are high explosives requiring no confinement for operation and are usually packed in small polythene bags, in 1 cwt fertiliser bags or in milk churns.

The main 'loyalist' improvised explosives are:

   a. A mixture of sodium chlorite and sugar

   b. A mixture of sodium chlorite, sodium nitrate and sugar

   c. A mixture of ammonium nitrate, sodium or potassium nitrate and sugar

   d. A mixture of ammonium nitrate and fuel oil.

The first two of these mixtures are normally used in small devices containing up to 15 or 20 lbs of explosive packed into a small gas cylinder, fire extinguisher or the like. Of the second two mixtures by far the most common is the mixture of ammonium nitrate, sodium nitrate and sugar which is usually packed into a beer barrel. This mixture, in common with the first two, is a low or devastating explosive requiring confinement in order to produce an explosion. They are often boostered with a small bundle of chopped up cordtex detonating fuse or a small charge of commercial explosive.

Most explosion residues of chlorates or chlorites will contain chlorides while nitrites will be present if nitrate is included in the original explosive.

The presence of nitrite in the foam rubber in case No. 2588/74 is strongly indicative of the use of a nitrate containing explosive in this explosion.

At the end of his report Dr Hall commented:

It has been my experience that identification of the explosive used to cause an explosion can be achieved in the majority of instances providing the correct samples are received for laboratory examination within 6 hours. The correct samples are fragments of the bomb container or closely associated articles, non-porous surfaces in direct line with the explosion or debris from an explosion crater. With larger devices it is often difficult if not impossible to recover fragments of the bomb casing and even the recovery of closely associated articles or non-porous surfaces in direct line with the explosion can require careful scene examination. It is for example of little value to examine fragments of the bonnet from a vehicle which has contained a device in the luggage compartment. With regard to the rapid analysis this is essential if the more volatile organic explosive components such as nitrobenzene and the nitrate esters are to be detected. While a low efficiency explosion may scatter sufficient unconsumed explosive to allow identification of nitrate esters on surrounding material for several days or longer a high efficiency leaves only the minimum amount of explosive and rapid analysis is essential. In the case of inorganic components speed is not so necessary, however, items should be analysed within a few days if success is to be assured. Interaction between residues and highly reactive bare metal surfaces can quickly reduce the value of analysis and physical contact can result in the loss of adhering residues. The results of the laboratory examination of the items from Detective Garda Jones must be viewed with these points in mind.

In Northern Ireland two distinct groups of terrorists have evolved each with their own distinct explosives and devices. Obviously in some instances the different development paths have led to similar end products but in general it is possible to identify the group responsible for an incident by identification of the explosives used or the method employed to cause the explosion.

The restrictions on the use of commercial explosives and the amount required to produce a significant explosion has resulted in comparatively few bombs using commercial explosives.

The presence of sodium, ammonium, nitrate, nitrite and possibly sugar in the one part of the surface of one of the fragments from case No. 2589/74 is indicative of an explosive containing those entities. Unfortunately the area of contamination was so restricted that a firm conclusion could not be reached since sodium is a relatively common ion and the sugar not confirmed.

The presence of the beer barrel fragments in case No. 2587/74 is perhaps the most significant feature of the whole examination even though no explosive residues were identified. They may not be so completely attributable as the explosive mixtures themselves but are similar to many recovered from 'Loyalist' car bombings.

Dr Hall did not find any explosive residue whatever on the samples from Talbot Street or Monaghan. On the Parnell Street samples he found 'small quantities of nitrate' in the 'foam rubber'. On the South Leinster Street samples he found 'the presence of sodium, ammonium, nitrate, and nitrate ions' and the 'presence of sugar strongly indicated but not confirmed'.

The handling of the technical side of the investigation by the management of the Technical Bureau - namely Chief Superintendent Tony McMahon and his deputy Dan Murphy - was nothing short of a disaster. What appears to have happened is that according as the fragments of material from the bomb scenes were sifted from the debris they were sent to Dr Donovan for analysis. However, after the Bureau received Donovan's first report a decision was then (apparently) taken to switch back to Dr Hall in Belfast and send nothing further to Donovan. We can only assume that the Bureau was unhappy with Donovan's analysis but Donovan was never informed of this, if it was.

In his first report Dr Donovan says he found three separate traces of sodium nitrate on the samples. He also found two separate traces of nitroglycerine. Nitrate is a substance formed from nitric acid and is often used as a fertilizer for agricultural purposes. Nitroglycerine is a constituent of gelignite. Over the last thirty years fertilizer has been used by all the paramilitaries in making what is known as 'home-made bombs'. These are distinct from gelignite bombs which, as the name suggests, are bombs constructed from sticks of gelignite. However, in the later years of the Troubles, apart altogether from semtex, many bombs were made from both fertilizer and gelignite.

It has long been accepted by the Gardai that the Dublin and Monaghan bombs were constructed from both home-made explosives and gelignite, with the gelignite being used in large quantities as a powerful booster to inflict the maximum damage possible. By stating that the samples contained nitrate, nitroglycerine, sodium carbonate and ammonium, Dr Donovan by and large established just that. Therefore, it has to be said that his laboratory tests were excellent. However, by omitting to mention the possibility of home-made explosives being used - 'the results suggest the use of gelignite/dynamite' - Dr Donovan appears to have upset the Gardai and, according to a source close to the technical bureau at the time, caused a split within the Technical Bureau which led to a 'fierce row' (almost akin to a power-struggle) which lasted for several days, between opposing personalities within the Technical Bureau, with Chief Superintendent Tony McMahon at the centre of the row, over where the samples should be sent.

But the decision to send the material to Belfast cost them dearly. By the time the samples were sent to Dr Hall eleven days after the bombings, the explosive residues were practically dead and the technical investigation in a shambles.

In his report Dr Hall says: 'It has been my experience that identification of the explosive used to cause an explosion can be achieved in the majority of instances providing the correct samples are received for laboratory examination within 6 hours.' The distance from South Leinster Street to the State Laboratory in Merrion Street is 400 yards, or five minutes walking distance. Yet Dr Donovan did not receive his first samples until three days after the bombings.

By the time the 1974 bombings occurred there had already been over a dozen bombings in the Republic, over the previous two years, all of them related to Northern Ireland. At least five of these had occurred in Dublin, the rest along the border. In each case the bomb scene had been examined by the army EOD and Technical Bureau personnel. It was not as if the Gardai were dealing with a new phenomenon that had not been encountered before when the 1974 bombs exploded. Yet for twenty-five years the sheer ineptitude and downright arrogance of the management of the Technical Bureau during the 1974 bombings investigation has been covered up and hidden from the public gaze - not to mention the victims' relatives. The delay in sending the samples firstly to Dr Donovan and latterly to Dr Hall are inexcusable, and responsibility for such a shambles lay fairly and squarely on the shoulders of the head of the Technical Bureau, Chief Superintendent Tony McMahon and his deputy Superintendent

Dan Murphy, who ran the Bureau. The six detectives who investigated the bomb scenes and collected the bomb fragments bore no responsibility whatever, as they were not consulted about such decisions.

Much has been made in recent times of the 'political insensitivity' of the decision to send the bomb samples to Belfast for analysis, where the bombs had just come from. Whilst the integrity, independence and professionalism of Dr. Hall who after all was an eminent forensic scientist and not a member of the security forces, cannot be called into question, the decision was not only insensitive, but downright stupid and is further evidence of bungling and blundering on the part of the Garda management in charge of the Technical Bureau. The bombs had just come from Belfast. In 1972/73 (as I have just mentioned) bombs had also exploded in Dublin city centre (see chapter 7) which had come from Belfast and the Gardai had suspicions of security forces' involvement. Northern Ireland was the last place on earth the bomb samples should have been sent to. The decision was a bare-faced insult to the relatives of those killed and to those who were injured.

Whether or not the outcome of the investigation would have been any different, had the samples been analysed in time, we will never know. But there is little doubt that the Gardai would have been able to find out much more about the bombings at an earlier stage. A clearer picture of how much material was used in each bomb - the Gardai could only ever stagger a guess that 150 pounds was used in Parnell Street, 100 pounds in Talbot Street, and 50 pounds in South Leinster Street - could have been established, as well as the background to the bombings. Exactly which loyalist group was behind the outrage; where and how the material was procured and stored, could have been established much earlier.

In 1979 Chief Superintendent Tony McMahon retired from the Gardai. In a blasé, but somewhat hubristic, interview with *The Irish Times* he talked about the bombings. 'I was sitting right here at my desk that evening when I heard a thump *in town*. I telephoned all the specialist sections here, like the photographers and the ballistics people, to be on stand-by so that when the call came through with details from Garda Communications in Dublin Castle we were ready for it… what the hell hope have you with all the technical and forensic evidence blown away. If a car was used which might normally have finger-prints, what will you be left with only a heap of rubble blown to atoms.' Concluding his little monody in which he appeared to feel sorry for himself, McMahon says: 'The file on the mass murder of that night five years ago is still open.'

Twenty-three years later McMahon is dead, and the murders are still unsolved. Whether or not the file is still open we are not quite sure. McMahon was the personification of an arrogant policeman who cared little about human suffering but who cared everything about his own reputation. In an interview with my colleague Glen Middleton of Yorkshire Television shortly before his death in the mid-1990s he talked about 'this thing', the Dublin bombings. In a separate interview that I conducted with him myself around the same time, he attempted to dissuade me from investigating the attacks. 'Why do you wish to start digging up old stuff from the past causing trouble. Isn't it better to let sleeping dogs lie?' he implored, fearing the unmasking of his own disgraceful role in the investigation. The fact that thirty-three families were still mourning their dead and awaiting news of the investigation from the man who was 'sitting in his office when he heard the thump' and who got his men 'ready for it' was of no import. The only thing that mattered was Tony McMahon's reputation.

On Saturday morning, the day after the bombings, the Gardai held their first news conference in Dublin Castle. The conference was attended by Chief Superintendents John Joy, Tony McMahon, John Sheehan and Eamonn Doherty. Joy, who was head of the Serious Crime Squad and who did most of the talking, said he believed the people who carried out the bombings were still in the Republic. All hotels and guesthouses were being 'checked out', road blocks had been erected around the city and all traffic was being monitored. Cooperation with the RUC was 'excellent' but he was less than happy with the inability of the owners of the 'stolen cars' to give a clear description of the hijackers. As I shall point out later in the book the majority of the Dublin bombing team left the Republic and returned north before the bombs ever exploded. The remainder returned that night before 8 p.m. Mr Joy's information was somewhat off the mark. And whilst the Gardai could be forgiven for announcing such a non-sequitur at such an early stage in what was, after all, an unprecedented investigation, the announcement sparked a torrent of speculation throughout the country that the bombers were hiding out in Dublin. The *Evening Press*, in a front page banner headline later that afternoon, speculated that the 'BOMBERS COULD STILL BE HERE'. And in a follow-up story it mused about how the bombers succeeded in parking their 'death cars' and escaping through a crowded city.

> The car bombers who caused such death and devastation in Dublin yesterday may still be in the city. This, the Gardai said today, is a clear possibility but no matter whether they are or not many hundreds of people must have seen them yesterday they said. A number of people interviewed by Gardai last night after the blasts have been released. Interviews were still going on today but a garda spokesman pointed out that these were routine procedures to eliminate suspects. However, at a news conference in Dublin Castle today, garda chiefs said that a prime suspect is being sought in the nationwide hunt for the bombers. The man was seen acting suspiciously by a civilian witness in the area of the South Leinster Street car bomb blast about 10 to 15 minutes before it devastated the area. No matter what method they had of getting away, they say, they needed alternative transport and it could be that they made their way out of the city to some surrounding area where they would lie low during the massive search and road-block system set up by Gardai. All the possibilities were being discussed today by top gardai personnel in Dublin Castle. Several points emerged:

The bombers could not have chosen their spots to park, considering the density of traffic and parking problems. Their main object was to park in the city centre area, and prime the bombs to go off at 5.30 p.m., the rush hour, in the centre city area. They must have driven around for some time looking for parking spaces. Therefore, the cars, two hijacked and one stolen in Belfast, must have been seen by thousands of people as they toured around looking for parking spaces. When they did get parking space they must have walked away through the crowded streets so that many more would have seen them. The gardai would be interested in getting information from anyone who saw the cars touring, or parking, or saw the men leaving the cars. The gardai believe the men were faced with several alternatives: They either had other transport somewhere else in the city for their getaway, or they simply walked. Again, say the gardai, somebody may have seen something suspicious in men getting into other cars. They had no more than an hour to get away from the death cars, and, it is believed, only minutes to spare in the case of South Leinster Street. They could have walked to Connolly Station, Amiens Street, to catch the 5.30 p.m. Enterprise to Belfast, but the gardai searched the train at Dundalk found nothing or no one suspicious. Another alternative is that they could have taken cars to Dublin Airport. This, too, was checked out. Nothing suspicious was found. They could have taken cars to a destination outside the city to lie low. Another theory, which the gardai say is a clear possibility, was simply to walk and stay somewhere in the city. So the possibility of them still being in the city is one of the theories being investigated by the largest force of gardai ever to take part in a murder hunt. Two people at least hold vital clues to the identity of the men behind yesterday's bombings in Dublin. They are the drivers of the cars which were hijacked in Belfast. The owner of the Hillman Avenger was first held up by three armed men. Two drove off with his car while the third held the owner hostage in a house, for six hours from 10 o'clock yesterday morning. Top detectives have interviewed the owner of this car. Police are keeping the name of the motorist a close secret and a high police official in Belfast today was not prepared to say if the gunman who held the motorist as hostage wore a mask or not. Certainly police have a description of sorts and this undoubtedly has been passed on to the gardai, with whom they are working in the closest co-operation. The owner of the Hillman Avenger had been stopped and his car taken at Torrens Road in the mainly Protestant Oldpark area. The second, crucial witness could well be the driver of the Austin car used to transport another of the bombs. This car was hijacked at 8 o'clock yesterday morning in Richmond Street, deep in the heart of the Protestant Shankill, but, in this case, the owner was not held hostage but allowed to go and apparently was content to get away with his life. He, too, has been closely questioned but again police decline to say whether he was able to identify positively one or other of the hijackers.

Continuing the press conference Chief Superintendent Joy said the Gardai were making enquiries about a man with an English accent who had spoken to a woman in the city centre shortly before the bombings. Miss Nora O'Mahony from Roscarberry in County Cork was on a shopping trip to Dublin when she asked a man for directions in Westmoreland Street. The man, aged between forty and forty-five, she believed, was the driver of the car that exploded in Parnell Street. He was clean-shaven, about 5 foot 10 inches in height and spoke with a 'clear English accent'. After speaking to her the man got into a frosted green Northern registered car with a mustard coloured number plate bearing the letters 'DIA'. The registration of the green car which exploded in Parnell Street was DIA 4063.

The mystery of the suspicious man whom Ms O'Mahony spoke to has never been cleared up. However, as I shall point out later, the man who drove the Parnell Street car was not English, but very much Northern Irish and he did not speak with an English accent. Nevertheless, it cannot be ruled out that Ms O'Mahony mistook his strong northern brogue for that of an English one. Whether or not he would have driven via Westmoreland Street to plant a bomb in Parnell Street, we shall never know.

Chief Superintendent Eamonn Doherty, who was the operational officer in charge of the South Central Division, then addressed the conference. He said the Gardai were 'quite happy' with the rescue operation following Friday's bombs and the way in which the 'Red Alert System' (Major Disaster Plan) had worked. The difficulties of the situation had been compounded on Friday because of the very heavy traffic resulting from the city bus dispute. Parking restrictions had been relaxed by the police to facilitate the public. In those circumstances, he doubted if any alert system could have worked more efficiently. Asked to comment on criticism that there had been undue delay, and some uncertainty, in the handling of the situation, he said he was satisfied that there had been no undue delay in mounting the rescue operation. He did not think that any alterations were necessary, to make the Red Alert System more effective, following Friday's explosions.

As the Garda investigation began to gather pace, criticism of the RUC for failing to alert the Gardai about the stolen cars earlier on Friday began to appear in the press. Stung by the criticism, the RUC, in a lengthy statement issued on Monday, May 20, attempted to defend its actions. The statement said:

If the gardai in Dublin were to make inquiries about every car reported stolen or hijacked in the North, the average man on the beat would need a suitcase to contain his lists of information. Cooperation between the two forces on the Dublin bombings was being organised at the highest level, but the prevention of bombings through an exchange of routine information could not be expected very often to succeed. Details of every vehicle stolen were conveyed by the RUC station in the area to police control in Belfast and from there to all other stations and to the gardai headquarters in Dublin Castle. Scores of vehicles were taken every day, however, and the gardai could not have been expected to anticipate that any one would subsequently be used in an explosion in Dublin. There was no precedent for what had taken place on Friday and to check out every report thoroughly would prove an impossible task. The gardai and ourselves have the same problems and we both have to deal with them in the same way. As with all crimes, the gardai in this case are assured of our fullest cooperation.

CHAPTER 3

OPERATION CROSS-BORDER

On Friday morning, 17 May, 48-year-old William Henry left his home at 5 Queensland Street in west Belfast to go to work at Ariel Taxis in Agnes Street off the Shankill Road. Henry arrived at the office before the designated opening time of 9 a.m. and parked his four-week-old lagoon-blue Austin Maxi 1800 taxi outside. Within minutes a man arrived and asked Henry to drive him to Sandy Row (a hardline Protestant ghetto near the city centre two miles away) to collect his wages. Henry agreed, locked the office and both men proceeded downstairs towards the street outside. As they approached Henry's taxi they were joined by a second man and all three climbed into the Austin Maxi with Henry at the wheel. As they drove down Agnes Street towards the Shankill Road one of the men asked Henry to pull into a side street to collect two more passengers. As Henry pulled up two men approached him from the footpath, dragged him from the driver's seat and bundled him into the back, where three men held him on the floor with their feet on his back. He was then driven to a city centre warehouse where he was held at gunpoint for almost five hours before being released. At 5.30 p.m. that afternoon Henry's car exploded in South Leinster Street killing five people and injuring over fifty others. When Henry was interviewed at Tennant Street RUC station in west Belfast late that afternoon, following his release, this is how he described his ordeal.

> At about 9am on Friday May 17 1974 I was at Ariel Taxis Agnes Street when one man came in and asked me to take him to Sandy Row. I said that I would. When I went outside to my taxi we were joined by another man. The man who came in to order the taxi was aged about 30 years and he was wearing a black jacket. He was about five foot four and I didn't really pay much attention to him. I got into the taxi and the one who

ordered the taxi sat beside me in the front and the other man that joined us got into the back. When I got started I asked the man beside me if he wanted to go down Northumberland Street but he told me to go to the city centre. Going down Agnes Street they asked me to pull into Woburn Street as he had others to pick up. Immediately when I stopped two men came around to my door, pulled me out and threw me into the back. The three passengers in the back sat with their feet in my back and made me lie on the floor to keep quiet. The car was driven around for three or four minutes then it stopped and a hood was put over my head and I was taken out, brought into a building that seemed to be off a gate way. I was put into a room and my hands were tied behind my back and I was told not to worry that nothing would happen to me. They only needed the car. I remained in this place till nearly two o'clock and then I was taken in a car and I was released at Boyd Street Peter's Hill. I got out of an 1100 car and one man drove it away and another followed me up Shankill Road, as I had been told not to go near my taxi firm and to go straight home till three o'clock and I was then to go to Tennant Street police station. After three o'clock I came to the police station and reported the matter. My taxi was a lagoon blue 1800 Reg. No. HOI 2487.

Before exploding in Dublin, Henry's car was spotted at least five times by members of the public after it crossed the border into the Republic on its way to South Leinster Street. It entered the South via an unapproved road near Forkhill, Co. Armagh, and was driven along remote country roads through Counties Louth, Meath and north County Dublin and entered the city via Dublin airport. This was the route travelled by smugglers ferrying goods back and forth across the border for five decades to avoid paying customs duties. Henry's car was first noticed after it crossed the Boyne river near Drogheda, Co. Louth, thirty miles north of Dublin. James Crocock, a local land steward from Drogheda, was jotting the numbers of strange cars crossing the Boyne into a notebook in an effort to catch salmon poachers. While driving his car in the townland of Sheephouse, a mile south of the Boyne, at 11.45 a.m., Crocock met the bomb-car. The following is an extract of an interview he gave to investigating Gardai after the bombings.

> As I was passing an Electricity Supply Board van I noticed another car coming towards me from the Sheephouse direction. I slowed down and pulled in close to my left hand side as far as possible. I was travelling at 10-15 mph. The car coming towards me was travelling at a heck of a speed. It didn't slow down. It was a peculiar shade of blue - an Austin 1100, I think. I took the reg. Number as HOI 2487 from the front number plate. I can't remember the colour of the plate. The driver, a man, was the only one in the car. He was about 35 to 40, with dark hair, sleeked back and slightly sticking out at the temples. He had a normal type of hair cut. He had a sallow complexion, stern appearance, sharp features. I can't remember anything else about him. I can't remember anything about his dress. I travelled towards Sheephouse...

When William Henry was bundled into the Belfast warehouse earlier that morning there were four men with him; when he was released there were two. When Crocock met Henry's car it contained only the driver.

Henry's car was observed by a second eye-witness in Drumcondra, a north Dublin suburb, at 1.04 p.m., seventy nine minutes after the Crocock sighting. Gerald O'Reilly from Walkinstown on Dublin's southside was leaving his place of work at Dargle Road, Drumcondra, on his lunch-break and driving northwards towards Whitehall, when he spotted the car with three men in it being driven northwards away from the city centre. This is what O'Reilly told Gardai.

> I closed my premises at 1 o'clock for lunch. I got into my car. I drove the car across Dargle Road into Carlingford

Road, and then into Hollybank Road. I turned right at Hollybank Road and drove in the direction of Drumcondra Road. It was approximately 1.04pm. Traffic was pretty heavy. Just as I got to the junction there was a motor car coming from the city direction, going towards Whitehall. I had to stop my car as I couldn't get out. The lane of traffic coming from the city was also stopped. Once I stopped I noticed a motor car on my right, an Austin 1800, dark green or blue. When the traffic began to move, I looked at the driver, thinking he would let me out but he didn't. I pulled out and got in behind him. I passed the remark to my friend, Mr. Jowthy, that this driver could have let me out. While travelling behind the car, which was from the junction of Hollybank Road to Botanic Avenue, into which street he turned, I made a mental note of the number. I did not record it as there was no apparent reason. The reason why I took particular note of this car is that the last car I had was an Austin 1800, and I take particular stock of any 1800 cars I see. The car was very dirty and had no wing mirrors. I particularly look for these. There was nothing unusual about the car. There were three men in the car....two in the front and one in the back seat. I had a good look at the two in front but only a rear view of the man in the back. The window on the passenger side was open and the passenger had his arm resting on the window. He was aged 23-24 with black hair, not worn long. He was clean shaven, had long features, very thin about 5ft 10ins or 11ins, I'd say based on the fact that I drove 1800's for three and a half years. The number plate was HOI 2487... That night I was in my home when a news flash came on the television in relation to the bombing.

When O'Reilly saw the Austin Maxi it was on its way to collect its deadly cargo at a carpark in Whitehall on the northside of the city (see next chapter). However, shortly after he 'got in behind' it, it turned left into a side road - Botanic

Avenue - off the main Whitehall Road and appeared to head towards the Glasnevin/Ballymun area of the city. An explanation for this diversion I contend may be found in one of two possible scenarios: either the driver, unfamiliar with Dublin city, took a wrong turning, or the occupants, aware they had been noticed by the men in the car now behind them, decided to get off side as quickly as possible for fear of being identified at a later date.

The next time the Austin was sighted was when it was being parked in South Leinster Street shortly before it exploded. Charles Chain O'Doherty was driving a coachload of students on holiday to Dublin from Northern Ireland when he saw a man parking the car minutes before it exploded. He gave the following details to Gardai.

> At 5pm I came down Kildare Street with passengers and turned right into Leinster Street. I double parked on the right hand side facing Westland Row. The passengers got out and went into the hotel. I sat in the bus waiting for a parking space. I saw a car, green and fairly large, drive in on the left hand side, looking for a parking space. He drove into the space which was vacant. I'd been watching that space in case another car would pull out and I could pull in and park across two bays. The space was about 50 yards up on the left hand side. I saw the car parking and I saw a man sitting in it for one minute. I saw him get out of the car, close the door. He looked up the street and down the street. He crossed to my side of the street, walked past the bus towards Grafton Street. I remained sitting in the bus for about ten minutes. Suddenly I saw a large ball of fire and an explosion. The windscreen of the bus was blown in and the bus was lifted up in the air. I got out of the bus with some difficulty and saw a woman who was a ball of fire. I extinguished the fire on her body and hair. I got assistance and we took her into some premises. I also saw two dead men in the street. I did see a cameraman come on the scene very quickly with a small camera. I

have no doubt that the car that parked in the space I was watching went up in the explosion. The man that parked the car that I saw walking away from it I could describe as follows: about 24 years, looked like an office man, blue short coat and dark trousers, possibly brown. Clean shaven, neat hair, long thin face, no glasses. He was between pale and tan, had black hair not long or short. Had a respectable appearance. My observation is that the man who left the car in Leinster Street looked very suspicious. The man who parked the car didn't lock the car. I'm not sure if I'd know him if I saw him again. I am suspicious of the cameraman, I saw him take a keen look at me. I've seen several explosions in Derry and seen two policemen blown up. I was present at Bloody Sunday and the march. Shortly after pulling into Leinster Street I saw people pulling luggage out of a car which parked near the car which exploded. Two people were talking to two people in the car. I saw the car pull away and the two people who talked to the people in the car walked away chatting and looked quite innocent. I could see no connection between these people and the car which parked, which I later knew contained a bomb.

Macdara Freyne worked as an estate manager in Dublin. He noticed the bombcar parked in Leinster Street a short time before it exploded, as he parked directly in front of it. This is what he told Gardai:

On Friday 17th May I finished work at 5.15 p.m. and walked to a building site in Nassau Street and collected my car, a red Austin Sprite. I drove to Nassau Street and on to Leinster Street where I saw a vacant parking space nearly opposite Chubbs [alarms]. I parked the car there. I didn't put a shilling in the meter as there were 35 minutes on the clock. I saw a white-coloured car in front of me - I don't know what make or registration. There was an Austin 1800 parked behind - it was a metallic blue. I don't know the registration number of this car. There was normal pedestrian and motor traffic at the time. There was no person in the green [sic] Austin. I heard the explosion in Molesworth Street and went back to Leinster Street and saw a scene of confusion. My car was in flames and the Austin behind was almost disintegrated apart from the engine.

If O'Doherty and Freyne are correct, the Leinster Street car bomb was driven into position sometime after 5.00 p.m. - probably around 5.10p.m. Another witness who saw it after it was parked was Norman Whelan, who worked as an insurance broker a short distance away. He told Gardai of seeing the car parked unoccupied at 5.15 p.m.

On 17/5/'74 I left my car down to Crooke's Tyre garage, Fenian Street to have the wheels balanced. At 5.15pm I went back to the garage for my car. As I emerged out of my place of employment my attention was drawn to a Morris 1800 car parked slightly to my left on the other side of South Leinster Street. The reg. Was HOI - I can't remember the numbers, but 2 was in the registration. The colour was metallic green. It was parked facing Clare Street. As far as I can recall there was an Austin Healy red Sprite in front of it parked. I can't recall what was behind. There was no one in the 1800. I noticed it because the colour was the same as I would prefer to have had on my own car, but was unable to have it. I would say with reasonable certainty the Austin 1800 was not parked there at 4.55pm, when I previously left the office building. At no time did I see anyone near the metallic green car.

William Henry died in bed of a massive heart attack in 1989 aged sixty-six following fifteen years of serious ill health. He never returned to work after his ordeal and spent years attending psychiatrists and taking tablets. During the months following his kidnap he was unable to sleep and spent nights

'walking the floor'. His widow says he was devastated when he discovered his car had been used in the explosions. 'He spent the evening of May 17 glued to the television as he was expecting bad news. When news of the bombings came through he was devastated. He always blamed himself as he felt if he hadn't his car there it wouldn't have happened. He never got over it and he never worked again'.

Today there is still confusion over the hijacking of Henry's car as well as Henry's contacts with police at Tennant Street Station, the station responsible for policing the Shankill area following his release by his kidnappers. RUC records show Henry reported the incident at 2.30 p.m. on the afternoon of 17 May. In his report Henry is alleged to have said he was released by his abductors shortly after 2.00 p.m. and told to go straight home and not to report the incident until 3.00 p.m. Henry's widow now disputes this version and says events ran much later than that. She telephoned the taxi office where William worked shortly after 1.00 p.m. when he didn't show up for lunch and was told by his work colleagues that he had failed to report for work that morning and that the office was locked when they arrived. It was a number of hours later, 'nearer to tea-time', before William returned home and related what happened. It was then he went to the police station.

Following the bombings and the appalling loss of life, police at Tennant Street subsequently visited Henry a number of times and took him to the station for further interviews. He was shown a number of photographs of loyalist suspects from the Shankill area but was unable to identify any of his abductors. As no member of the gang was masked, police expected Henry (as a taxi-man out and about on the Shankill) to identify at least some of the four men. The full truth of what happened between Henry and his abductors may never be known. His new four-week-old car was ideally suited to the bombers' requirements. Were they aware of this in advance and if so by what means? It was also considered unusual, in an area like the Shankill Road where most terrorists were well known to the police and their photographs kept on file, for four men to present themselves to William Henry unmasked. At least one of them spoke to him at some length and sat beside him in the front passenger seat issuing instructions. One theory is that the kidnappers threatened Henry at gunpoint never to identify them, even from police photographs. Failure to comply would result in severe retribution against him or his family. Another theory put forward (based on the fact that he was suitably available with his new car before his colleagues arrived for work) was that Henry agreed beforehand under duress to loan his car to the kidnappers but had no idea it would be used in a bombing. One way or another there is little doubt that the gang had earmarked Henry's car well in advance and that they had some prior arrangement with him. What if Henry had failed to show up for work that morning? - the entire bombing plan would have been thrown into disarray.

As William Henry and his captors were settling into their warehouse near Belfast city center, victim number two, William Scott, was about to begin a similar ordeal a number of miles away in the Oldpark area in the north of the city. Scott, aged sixty-two, was a night security man with the security company Securicor. He was held at gunpoint while his car was stolen and driven to Dublin, where it exploded in Parnell Street, killing twelve people and injuring almost 150 others. At 5.00 p.m. that afternoon, following his release, Scott gave the following account of his experience to the RUC.

> I'm a security man employed by the Ministry of Finance, Public Records Office, 66 Balmoral Avenue. I live alone at that address, 27 Torrens Road. At about 8.30am on the 17 of the fifth, I returned home from work. At 10.00am I was upstairs changing my clothes and the front door was open. I heard a step on the stairs and two men came into my bedroom. They were both wearing some sort of mask. The big fella came in and pushed me on the bed. He had a pistol in his right hand and he said we are taking the car. He said we want no trouble we are taking your car. He was tall, he was thin, he was about 5ft 10ins or 11ins. I think he was wearing a grey coat and a green jersey. He seemed to have a

sallow complexion. The other fella was stoutish, about 5ft 7ins. He seemed to be in his 20's as well as the first. He was carrying a pistol as well. A third one came up. He was about the same size as the second one. I don't know how he was dressed and he didn't have a gun. The tall one took the keys to my car and went off. He said I would get my car back in two hours, but they kept me in there all day until 4 o'clock. They made me stay upstairs while they played cards downstairs. At 4 o'clock they said they were going and he told me not to come out for half an hour or I'd be shot. I came out at 4.20pm and informed the police. They said I'd get my car back either in Buller St. [is there such a place?] or Bottle St. My car was a 1970 Hillman Avenger DIA 4063, metallic green colour. I got her filled up with petrol yesterday. I was not injured by any of these men. Two at least of them were wearing black gloves, but they had them off when they were playing cards.

Like Henry's car, Scott's Avenger was seen a number of times by eye-witnesses throughout the day before it exploded in Parnell Street. James Crocock, who had seen Henry's car, also saw Scott's Avenger in the same area, establishing that both cars had travelled the same route (the smuggler's route) across the border. This time the sighting was at 1.00 p.m., an hour and a quarter after the first sighting, and in keeping with the time Scott's car was stolen in Belfast, which was approximately an hour after Henry's. This is how Crocock described the second car:

I was travelling slow as the road is narrow. I'd just come round the right hand bend. I saw a green Hillman immediately behind a van towing a car. The front number plate of the Hillman was DIA 4063. There were two male occupants in the car and the driver was anxious to pass. The driver was 38-40, stout, full face, his hair was darkish fair and combed to the right. It was an ordinary hair style. He was clean shaven, full face, outdoor complexion. His nose was slightly turned up at the end. I had a full view of this man. I think I would know the driver again if I saw him. He was wearing a light grey suit. He had a crouched appearance behind the steering wheel. The passenger was sitting alongside the driver. Male 25-30, dark hair, high on forehead, seemed to be a quiff-style in front. He had a pale complexion, very sharp features. He wore a darkish suit and darkish overcoat and a collar and tie. The incident took place when I was almost stopped in the roadway. The Hillman was a beautiful apple green. There appeared to be clothes strewn over the back seat of the car. I'm not sure if it was two or four door. I saw the rear no. plate, mustard colour, DIA 4063. I'm satisfied of this.

As Crocock had already observed the first car speeding through Sheephouse, he was obviously much sharper and more on the alert (in his hunt for poachers) by the time he met the second one. As the suspect car was 'directly behind a van towing a car' on a very narrow by-road when Crocock met it ('the incident took place when I was almost stopped in the roadway'), he was obviously in a good position to acquire mental detail of the car and its two occupants. However, it is highly unlikely he could acquire such detail of both occupants plus the car from a passing glance. Within minutes of Crocock seeing the Avenger, his 32-year-old cousin, Brian Crocock, a gardener who also lived locally, noticed the car travelling ahead of him as he rounded a bend near the Boyne River. This is what he told Gardai:

Two or three minutes past 1.00pm on Friday 17 I left my place of employment and went to Sheephouse for dinner, driving my own car. As I drove up a straight path after negotiating the junction at the canal, I saw a shiny green car ahead of me up the road travelling towards Sheephouse. Ahead was a big van towing a car travelling in the same direction The car immediately ahead of me was a distinct green, mustard plate with black lettering on the rear. I was satisfied it was a Northern Ireland registration plate, but I didn't take a note of the reg. plate or numbers.

If William Scott and the Crococks are correct, the Hillman Avenger made little delay on its journey between Belfast and Sheephouse. According to Scott, the bombers left his house shortly after 10 a.m. Under three hours later the car was being driven through north County Louth, seventy miles away, the driver having negotiated his way through Belfast city (paralysed by a workers' strike) and an intricate network of backroads on both sides of the border.

The Avenger was next observed being driven at high speed through Glasnevin - a north Dublin suburb three miles west of the Whitehall carpark, towards the city centre. The time was 3 p.m. and the Avenger was travelling at '55 to 60 mph'. Peter Flanagan of Ratoath, Co. Meath, was driving towards the city centre when he saw the car. These are the brief details of the sighting which he related to Gardai.

> At about 3pm Friday 17/5/'74 I was driving a Landrover from Finglas to Dublin. As I was going past Glasnevin cemetery (I was travelling at 30mph and it was raining) I noticed a Hillman Avenger passing me and also going to Dublin - passing me at about 55/60mph. At the time of his overtaking, I'd indicated to my right, passing either roadworks or parked cars and I said to myself the driver of the Avenger must be in a hurry. I can give no details of the driver or if there were any passengers. The Avenger was metallic blue - I'm sure of the colour. The no. plate was Northern Ireland and I remember the letters DIA.

Flanagan's account of the sighting is scant. However, experienced detectives within the Garda murder squad considered it relevant enough to include in the investigation file.

The next sighting of the Avenger was in Dublin city centre a short time before it exploded and close to its designated target - the Welcome Inn pub on the corner of Parnell Street and Marlborough Street. Parnell Street runs perpendicular to the northern end of O'Connell Street and is one of the busiest shopping thoroughfares in Dublin city centre. Again the driver (who by now was the only person in the vehicle - the passenger having disembarked somewhere between Sheephouse and the city centre) was unfamiliar with Dublin and was having difficulty negotiating his way through the city streets. He was driving the wrong way up a one-way street and apparently believed he was already in Parnell Street. This time the witness was a shop assistant, Eileen Kavanagh, who worked in Tyler's shoe shop in Cathedral Street, a tiny side street off O'Connell Street but which runs close to and parallel to Parnell Street. This is what she told Gardai:

> At 5pm on 17/5/'74 I was in Tyler's shop. I saw a green car go up Cathedral Street the wrong way. He drove up fast as far as Thomas Lane, then reversed quickly and drove back down Cathedral Street the right way. He turned left into Marlborough Street and went towards Parnell Street. The green car is like the car the detectives drive. I went out to the door when I saw him driving up and I saw the driver of the car. He tried to drive up Thomas Lane but he could not get up because it was blocked with cars at the back of the Gresham hotel I expect. There was a bus strike and cars could park anywhere. Then he reversed back. He seemed to be tall sitting in the car. He had sleek combed-back, fairish hair (blonde) short cut, very neat. He was sitting in the car and I only saw his profile because he was sideways on. He seemed to be very nervous. I'm sure it was around 5 o'clock as I was checking the post. I have a photograph of the driver in my mind. It didn't take three minutes. I didn't see the number plates so I don't know if it was Northern Ireland or not. There was one person in the car, that's all. When I saw it I said to the fellow next to

me what I'd seen. I'll never forget that day. We went out and we didn't know what to do.

Following the explosion detectives visited Eileen Kavanagh a second time with a piece of the green Hillman Avenger to establish if the vehicle she saw was the bomb-car. This is the brief statement she made to Gardai the second time around.

I now see a piece of metal produced - dark green. This was the colour I saw on the car driving up Cathedral Street fast and turn down Marlborough Street on Friday 17 May. I didn't see the way he turned when he got to Marlborough Street.

Eileen Kavanagh's second statement differs from her first in that this time she can't remember which way the driver turned when he got to Marlborough Street. She is also unfamiliar with car models and describes the car as 'like the car the detectives drive'. Her observation is nevertheless sharp as the unmarked cars mostly used by the Garda detective branch throughout the 1970s and 1980s was the Hillman Avenger, usually black or blue in colour. Ms Kavanagh was also strategically positioned to observe the car as it 'drove back down Cathedral Street' as she had gone 'to the door' when she first saw it.

As the Avenger entered Parnell Street in search of a parking bay outside the Welcome Inn pub, it was seen by a number of eye-witnesses, some with vague recollections of seeing it double-parked as it waited for a bay. Others remembered it parked where it later exploded, and gave a clear description of the driver to the Gardai. Mortimer O'Loughlin from Templeogue on Dublin's southside was in Parnell Street shopping with his wife. Following a visit to his tailor he returned to his car and noticed a vehicle double parked, which he believes moved into his parking bay. He gave the following vague details to Gardai.

At 5pm on Friday evening I parked my car outside the Welcome Inn. I parked outside the Lounge door -

immediately outside. My wife remained in the car while I went to Saville Row Tailors at 150 Parnell Street. While I was in the shop I saw the car and I looked over towards the car a few times [his own car]. I didn't notice anything. At 5.10pm I returned to my car and sat there for one or two minutes. Just before I pulled out of my parking space I became aware of a car double parked just in front of me. He (the Avenger Driver) was looking for a space to park. I can't recall the make, possibly an Opel Rekord or similar. I pulled out and I assumed he took up my space. The driver of the car, who was alone, was in his mid 40's, a broad-shouldered fellow.

Mortimer O'Loughlin is unable to identify the make of the car but his description of the driver, double parked, waiting for a space, tallies with other eye witness accounts, notably that of his wife, Teresa, who waited in the car while he went shopping. This is her account.

At 5pm on 17th May '74 I was with my husband when we parked our car, a grey Anglia, outside the Welcome Inn, in Parnell Street. We drove from Summerhill and parked the car in the second parking bay on the left, after passing Marlborough Street directly outside the Welcome Inn. When we parked the car my husband left and I remained in it. A few seconds later a nun pulled in, in a car in front of us - that is on the Parnell monument side of us, and parked. This car was a dark blue mini and the driver was the only person in it. She left and crossed the street and had not returned when we left about ten minutes later, when my husband returned. About a minute before we left, at 5.12pm, a dark green car stopped directly alongside the nun's car in front of us. The driver, a man aged between 45-50 years, was the only person in the car. He was not wearing a head-dress and he had greying hair. I did not notice how he was dressed. As far as I can recall there was a vehicle parking space behind our car, but this man did not appear to want to use it. As we pulled away this car reversed into the space that we were leaving. It did not move until my husband had reversed our car into the parking space behind us, and then it reversed very fast into the space we had left. We then drove on into O'Connell Street, stopped at Easons [city centre book shop] for a few minutes and then drove along D'Olier Street, College Street, Grafton Street, Nassau Street, South Leinster Street and on to the canal. I did not hear or see anything unusual for the remainder of our route through the above mentioned streets. There was a green coloured Rover parked on O'Connell Bridge with the bonnet raised. The car that pulled into our parking space at the Welcome Inn had a high back like in the Opel models, but I do not know what make it was. It was a fairly large car. I did not notice the registration number. I do not think I would recognise the driver again, but he appeared to be fairly stout. The only other car I can recall in Parnell Street was a blue Opel parked for some time behind where we were. It only stayed for a few minutes… I'm sure of the time we left Parnell Street as my husband and I checked our watches and it was 5.12pm. We wanted to get to Easons before half five. The traffic was very heavy.

Gardai visited Teresa O'Loughlin on two further occasions in early June with two separate albums of photographs of loyalist suspects from Northern Ireland supplied by the RUC in an effort to establish the identity of the Parnell Street bomber. In mid-June she made a second statement to Gardai:

Further to the statement on 25th May '74 in relation to the bomb which exploded in Parnell Street on 17th May, I now wish to say that on 3rd June 1974 two Gardai called to my home and produced to me an album of photographs. I examined these photographs and I picked out two photographs of a man, who in my opinion, closely resembled the man I saw in the green coloured car at Parnell Street at 5.12pm on 17th May '74, as referred to in my previous statement. On 8th June Detective Inspector Mulready again called to my home and produced a different album of photographs and I examined them. On this occasion I picked out a photograph of a man who, in my opinion closely resembled a man who I saw in the car in Parnell Street on the 17th May. The three photographs of the man I picked out in the albums were very like the man I saw in the car in Parnell Street.

From the first Garda album, which contained nineteen photographs, Teresa O'Loughlin picked out two different profiles of David Alexander Mulholland, a leading UVF activist from Portadown in County Armagh, as the driver of the green Avenger she had seen pulling into Parnell Street. From the second album, which largely contained pictures of different people from the first one, but with Mulholland included in a different and more obscure profile, she again picked him out. In 1974 Mulholland was thirty-six years of age, tall, broad-shouldered with fair hair. Her description is not far off the mark.

A young man who was seriously injured in Parnell Street while serving petrol in a filling station just yards from the scene of the explosion remembered a green car parked nearby. Derek Byrne, who was fifteen years old, told Gardai in a statement from his hospital bed what he'd seen:

On or about 10th May 1974 I started work as a petrol pump attendant at Westbrook Garage, Parnell Street. I was working there on Friday 17th. I started work at a quarter to nine and worked till 11.45am and then I went to my dinner. I left home at 12.45pm and walked back through North Street, Diamond, Gardiner Street and into Parnell Street I went into the KC Shoe Shop and bought a pair of canvas shoes. I was back in the garage at about three minutes to 1 o'clock. I was serving petrol for the remainder of the evening. There were three petrol pumps on the pavement outside the garage - two on the O'Connell Street side and one on the Marlborough Street side. There was no petrol in the pump on the Marlborough Street side and I was working the other two pumps on that day. At about 5.25pm on that date a man I knew to see pulled in for petrol. This man came from O'Connell Street direction and pulled into the garage facing the Summerhill direction. He was driving a yellow Volkswagen car. I was sitting on a chair outside the garage door when this man pulled in. He got out of the car and asked me for £1.50 worth of petrol - regular brand. I started to put in the petrol. I had about a £1's worth in when a dark red Morris 1100 pulled into a parking space between Barry's and the butcher's shop on the Marlborough Street side of the garage. This car came from around the corner at the Welcome Inn and had no front number plate. It had two small wings at the back. I continued filling the customer's petrol and when I had finished the customer handed me £2 and asked me for small change. As the customer was handing me £2 the man driving the Morris got out, pressed the button on the handle of the door and closed it gently. He had something white in his hand like a handkerchief or a bandage and he wiped the handle of the door when he closed it. He then turned and ran fast across the road and turned into George's Street. When the man was running across the road the customer said to me he must be in a terrible hurry. I then walked into the garage, got the customer's change, which was made up in four 10p pieces and two 5p pieces, and walked out and gave it to the customer. I had given the £2 to a man named Jim in the garage and he had given me the change. The customer was just about to give me a 5p tip when I heard a loud explosion, which I thought came from the back of the garage. I was thrown back two or three yards towards the pump and collapsed. I remember waking up two or three minutes later and seeing a customer I had just served lying on the path with holes in his face and smoke around the doors. Then I saw a priest coming over blessing me, then a policeman and four others came over to me. One of the men was carrying a white coat and he put it over me, covering my head, I thought I was dead. I was able to pull the coat off my eyes and then I was put on a stretcher. When I was on the stretcher I saw a lot of bodies lying along the road. Then I was put in an ambulance and brought to Jervis Street hospital and have been here since. I would describe the man who parked the Morris car between Barry's and the butcher's shop while I was filling the petrol as follows: 20-25, 6ft, black hair, wavy and black colour, stout, broad. The hood was down and there was black and grey on the edge of it. He was wearing creamy white trousers, with wide bottoms. That's all I can remember. I would know the man again if I saw him.

A number of days later Gardai visited the boy in hospital a second time with a piece of wreckage from the Avenger to ascertain if he'd seen a car of that colour in the filling station precincts. This was his reply:

Further to my statement I now wish to say the following: I have been shown a piece of metal by Garda Neelan on this day. On the 17th May '74 I saw a car of the same green colour parked outside the Welcome Inn in Parnell Street. I did not see the car come there. I did not see anyone sitting in this car or going away from it. I first saw this car was there about 5 o'clock on the 17th. I did not see the number plate of the car. The red Morris I told you about was parked about two cars ahead of the green car, which was still there when the red car came. I don't know which car exploded. I thought the explosion was in the garage. I only heard since that it was a car that exploded. The green car was the last car before the junction of Marlborough Street and Parnell Street.

Clearly the young man, due to his horrific injuries, was unable to recall with any degree of clarity the sequence of events at the filling station forecourt immediately preceding the explosion. His story of the 'Red Morris' confused investigating Gardai and the driver was never traced. Some Gardai wondered if it was not the Avenger driver he saw wiping the car door handle and running across the road.

Kevin Browne, a motor mechanic from Dublin's South Circular Road, parked his car near the scene shortly before the explosion and remembered seeing the Hillman Avenger.

> At 5.10pm on 17th May I parked my car, a Consul Automatic outside the Bell and Swastika Laundry in Parnell Street. I saw three cars parked between the Westbrook Garage and the Welcome Inn pub. One was definitely a Hillman Avenger - I can't say what colour. I thought one of the cars was a white one. The car parked outside the Welcome Inn was, as far as I can remember, a Morris Minor, black colour. I have no idea of registration. The Morris Minor was the last car parked in Parnell Street between Marlborough Street and the Westbrook Garage. The car beside it was, I think, a white Hillman Avenger. I don't know what the registration was. The third car I can't give a description of. I can remember looking at my watch between 5.15pm and 5.20pm Five mins. later I heard the explosion. I went out and saw a man from the Italian restaurant lying in the street. I think he was dead.

At first Kevin Browne is unsure of the colour of the Avenger but later suggests it might have been a white one. Another witness who saw the bomb-car 'badly parked' and had no doubts about its make or colour was Patrick Kirby, who worked in the city centre.

> At 5.15pm I left my place of work and drove up Gardiner Street and turned left into Parnell Street from

Marlborough Street. I parked my car in the first parking bay outside the Welcome Inn. I got out and went to the laundry, collected some laundry and walked back to my car and pulled out of my parking bay. I noticed a green Avenger parked two bays up. It was badly parked and I had to pull out around it. I didn't see anyone near the car.

It is clear from the evidence of both Teresa O'Loughlin ('then it reversed very fast into the space we had left') and Patrick Kirby ('it was badly parked and I had to pull out around it') that the bomber was running out of time and was anxious to get away fast.

Back in Belfast William Scott, freed by his captors, learned that his car had been used in the bombings. Next day he spoke to one of his neighbours and related his ordeal and spoke of his 'shock' that his car was used to 'kill all those children in Dublin'. As happened with William Henry, the RUC visited Scott a number of times as the enormity of the tragedy unfolded, but he was unable to identify his captors from police photographs. Like Henry, Scott's role in the affair has never become clear. During research for this book I discovered that for some time prior to the bombings he developed close links with the British army and turned an upstairs room in his house into a drinking 'shebeen' where soldiers based at the local army camp visited regularly for late night boozing sessions. It also emerged that soldiers returning to Northern Ireland from tours abroad brought him souvenirs and presents. One close neighbour, who knew Scott for years, told me of the relationship:

> He was very great with the army. Soldiers returning from abroad and particularly Germany, who had served here on earlier tours, brought home scores of presents. You'd see them going up for the booze late at night and they could be there half the night. He turned one of the upstairs bedrooms into a sort of a shebeen and sound-proofed the walls. He was really very close to them.

A year after the Dublin bombings Scott left Northern Ireland for Yorkshire, in north-east England. He had separated from his wife in earlier life and moved to be near his married daughter, where he remained until his death a number of years later. In the late 1970s his house was pulled down and replaced by new housing, which was built as part of Belfast's urban renewal programme. In recent years Torrens Road, where Scott lived, has been quiet and trouble-free, despite its proximity to the notorious Protestant enclaves of Oldpark and Ballysillan in north Belfast. Neighbours say Scott was used and manipulated by 'evil men' smarter than himself and that it was an open secret in the area where the hijackers came from that morning. One local man told me:

> Scott was a vulnerable man. He lived alone and made his own home brew for the boys and they knew he was easy prey. For years he went around on a bicycle and then suddenly he got this car which he became obsessed with. Everyone knew the gangsters came from that other shebeen down the road there in Wheatfield when they stole his car'.

The 'shebeen' he referred to was a social club on the Alliance Road, between Oldpark and the Ardoyne, which was used by a congeries of UVF/UDA and Red Hand Commando terrorists from the loyalist nexus in the 1970s to plan murders and robberies. It was also used for drinking and 'rompering'. This was a practice whereby, during the worst period of assassinations in the 1970s, Catholics were picked up from the streets at random and tortured before being killed and their bodies dumped on waste ground. Like Henry, there is little doubt that Scott was in some form of cahoots with the bombers and that they had earmarked his car well in advance. If not and if by some stroke of luck he had failed to return home from his night-shift that morning, the bombers' plan would again have been badly disrupted.

On the same morning (17 May) victim number three, William Hamilton Shannon, left his home in County Down, at 7.30 a.m. to travel to Belfast docks, where he worked as a motor mechanic. He arrived at his place of work at 8 a.m. and parked his metallic blue Ford Escort nearby. He returned to the car at 10.30 to lend it to a workmate but discovered it missing. Shannon immediately reported the theft to the RUC. At 5.31 p.m. that evening a bomb in Shannon's car exploded in Talbot Street, killing nine people and injuring almost 100 others. This is what Shannon told police.

> On Friday 17 May I drove to work from my home arriving at 8am. I parked the car and locked the car. I went to work and on returning to the car at 10.30am in order to lend it to a work mate, I found it was missing and I reported it to the police. Another employee who commences work at 9am passed a comment to me at 9am that my car was not outside, but I treated this as a joke at the time. I therefore think it is possible that the car was stolen between 8am and 9am. There was only one other car on the Motorway area at 8am on that morning. It was a yellow Ford Capri with a black roof and there were two men, aged approximately 60 years of age in the car. I do not think this car was acting suspiciously but it was the only one in the area at the time.

The movements of Shannon's car immediately following the theft have never been traced. Based on the assumption that it went missing before 9 a.m. (possibly around 8.30 a.m.), it was the first of the three Dublin bomb-cars to be taken that morning. It was later established, however, that Shannon's car was the only one of the three not driven the smuggler's route across the border to Dublin. Like the others it too was observed by a number of eye-witnesses after it crossed into the South. It was first sighted shortly before 12.30 p.m. being driven through the town of Drogheda, along the main Belfast-Dublin road. Uniformed Gardai, manning a 24-hour security hut outside the town's police station, logged its registration number as it passed through the town. Because of previous attacks in the area, Gardai in Drogheda had received intelligence that an attack on their station was possible. As a precaution a security hut was erected in the station's forecourt, adjacent to the main road, manned by Gardai round the clock with instructions to log all Northern Ireland cars travelling north or south. As there was nothing unusual about Shannon's Escort - it was not reported stolen to Gardai by the RUC until much later in the day - no action was taken.

A short time later Shannon's car was observed a second time by a civilian eye-witness as it made its way south of Drogheda towards the Dublin suburbs. Michael Thornton, a company rep. from Carlingford, Co. Louth, was on his way to Dublin when he noticed it. This is what he told Gardai:

> I was on the south side of Drogheda at 12.30pm. I was approaching the Nos Na Ri hotel and slowed down as I intended going into the hotel for a meal. A car passed me at this time. I thought it was a white colour. It was an Escort. I made a mental note of this reg. plate and as far as I can recall I feel this vehicle was 1385 WZ.

The next sighting of Shannon's Escort was at 4 p.m. in the afternoon as it made its way from the north Dublin suburbs towards the city centre. Eamonn Ennis, a haulage driver from Coolock on Dublin's northside, was driving his lorry at a well-known Dublin landmark, Doyle's Corner, when he saw the bomb-car. This is what he told Gardai:

> On Friday 17 May about 4pm I was driving my firm's truck along the Phibsboro Road from Cross Guns Bridge. I was alone. When I got to Doyle's Corner I intended going straight ahead and down Church Street to the Quays. When I got to Doyle's Corner the traffic lights showed green in my favour, but there was a traffic jam on the far side of the junction, so I decided to pull up as I didn't want to stop on the middle of the

road. The red light was on at this time showing against traffic coming from the Phoenix Park direction, so that in fact when I pulled up there was no movement of traffic at all at the junction of Doyle's Corner. I pulled up at the right centre of the roadway as I was going straight ahead. There was a double line of traffic on the North Circular when I pulled up [the road in front of Ennis to his right and left]. They were coming from the Phoenix Park direction. The inner lane was signalling their intention of turning left at Doyle's Corner and the outer lane was going straight ahead towards Mountjoy. In fact there was no right turn at this point. I noticed the first car in the outer lane of traffic that had stopped coming from the Phoenix Park direction as a Ford Escort, registration number 1385 WZ or UZ. I'm fairly sure it was WZ. It was a bright colour. I cannot be sure of the colour, the only thing I can say is that it was bright. I am definite about the figures of the registration number. My reason for remembering the figures is that some time ago I owned a motor car and the figures of the registration were 751 and a friend of mine mentioned these figures totalled 13, which is an unlucky number. So you know what that is. Since then I have a habit of adding up the registration of cars. I saw this at the Earl's Corner or Doyle's Corner. The Escort was coming down from Phibsboro and heading towards town. There were two men in the car. They appeared to be aged between 25 and 30. The driver had a black anorak with a red stripe on it. I didn't notice anything else about either of the two men. The car headed on down towards Mountjoy. That is all I noticed about this car or the men driving it.

Ever since the bombings, it has been widely assumed that all three bombs were planted around the same time - 5.00 p.m. or thereabouts. The driving distance from Doyle's Corner - where the Escort was spotted by Eamonn Ennis at 4 p.m. - to Talbot Street in the city centre, in 1974, allowing for extra traffic due to the bus strike, was decidedly less than an hour. In contrast to the other two cars, no witnesses came forward to say they saw the Escort being parked. Talbot Street is an extremely busy thoroughfare, with a train station at one end and a bus terminus at the other, and is more difficult to reach than Parnell Street or South Leinster Street. It can therefore be assumed that the bombers took no chances with traffic and arrived ahead of schedule. Gardai now estimate the Escort was parked as early as 4.45 p.m. or 5 p.m. at the latest.

Unlike their co-bombers, the Talbot Street bombers displayed extreme guile and astuteness and apparently managed to park their deadly cargo and escape without being noticed. Their vehicle was observed parked, however, by one male witness who, accompanied by his family, parked his car directly in front of the Escort shortly before it exploded. Christopher Smith from Beaumont, on Dublin's northside, was shopping with his wife Marie, three children and a family friend, Jane Hegarty, in the city centre when he noticed the Escort. Following his, and his family's, miraculous escape from almost certain death, this is what Smith told Gardai:

> I drove up Talbot Street from Amiens Street looking for a parking space. I saw a parking space in a meter opposite the Talbot Bar, outside the shoe-shop loading area, and backed into the space. My wife Marie was in the rear seat and guided me into the space by looking out the rear window. There was a slate blue car behind me. There was no person in this car. I looked at my watch and saw it was 5.15pm We then went shopping to Marlborough Street. I heard the explosion in Marlborough Street and I knew my car must be near the explosion, but I wasn't allowed down by Gardai. I subsequently identified it as the same colour as the car I observed parked behind me.

CHAPTER 4

PREPARING TO BOMB

Regardless of the fact that no organisation had claimed the attacks and despite the paramilitary denials, they were immediately blamed on the Ulster Defence Association (UDA), the largest loyalist paramilitary grouping and the organisation most involved in the strike. But, as mentioned in chapter two, the bombings were, of course, carried out by the Ulster Volunteer Force (UVF), a sister (but much smaller) organisation of the UDA.

The reason was simple. When the conflict started, the UVF was the only credible loyalist paramilitary organisation in the province, having been re-activated in 1966 by Gusty Spence, who was sentenced to life for the murder of a Catholic barman in the same year. Throughout 1969, and following the start of the civil rights campaign, the UVF was responsible for blowing up the main water pipeline between the Mourne Mountains and Belfast as well as part of the electricity pylon in County Armagh. It was also behind an abortive attempt to blow up an electricity pylon in Ballyshannon, in Donegal in the same year, in which one of its members was electrocuted. In 1972 and 1973, and two years into the IRA bombing campaign, the UVF was also behind a number of minor bomb attacks in Dublin city centre in which three people were killed and several others injured (see chapter 7). The UDA, which was formed in 1972, was seen as too big, too cumbersome and lacking in experience to carry out the 1974 Dublin bombings. When the time arrived for the big hit the UFV was the obvious choice for the task. It had bombed Dublin before and got away with it - it could do it again. The 1972/73 attacks were carried out by members of the UVF Brigade staff on the Shankill Road in Belfast. At the time the organisation was still small and largely confined to the city. The 1974 operation was by and large organised from County Armagh.

Around the middle of 1972 Gusty Spence was freed on parole from prison to attend a family engagement. On the day he was due to return he was 'kidnapped' by the UVF and taken to a secret hiding place. Over the following months Spence, who by this time had become something of a folk-hero in loyalist circles, travelled the length and breadth of the province organising and training the UVF, accompanied by other senior UVF men from the Shankill Road. Eventually he was 're-captured' by the security forces and returned to prison. One of the places he visited while on 'parole' was Lurgan in County Armagh, where a 42-year-old unemployed plumber by the name of Billy Hanna had recently set up a unit of the UVF in the town. Hanna was a part-time member of the Ulster Defence Regiment (UDR), a recently established regiment of the British Army, and was beginning to flex his muscles as a hard man, robbing banks and post offices and intimidating local business people into paying over money to the UVF. Like Spence he had been a former soldier in the British Army and received a medal for bravery following his service in the Korean war with the Ulster Rifles, a regiment of the British army. He and Spence had much in common and both knew how to make bombs and handle guns.

When the decision was taken to bomb the South in a serious way, Billy Hanna, now the UVF's Brigadier in mid-Ulster, which also covered the border area, was the man chosen by the UVF (and its advisors in the security forces) to lead the operation. Hanna, who by this time had gathered round him a coterie of young men from the Lurgan/Portadown area who were prepared to defend Ulster at any cost, was considered an able leader and an experienced tactician. He was born into a Protestant working-class family of nine children in Wellington Street in Lurgan, where many of his closest neighbours were Catholics. His father abandoned the home at an early stage to work in England, leaving his wife to bring up a large family on her own. From an early age Billy's abiding interest was guns and military paraphernalia in general. On his return from the Korean war in the 1950s he took a job as a plumber and also joined the B. Specials - the RUC's reserve force until it was disbanded shortly after the outbreak of the Troubles. When the UDR was formed in 1970 Hanna applied for a full-time job but was rejected. He was then offered part-time service. He had by this time also married his wife Ann and settled down to bring up a family in a Council housing estate in Lurgan. He later had five children, four girls and a boy. At the time of the bombings the boy, the youngest of the family, was twelve. None of his family ever became involved in terrorism. But like Spence, Hanna was never considered a sectarian bigot (a hater of Catholics), nor was he a particularly malevolent person. But he was certainly a militarist and believed in the power of the gun and the use of violence to achieve his aims. He was also, like Spence, a passionate believer in the Union and the trappings of empire and royalty in general.

When the British army arrived in Northern Ireland it set up headquarters in the Protestant town of Lisburn, ten miles south of Belfast. A short time later it moved 39 Brigade - which would be responsible for security in the greater Belfast area - into the same building. 8 Brigade was installed in Derry to look after the West of the province and 3 Brigade, which would patrol the southern half of the province including 150 miles of border with the Republic, was moved into a vacant building known as the 'knicker factory' (women's underwear had been manufactured there in earlier times) in Kitchen Hill in the Mourneview estate in Lurgan. Mourneview is a large, sprawling, working-class Protestant housing estate on the southern side of Lurgan town. Also living in Mourneview estate, with his family, was Billy Hanna.

Like most ex-service men, Hanna's social life centered mainly round the two British Legion clubs (social drinking clubs for ex-members of the armed forces and their families), which were situated in the Mourneview estate. He and his wife spent most weekends socializing in either one and fraternising with other ex-service men and their wives. There Hanna also became friendly with members of 3 Brigade, who had recently arrived in the town and who also became frequent visitors to the clubs. In the beginning these were mostly squaddies who carried out foot patrols around the town, or 'drivers' who drove armoured vehicles around the place. As time went by Hanna became more friendly with the soldiers, including intelligence personnel, and began inviting them to his home in Huston Park for 'cups of tea'. One of these, William Appleby, who was a driver in 3 Brigade, became a frequent visitor to Hanna's home and began supplying Hanna with guns and free petrol for his car from the Kitchen Hill depot. He also started taking Hanna, who was a keen fisherman, on fishing trips to Tarbot lake outside Banbridge in County Down. Also visiting Hanna's home from Kitchen Hill was 'I.B.', a low-sized stocky man from the intelligence cell whose official army title was 'Finco'. I.B. was a keen fisherman and he too took Hanna on numerous fishing trips. All of this while Hanna was commanding officer of the illegal Ulster Volunteer Force in mid-Ulster, which was carrying out murders and bank robberies on a grand scale.

As time progressed, Hanna was introduced to more important members of the British army. Middle-ranking officers of the intelligence corps based at army H.Q. in Lisburn began visiting Hanna's home in Lurgan on a regular basis. They also took him on 'fishing trips' to Tarbot lake, and on numerous occasions invited him to Thieval Barracks army H.Q. in Lisburn. Ann Hanna, who still lives in Lurgan, told me during a taped interview for this book that she remembers the soldiers coming to her home to visit Billy on a regular basis between the years 1972 and 1975.

> I made tea for them regularly and I distinctly remember Appleby, who was very tall, well built and very pleasant. I knew him by name and a friend of his, whose name I can't remember now, from meeting them in the Legion club and from visiting our home. I knew they were local guys who were stationed with 3 Brigade.

But there were others too who kept their distance and whom she never got to know very well, who visited Billy at home and took him fishing to Tarbot lake.

I knew they were soldiers but I didn't know where they were from. Whenever they arrived Billy took them to another room where they chatted but I had no idea what they talked about.

Other members of Hanna's family, including his younger brother, Gordon, who was also a member of the UDR, and his sister also confirmed to me during research for this book that they were aware of Billy's friendship with the soldiers. They both saw soldiers with Billy in his home on a number of occasions while they were visiting there and they were aware that they took Billy fishing to Tarbot lake. All of Billy's family admitted they knew he was in the UVF but they were not aware of the extent of his involvement and they did not believe at the time that he was actually engaged in violence or killing people. No other member of Billy's family was ever involved with paramilitaries.

One former UVF man, now in his seventies, who was a member of Billy's squad and whom Gardai named as having been involved in the Dublin bombings, told me during research for this book that Billy worked as a UVF agent for army intelligence officers in Lisburn. He said two middle-ranking officers in plain clothes travelled down from Lisburn once a fortnight in a van to meet Billy and give him instructions on what they wanted done.

They would visit his house from time to time and they took him fishing to Banbridge. I saw them in his house a couple of times through the window as I approached but as no member of the unit was allowed to meet them I turned and went home and saw Billy later. But mostly they met him away from his house; in carparks or the like. They would meet him in Portadown, Lurgan, Banbridge or out the country somewhere. Occasionally when our unit met to plan operations someone might ask Billy a question about some aspect of the operation. If Billy did not know the answer his reply would be: 'I'll have to take advice on that.' No one pushed the matter further but everyone knew Billy was talking about the army.

The UVF man said he regarded Billy as a brilliant strategist.

> He could plan an operation so well that two of us from the unit could be designated to carry out specific functions in the same area at the same time without either of us knowing of the other's presence. There will never be another like Billy again.

Throughout the early months of 1974, as the new Northern Ireland executive began to function with a number of nationalist government ministers in its ranks, the two army intelligence officers whom Ann Hanna had made tea for, began to plan its downfall. They took Billy on regular 'fishing' trips to Tarbot lake, where they outlined their plan to bomb the South. By choosing the open air, particularly at a lake, there was virtually no risk whatever of their highly sensitive discussions being taped or overheard.

Having received his instructions from the army, Billy Hanna, in consultation with UVF Brigade Staff headquarters in Belfast, was left to assemble his own team to carry out the bombings. As commander for mid-Ulster, Hanna was automatically a member of the Brigade Staff, and as such was subject to its authority. However as far as the leadership was concerned, the proposed onslaught against Dublin was primarily a border operation and as such was the responsibility of the border brigade. The Belfast brigades had their own turf to cover but they would help out Hanna in whatever way necessary.

Between January and April planning meetings were held in Belfast, Lurgan, Portadown, South Armagh and in some instances in pubs and restaurants in Dublin. The operation was the biggest ever terrorist attack to be undertaken by the loyalist group since its formation in 1912. In Belfast, meetings were held in the Windsor Bar on the Shankill Road, the Rumford Street club, a loyalist drinking den off the Shankill Road, and in a loyalist club in Wheatfield in the north of the city attended on occasions by Hanna and other mid-Ulster loyalists. By and large the bombing team was chosen from UVF battalions (mainly brigadiers or commanders) from Belfast and mid-Ulster, but in some instances UDA men were also chosen, primarily for their paramilitary experience.

Because Lurgan and Portadown were small country towns and loyalists living there were vulnerable to retaliation by republicans, and possible apprehension by the police, a decision was taken at an early stage to conceal, as far as possible, their involvement in the bombings. Therefore, the cars to be used in the explosions, which were certain to be identified publicly by the Gardai in their follow-up investigation, would be 'acquired' in the loyalist heartlands of north and west Belfast. Such areas were well nigh impenetrable to Republican attacks, and less vulnerable to police scrutiny. The decision to bomb Monaghan was taken as an afterthought, in the days immediately preceding the operation, and was never part of the original plan. As plans for the Dublin end of the operation, particularly the acquisition of the cars, were already delicately in place, it was too late to change the plans and an order was given by Hanna to steal a car in Portadown for use in the Monaghan explosion.

In Belfast a team of loyalists known as 'Freddie and the Dreamers', named after the 1960s pop group, was chosen to hijack two of the cars. The team was led by a Shankill UVF commander, William 'Frenchie' Marchant, who became notorious throughout the 1970s for his involvement in murdering Catholics. He was detained in the early 1980s on the word of a supergrass but later walked free when the evidence against him collapsed. He was shot dead from a passing car in 1987 by a republican hit-squad, while standing on a footpath on the Shankill Road. Also part of the Dreamers was John Dowey Bingham, another notorious assassin who was also shot dead by a republican hit-squad who broke into his home in the middle of the night in West Belfast in the late 1980s and shot him in front of his family. In the mid-1980s Bingham was one of a handful of senior loyalists directing the operations of Michael

Stone who shot dead three people at a republican funeral in Milltown cemetery in Belfast in 1988. In 1983 Bingham, from Ballysillan Crescent in north-west Belfast, was sentenced to twenty years for conspiring to import arms from the US as part of the supergrass trials. He was also convicted of possessing an M60 machine gun, an RPG7 rocket launcher, and membership of the UVF. Shortly after being sentenced, however, Bingham was released when the supergrass trials collapsed and he went on to kill more Catholics. After Lennie Murphy (the Shankill Butcher), Bingham was considered the most notorious loyalist assassin in Belfast.

Also with the Dreamers was a north Belfast UDA commander, Davy Payne, who in 1973 was involved (but not charged), with John White, the present-day UDA hardman (see chapter 9), in the murder of Paddy Wilson, Gerry Fitt's election agent.

Responsibility for 'acquiring' the third Belfast car was given to Billy Mitchell, a senior UVF Brigade Staff man who had been involved in the 1972/73 Dublin bombings. From Carrickfergus in north Antrim, Mitchell, known as 'mad Mitch', was considered a bright, intelligent operative who subsequently played a key role in the overall planning and execution of the operation. He was the principle link-man between the 1972/73 and 1974 bombings and played a key role in mapping out the streets to be hit in Dublin.

Having chosen his Belfast team, Hanna switched his attention back to his home base of mid-Ulster. The task of choosing the routes to be travelled across the border, to and from Dublin, he designated to three senior UVF men - Robin Jackson (the Jackal) from Lurgan, Harris Boyle from Portadown and Wesley Sommerville from County Tyrone. Jackson and Boyle, both of whom lived close to Hanna, became his two principle assistants on the operation from beginning to end. Both of them had been heavily involved in murders throughout mid-Ulster over the previous two years and their credentials for the task were second to none. They were also given responsibility for finding a suitable 'launching-pad' in or near Dublin which could be used as a kind of transit site where vehicles could be parked and the bombs loaded on to the bomb-cars on the day of the bombings. They were also told to familiarise themselves with Dublin city, with its intricate network of city streets, and to find suitable restaurants and pubs which the team could use for refreshments during the months of planning and on the day itself. In his day job Jackson drove a chicken lorry round Ireland for an egg production company called Moy Park in Moira, Co. Antrim, and he was already familiar with the South and Dublin city in particular.

From contacts with local Protestant smugglers around Armagh, Hanna discovered that the route the smugglers travelled back and forth across the border to Dublin avoided all security checks and by and large was ignored by the authorities, North and South.

He also became aware that the smugglers regularly used the same well-known pubs along the route for eating and drinking. These pubs, which became part of the smuggling culture going back over decades, all had large car parks, from where the smugglers plied their trade. Two of these were The Boot Inn, at the back of Dublin airport in north County Dublin, and The Coachman's Inn, a large pub with a sprawling car park to the rear, two miles north of Dublin airport on the main Dublin-Belfast road. On most days of the week, but particularly on a Friday, smugglers crowded the car parks with lorries, trucks and vans from which they bought and sold goods to each other - 'everything from a needle to an anchor', one smuggler once told me. As much as half of the vehicles in either car park at any one time had Northern Ireland registration markings and as many again of their drivers had Northern Ireland accents. For Hanna it was the ideal setting, and provided the perfect cover from which to load and off-load bombs.

Between January and early May, Jackson, Boyle and Wesley Sommerville made numerous trips along the smugglers' route from Armagh to Dublin, crossing the border at Hackballs Cross between Dundalk and Carrickmacross in the Republic, reconnoitering the countryside and the streets of Dublin city centre. On at least one occasion, according to Dundalk Detective Owen Corrigan, they were stopped and questioned by Gardai manning a checkpoint near Hackballs Cross who recognised them from photographs supplied by the RUC. As they were not breaking the law, they were allowed to proceed. On several occasions they visited the Coachman's Inn, where they ate and drank in the bar and surveyed the car park to the rear. On occasions they were joined on the trips by Hanna and other loyalists from mid-Ulster and Belfast, who were being groomed to drive the bomb-cars and the getaway cars.

As well as the Coachman's car park Hanna chose a second car park close to the Holy Child Catholic church in Whitehall, a north Dublin suburb, adjacent to a major four-roads junction linking the Dublin-Belfast road with Collins Avenue. This car park is positioned approximately three miles north of Dublin city centre and two miles south of the Coachman's. It is owned jointly by the church and Dublin Corporation and is used as a facility for the annual circus in the area as well as Massgoers and the public in general. Hanna's idea was to use this car park for parking get-away vehicles, which would also be used as scout cars, and use the Coachman's Inn car park as a transition point for the bombs.

Back in Armagh, Hanna appointed Billy Fulton, a Portadown UDA commander and a close friend of his own, as quartermaster for the bombings. Fulton, a 32-year-old unemployed bar waiter, was an uncle to Mark 'Swinger' Fulton, the former leader of the Loyalist Volunteer Force (LVF), the loyalist splinter group set up in Portadown by Billy 'King Rat' Wright in 1997. Billy Fulton was a low-sized, stocky, impulsive man who was not a particularly evil terrorist but who got involved with paramilitaries more out of bravado than political ideology. In 1987, during research for a project on the murders of three members of the Miami Showband for the RTE current affairs programme *Today Tonight*, Fulton gave me my first break on the bombings. He was not prepared to reveal the full story nor was he prepared to admit his own involvement in the outrage but after much cajoling he revealed that the operation was led by Hanna, that a car park beside a church in Whitehall was used for parking cars and that a group of loyalists from north and west Belfast known as 'Freddie and the Dreamers' had played a key role in the operation. 'That's it, Joe, I'm not prepared to say anything more about it.' Later senior Garda sources from C3 in Garda headquarters in Dublin confirmed that Fulton's information was correct and that on the day of the bombings the church car park was used as part of the operation. In the seventeen years since I first interviewed Fulton, I checked out numerous other stories (not connected to Dublin) that he told me, and each one turned out to be accurate. I found him the most truthful terrorist I have ever interviewed.

Meanwhile for Hanna work continued apace on the Dublin plan. From his own town of Lurgan Hanna chose Robin Jackson and a Portadown UDA man who we shall call G.J. All three lived within a stone's throw of each other and also close to the Kitchen Hill army base. From the neighbouring town of Portadown Hanna chose Billy Fulton, David Mulholland (whom Teresa O'Loughlin identified as the Parnell Street bomber) and Harris Boyle. Again, all three lived close to each other in the working-class housing estate of Killycomaine. Mulholland was born in Mourneview Street, on the opposite side of Portadown but moved to Killycomaine, a newly built estate of housing executive houses, after marrying. He worked as a butcher in Portadown and was a part-time member of the UDR. Fulton was appointed quartermaster with responsibility for procuring the explosives, while J.G. was appointed his assistant.

Mid-way through the planning stages Hanna moved his operation from Lurgan to the farmhouse of an RUC reservist called James Mitchell in a loyalist area of south Armagh called Glenanne, a number of miles south of Markethill. Attached to the farmhouse was a large sprawling farm where cattle, sheep and pigs were raised. Before the Troubles, Mitchell, who lived in south Armagh all his life, was a member of the B. Specials. Following the disbandment of the Specials and the onset of the conflict he joined the RUC reserve force and served as a part-time policeman in local stations in the area. Throughout the early 1970s he met up with other members of the security forces who held similar hardline unionist views to his own. Amongst them was a part-time UDR captain serving in the Armagh area,

John Irvine. Later Irvine would play a key role in Hanna's Dublin operation.

The farmhouse, which for a period of over five years in the 1970s served as a kind of engine-room for murder and mayhem in mid-Ulster, is a large, two-storey country house with numerous sheds, barns and other outhouses and was an ideal setting for hiding guns and explosives and manufacturing bombs. Under the cover of the rural setting of the farmhouse, huddled over street maps of Dublin and Ordnance Survey maps of the countryside between Belfast and Dublin, Hanna, Jackson, Boyle and Sommerville worked out the details of their plan.

Transport for the operation - that is, cars to travel back and forth to Dublin during the planning stages, as well as scout cars to transport the bombing team to and from Dublin on the day of the bombings itself - was provided by a County Armagh businessman. According to Billy Fulton this man, who in the years following the bombings expanded his business considerably, 'did well out of Dublin'. In other words he was paid a small fortune by the UVF for his contribution.

Two weeks before the bombings Fulton and his UDA colleague G.J. delivered a van-load of home-made explosives to another isolated farmhouse five miles south of Portadown, with the permission of the owner, who had been a supporter of the UVF from the 1960s. They hid the explosives under hay in a windswept hayshed to the back of the house. A week later both men returned with the van, collected the explosives and delivered them to Mitchell's farmhouse. A short time later the three Dublin bombs were constructed in Mitchell's yard to the back of the house by Irvine and Mitchell. The bombs were made from a mix of both home-made explosives and gelignite. The gelignite was stolen earlier by Irvine in small quantities over a period of time from quarries across mid-Ulster. The gelignite was being used legally by commercial companies for quarry blasting. Irvine then delivered the gelignite to the farmhouse in a Land Rover and was paid £1,000 for each bomb by Mitchell.

On the morning of the bombings the three bombs, which were packed in suitcases, were collected by Robin Jackson in his chicken lorry from south Armagh and transported to the Coachman's Inn car park in north Dublin. It is not certain if the bombs were stored at the farmhouse up to the last moment or if they were moved to a second farmhouse a number of miles away a day or two before the bombings for security reasons. According to a Garda Chief Superintendent who was serving on the border at the time and who was involved in the investigation, the 'Dublin bombs were collected in suitcases from the Newtownhamilton area and transported to Dublin'.

According to a disaffected former RUC Sergeant, John Weir, who served a life-sentence for his part in the murder of a County Antrim shopkeeper in 1977 and who operated as a terrorist from the farmhouse between 1975 and 1978, two Belfast members of the Dublin bombing team slept at the south Armagh farmhouse the night before the bombings. When in August 1975 Billy Hanna was shot in Lurgan, Mitchell, who was profoundly shocked at the news, talked to Weir about his long-time friend.

'That's a great tragedy. Hanna was a great man you know, decent, quiet, not like some of the riff-raff you get around the place. You know he carried out the Dublin bombings'.

'Was he one of the men who slept here the night before the bombings?' Mitchell's girlfriend, Lily Shields, enquired. 'No, those were two Belfast men,' replied Mitchell. Shields then turned to Weir.

'You know those two guys shook hands with me that morning before leaving, saying they "might never make it back".

Because the subject was so sensitive the conversation ended there, Weir says.

Meanwhile, back in Belfast, as William Scott and William Henry were having their cars hijacked, Billy Mitchell accompanied by a local UVF commander, was on his way to Dublin in the car he had stolen from William Shannon at the Belfast docks. Stealing Shannon's car was a separate and different type of operation from the other two. No violence or threats of violence were used against Shannon and he never saw the thieves.

There were other dissimilarities too. Shannon's was the only car which was not driven the smuggler's route to Dublin, but instead was driven the main road (or at least part of it) through Drogheda towards Dublin. It was the only car seen with two people in it as it approached Dublin city centre with its bomb on board, and it was the only bomb-car that was almost certainly parked in position at least thirty minutes (possibly even more) before exploding in Talbot Street. And, finally, it was the only bomb-car of the three which was not seen (or reported seen) being parked by its driver at the bomb site.

Shortly after 10 a.m. on the morning of the bombings a local woman, Esther Drumm, was in the vicinity of the large bleak car park that forms two sides of a rectangle with the Belfast Road and Collins Avenue near the Whitehall church in Dublin. Mid-way up the car park she noticed a number of cars with mustard-coloured (what appeared to be Northern Ireland) registration plates. At the same time she noticed a number of men 'walking away' from the cars towards the exit gate.

According to a senior Garda Special Branch officer who spoke to Ms Drumm and whom I interviewed for this book, Ms Drumm took no further notice of the men or the cars, as there was nothing unusual in strangers parking cars in the car park. What did strike her as odd was the number of men together parking a number of cars so early in the morning. When news of the bombings broke that evening, particularly the news that all three bombs had been planted in Northern registered cars, Ms Drumm became suspicious and reported the matter to the Gardai. According to the Special Branch man, the men were also seen by an un-named lorry driver who was driving his lorry on the main road at the time but who was unable to give precise details of the sighting due to the distance. Initially, of course, there was nothing in either sighting to connect the men to the bombings. However, as Gardai received further authenticated intelligence that the car park was indeed used, the witnesses' stories began to fall into place.

I have researched the Dublin and Monaghan bombings, on an ongoing basis, now for almost sixteen years. During that time I researched one major documentary on the subject for Yorkshire Television. I also did research for RTE and Channel 4 television and wrote widely in newspapers on the subject. I have interviewed many members of the Gardai (up to the rank of former Commissioner) who were involved in the investigation, as well as numerous members of the RUC. I have interviewed dozens and dozens of loyalists (possibly as many as a hundred) about the subject, some of them directly involved. Despite all of that I do not possess the full picture of what happened and there are still many gaps to fill. However, almost all of the information contained on the subject in this book either comes directly from or has been confirmed officially by Gardai in Garda headquarters in the Phoenix Park.

Therefore, the sequence of events on the morning of the bombings, is approximately as follows.

a) Robin Jackson transported the explosives from south Armagh to the Coachman's Inn car park in a chicken lorry.

b) William Henry's blue Austin Maxi 1800 was driven directly to Dublin (without any stops on the way save delays due to the UWC strike) by one of the four men (the 'Dreamers') who hijacked it that morning. It took the driver approximately two and a quarter hours to travel from Belfast city centre to Sheephouse south of Drogheda. As Belfast city and many of the roads leading to the border were in chaos due to the strike, the driving time was extremely short and begs the question: did the driver have some kind of security clearance?

c) William Scott's green Hillman Avenger, which was taken around 10 a.m., was driven to County Armagh alone by one of the 'Dreamers', who collected David Mulholland on the way. As Hanna wished each bomb driver to become as familiar (and comfortable) as possible with each car, which after all had to be driven through the chaos of Dublin city, Mulholland took over the wheel and drove Scott's car to Dublin with the 'Dreamer' in the passenger seat.

d) The 'group of men' Esther Drumm saw walking from the car park were the people who scouted the bomb-cars into the city in the cars they had just parked and later that evening collected the bombers and ferried them home to Northern Ireland. The cars which were driven to Dublin that morning from the businessman's premises in County Armagh were 'legitimate' (not stolen) and did not pose a threat to the operation The two passengers Gerald O'Reilly saw in William Henry's car in Drumcondra were two of that 'group of men' who had just walked the one mile distance from the car park to Drumcondra. They had just boarded Henry's car shortly before O'Reilly saw it.

e) Each bomb driver collected his bomb separately from Hanna in the Coachman's Inn car park between approximately 1.30 p.m. and 3.30 p.m. in the afternoon, with a time lapse of approximately 40 minutes between each collection. According to explosives expert Paddy Trears, the three Dublin bombs were probably deposited from the suitcases (without a container) in the boot of each car, with sticks of gelignite, surrounded by home-made explosives, standing in the boot of each car. (Gardai did not find fragments of a container at the site of either bomb and the absence of such fragments made it all the more difficult for Gardai to trace the source of the bombs.) Trears says the bombs were extremely well constructed; so well that practically 100 per cent of each bomb exploded with the detonation. 'This is the hallmark of a bomb-maker who knows what he is doing,' Trears says. One customer I spoke to in the Coachman's Inn during research for this book said it was 'common knowledge' in the pub in the weeks and months after the bombings that the bombs had been loaded and 'wired up' in the car park. 'It was so well known around here afterwards that it became something of a joke. They were seen by people loading the stuff into the boots of the cars and wiring them up but no one suspected anything until after the explosions occurred,' the customer said.

According to a senior UVF man in mid-Ulster who was a close friend of Billy Hanna's, Hanna later told him he was standing in the car park in Whitehall that afternoon 'handing out bombs to the drivers as they came along'. This UVF man, who was heavily involved in terrorism in Armagh but was not on the Dublin operation, said Hanna later regretted the bombings. 'He used come to my house here, lean his head on his hand on the table and start to cry about "all those children killed in Dublin".'

Throughout the operation in Dublin that day, Hanna became paranoid about the Gardai, fearing his men might get caught at a checkpoint. He could not be certain that an informer within the ranks had not spilled the heap. Therefore he was taking no chances. He instructed all drivers who drove a vehicle into Dublin that morning to travel separate routes to check that the roads were clear. It was a kind of blanket sweep of the north side of the city: taking the early morning temperature. Thus when Henry's car was seen by Gerald O'Reilly in Drumcondra driving out of the city towards Whitehall it had just been on an extended detour to check that that particular part of the city was clear. As it proceeded towards the Coachman's, its two passengers disembarked at the church to collect a scout car. As the driver of Henry's car collected his bomb and emerged on to the roadway he was joined by the scout car which then preceded him to South Leinster Street and collected him after he alighted from the car. When Charles Chain O'Doherty, the Derry bus driver, saw the man alight from the car and walk in the 'direction of Grafton Street', he was about to board his get-away car which had pulled up a short distance back on the opposite side to the bomb-car. It was easier to double park on that side of the street. O'Doherty was obviously not to know this and presumably assumed the man - whose identity is known to me but who cannot be named for legal reasons - continued walking towards the city centre.

Equally when the drivers of Scot's and Shannon's cars arrived at the Coachman's to collect their bombs they, too, were joined by scout cars from the church car park which preceeded them to their destinations. As much activity had now taken place at both car parks, Hanna, fearing the Gardai might have been alerted to the fact that something suspicious was taking place and erected checkpoints on the main road to Dublin, instructed all three bomb-drivers and their scouts to spread out and take separate roundabout routes to the city. Thus when Shannon's Escort was observed at Doyle's Corner by Eamonn Ennis - the Coolock haulage driver - at 4 p.m. with two men on board, it too was being preceded by its scout car, having travelled 'round the world' through north county Dublin to avoid the main road to the city. And like the driver of Henry's car its occupants, Billy Mitchell and his local commander, were ferried to safety from the Talbot Street bomb scene by the scout car. However, when Scott's car was observed in Glasnevin at 3 p.m. by Peter Flanagan doing '60 mph' it had still to collect its bomb and was on its way to Whitehall to do so. Two hours had elapsed from when it was last reported seen at Sheephouse - at 1 p.m. - little more than a half hour's drive from Glasnevin. There can, I contend, be only one of two explanations for this delay. Either its driver, David Mulholland, lost his way or he sustained a breakdown of some sort, such as a puncture. One way or another it is obvious he was beginning to panic and feared he might miss Hanna in Whitehall, who was anxious to load the bombs as early as possible and return north before they exploded.

As the bombers left the Coachman's with their bombs on board they still had over two hours to spare before planting their bombs. Hanna stipulated that the bombs should be planted nothing more than fifteen to twenty minutes before exploding - perhaps thirty minutes in the case of Talbot Street. Cars with Northern Ireland registration markings parked in Dublin city centre for any length of time would arouse suspicion, he believed. His overriding objective was to bomb Dublin and he did not wish the cars to be discovered and the bombs defused. But neither did he wish to hang around in the Coachman's car park into the late afternoon with the attendant risk that that presented to him personally if the bombs exploded before he left the South. He concluded, therefore, that the most practical strategy for him personally was to load the bombs early, send the bombers on their way and get back across the border before the bombs exploded. The risk of the bombers being apprehended as they 'wandered' round in their cars in north County Dublin with their bombs on board was minimal, Hanna believed.

Contrary to speculation in the press in the days following the bombings, the bombers did not have 'relief cars' parked ahead of them in each street. Hanna did not wish Northern cars, stolen or otherwise, to arouse suspicion or worse still the bombers to be arrested. But the issue did not cause a serious problem. If the worse came to the worst they were prepared to 'dump' the deadly cargo by simply abandoning the cars (as their co-bombers in Monaghan did) double parked or otherwise in the same locations. They would still have caused the same death and destruction: possibly even more if they were double parked.

Nothing is known for certain of the route the bombers travelled home. What is known is that Billy Hanna and his accomplices in the car park left Dublin before 4 p.m. and with little more than an hour's travelling time between that and the border were safely back in the North before the bombs exploded. It's believed, however, that the bomb-drivers and their accomplices escaped by driving directly through Dublin city centre (in the case of the Leinster Street bomber and his accomplice directly through O'Connell Street) back along the smuggler's route from whence they had come. Having planted their bomb at approximately 5.10 p.m., the Leinster Street bombers would almost certainly have reached the northern end of O'Connell Street - possibly even further - by the time the bombs exploded. It must not be forgotten that the Talbot Street and Parnell Street bombs were planted on one side of O'Connell Street only. This, say military experts, was highly intelligent military planning by people who knew what they were doing. It meant that in the immediate wake of the bombings the chaos and confusion would largely be confined to one side of O'Connell Street and would not block the escape route of the bombers fleeing north. It would be reasonable to expect a delay of at least twenty minutes, possibly even longer, before the Gardai in north city stations got around to erecting their first checkpoints, having received information from communications in Dublin Castle as to what had actually happened. By then the bombers were almost certainly outside what could be described as the inner city and its precincts and were well on their way towards the back roads of north Dublin, heading towards the smuggler's country.

Each getaway car, as it fled the scene from Dublin city centre, contained three men (in the case of Talbot Street possibly four) including each bomb driver. Some, and possibly all, of the occupants of each car were heavily armed. They did not intend giving up without a fight if stopped at a Garda checkpoint.

Precisely where and at what time the bombers crossed the border will probably never be known, but it is accepted they were home before 9 p.m. Gardai say the Monaghan bomb was planted to coincide with the time the bombers reached the border and that the tactic was used to 'pull their men away' from that stretch of border where the Dublin bombers intended to cross in making their escape: the area mentioned is that stretch of border around Hackballs Cross between Dundalk and Carrickmacross. The Gardai are prepared to admit that the tactic worked and that the bombers did escape around that time but no one is prepared to elaborate. However, mystery surrounds precisely what happened that fateful evening. For years rumours have abounded that Gardai manning a checkpoint at Hackballs Cross found themselves confronted by heavily armed men returning from Dublin and, threatened with instant death, were left with no option but to let the bombers through. It was feared the incident would cause a public outcry and as a result was concealed from the public. However, such an allegation has never been confirmed.

Throughout the 14-day UWC strike Billy Hanna, Jackson, Boyle and other UVF men from Lurgan operated a kind of 'soup kitchen' from a bingo hall in the Mourneview estate in Lurgan. Because the economy was virtually paralysed many essential items necessary for simple day-to-day survival in homes across the North were in short supply. One Lurgan woman remembers the bingo hall and says the UVF men were handing out coupons on a rota basis to the people, allowing them to collect their rationings. They were also handing out food parcels to people in need. She distinctly remembers Hanna and Jackson and says Hanna was the 'head buck cat' in charge of the bingo hall throughout the duration of the strike. Neither she nor anyone else in the Mourneview estate however can remember Hanna or Jackson going missing for a day (or even half a day) to hand out different kinds of parcels in the car park of a pub in Whitehall in north Dublin.

CHAPTER 5

INVESTIGATION CUL-DE-SAC

'This is the bastard we are looking for and we have enough evidence on him to stick him away.' Detective Superintendent Dan Murphy had worked night and day on the investigation and he was now confident he had the right man for the Parnell Street bomb. According to a number of gardai present he paced up and down the floor at the Garda conference holding aloft a photograph of David Alexander Mulholland, the 36-year-old part-time UDR man from Killycomaine in Portadown.

'So what's holding us; can't we get cracking and have him extradited?' asked a detective sitting on a chair within feet of Murphy. 'Do you want to get us all fucking sacked?' barked Murphy as his face reddened and the veins in his neck swelled out. Officers could only speculate that the case for extradition was being blocked somewhere higher up the line.

Mulholland had been easily identified as he parked his bomb-car in Parnell Street. Teresa O'Loughlin had picked him out twice from two different photographs and two other male witnesses had also picked him out. They had given Murphy his biggest break on the investigation and Billy Hanna his biggest headache. After Mulholland's identification, the Garda investigation began to snowball and their enquiries moved uncomfortably close to Hanna and later proved his undoing. He had allowed all four bomb-drivers to drive the bomb-cars undisguised. For Hanna and the bomb-team it was a recipe for disaster, particularly in the case of Mulholland, who operated on the border and whose identity and photograph were certain to be - and were - in the possession of the Gardai.

Mulholland was tall (well over six feet) weighed about 14 stone, had fairish hair sleeked back over his ears, and was strikingly handsome. He was chosen by Hanna to plant the Parnell Street bomb, not because of his intelligence as an operative but because he was courageous and could fight his way out of a tight situation if cornered. But it was Hanna's great mistake, not only to use him undisguised, but to use him at all. Mulholland was an irascible character with a short temper. He drew attention to himself by driving the wrong way up a one-way street and showing impatience while attempting to park his bomb-car. He was entirely the wrong man for the job. Shortly after Mulholland's identification he was arrested by the RUC in Armagh, following a request from the Gardai, and interrogated about the Dublin bombings. He denied everything and was released.

Three weeks after the bombings, the British army undercover operative Fred Holroyd, who was based in Portadown at the time, wrote in his diary: 'David Mulholland seen in Portadown after his accident.' Twenty-eight years on Holroyd cannot remember what the entry meant or where he got his information from. He was not aware at the time that Mulholland was involved in the bombings or indeed that Portadown played a significant role in them.

As the pieces of the jigsaw began to fall into place, Dan Murphy and Colm Browne visited Belfast to investigate the background to the car hijackings. Arrangements were made with the RUC for the two men to visit Tennant Street police station, which polices the Shankill area where two of the cars were hijacked. But the visit turned out to be a disaster. Murphy and Browne were asked by the duty officer to sit in the station's waiting room while he went to look for a senior officer. Twenty minutes later he returned to say no one was available to see them. When they asked if they could visit the areas where the cars were hijacked and speak to the owners they were told it was dangerous and were advised not to go. Angered and frustrated at the lack of RUC cooperation, the two men left for Derry to investigate reports (which turned out to be false) that the explosives used in Dublin had first been delivered to Derry, where a senior UDA man there was supposed to have delivered them to Dublin. Dan Murphy later told colleagues that the visit to Tennant Street was one of the worst experiences of his life. The atmosphere in the station was so hostile he feared he and Browne would not get out alive.

But the refusal of the RUC in Belfast to cooperate did not deter the Gardai. The identification of Mulholland from file photographs was a significant breakthrough. According to a former high-ranking garda officer (now retired), Mulholland, shortly after his release from RUC custody, was approached by RUC Detective Inspector Frank Murray, who was based in Lurgan. Murray, a Catholic, was a close friend of the Gardai and visited Garda headquarters in Dublin regularly. At the request of the Gardai Murray persuaded Mulholland, due to the overwhelming evidence against him from witnesses in Parnell Street and the threat of extradition, to turn informer on the bombings. A short time later a similar approach was made to Hanna - after Mulholland named him as the leader of the gang - and he too agreed to cooperate. In return for their 'full and frank' cooperation both men were offered immunity from prosecution. The deal was worked out by Ned Garvey in Garda headquarters with Frank Murray acting as go-between, but it did not have official RUC approval and was merely a personal thing between Murray and Garvey. Because of the great sensitivity surrounding the deal, Garvey, who was effectively running the investigation from his office in the Phoenix Park, did not inform his boss, Commissioner Patrick Malone. Malone was a weak leader and during his term of office effectively did what Garvey instructed him to do. During an interview with my colleague Glen Middleton from Yorkshire Television in 1992, Malone admitted that Garvey ran the bombing investigation and that he knew little of what was happening on it.

As a quid-pro-quo for Murray's involvement in the investigation, Garvey invited Murray to visit a republican arms dump in Donabate in north Dublin, which the Gardai had uncovered a short time earlier. According to Fred Holroyd he and Murray visited Garvey in his office in the Phoenix Park (where Holroyd was introduced to Garvey for the first time) in early 1975 and later that day visited the arms dump accompanied by armed Garda detectives. The purpose of the visit was to determine if the weapons had been used by republicans in attacks in the North. That night Murray returned home but Holroyd was booked into a guesthouse near Garda headquarters by a Garda detective, who paid the bill and asked

Holroyd if he wished to be 'fixed up' with the landlady's daughter. Holroyd declined the offer however. As Holroyd was not involved in the bombing investigation he was not informed of the real purpose behind Murray's visit.

By the end of July the Gardai had pieced together 95 per cent of the entire operation. From Armagh they had the names of Hanna, Jackson, Boyle, Wesley Sommerville, Fulton, Mulholland, Fulton's co-quartermaster, G.J., James Mitchell and the businessman who supplied the cars. From Belfast they had the names of Marchant and Bingham, who were involved in hijacking the cars. Along with Mulholland the information supplied by Esther Drumm and customers in the Coachman's Inn had given them almost the entire picture of the Whitehall end of the operation. But apart from Mulholland the evidence against the remaining suspects was unproveable. They had been fingered by loyalist colleagues who were not prepared to go to court to give evidence against them. And there was no forensic evidence against any of them.

For their part Hanna and Mulholland paid a heavy price for their cooperation with the Gardai. On Sunday night, 27 July 1975, thirteen months after the bombings, Hanna was shot dead as he returned to his home at 45 Huston Park, Mourneview, with his wife Ann from a night out in the nearby Legion club. As he alighted from his car outside his gateway a man wearing a mask, but whom Hanna recognised, approached from a nearby laneway and pointed a gun at him. 'What are you playing at, Robin?' Hanna enquired calmly, treating the matter as something of a joke.

The man was Robin Jackson who was accompanied by Harris Boyle, Wesley Somerville and Stewart Young, another senior Portadown UVF man. Jackson later told William McCaughey, a crooked RUC man convicted of murder, that he shot Hanna as a result of information he'd received that Hanna was selling guns to the IRA. However, it is believed by loyalists now in mid-Ulster that Hanna's murder was set up by the army, who found out about his contacts with Murray and hence the Gardai but who decided to conceal the truth from

Jackson, in case Jackson decided to follow suit and also start informing.

Twenty-four hours after Hanna's death, Mulholland fled his home at 113 Ulsterville Park, Killycomaine, with his wife and family and has lived in Chester in England ever since, where he is said to suffer chronic bad health. A colleague, Billy Cooper, who grew up with Mulholland and lived a few doors away, told me of his departure:

> He received word that he was about to be shot and he fled literally overnight. I tried to persuade him to wait a few days so that he could organise things properly but he would have none of it. He was very scared. In the end I loaned him some money to help him settle in on the other side of the water.

The same loyalist sources believe Jackson had already marked Mulholland's card and that he just got out in time. (In 1993, following the Yorkshire Television programme on the bombings, two Garda special branch men from Dublin, Detective Supt. Sean O'Mahony and Det. Sgt. Pat Raftery, flew to Chester to interview Mulholland at a local police station where he had been detained by local police following a Garda request. He flatly denied involvement in the bombings and was released.

Shortly before the publication of this book I spoke to a former high-ranking Garda officer who was involved in the 1974 investigation. In the years afterwards this officer went on to achieve even higher rank within the Gardai, and had access to Garda files at the highest level. He was not aware of Dan Murphy's remark vis-a-vis David Mulholland's extradition, nor was he aware that his extradition was allegedly being blocked at a high management level - namely the Assistant Commissioner Ed Garvey. But he offered this comment on the matter and the Garda investigation in general. He asked not to be named as he feared he might be called to give evidence to the bombing enquiry.

Any important information on the bombings would have come through Garda Special Branch. With regard to David Mulholland's possible extradition, if Mulholland was an informer and if Dan Murphy went to C3 in Garda headquarters and said, 'Look, we've got enough on this guy, can we start moves to have him extradited,' he could very well have been told 'Forget that one, that one goes no further.' There was nothing Murphy could do in those circumstances.

After the first three-month burst, the Gardai began to scale down their investigation and by the summer of 1975 it was, for all intents and purposes, at an end. The RUC had officially pulled down the shutters and the Gardai appeared helpless to press the issue. Despite the overwhelming success of the investigation in unearthing the names of the bombers and their *modus operandi*, the government was not informed of the developments. The Minister for Justice, Mr Cooney, was not told that the Gardai had a list of suspects - with solid evidence against one of them - nor that the RUC were refusing to cooperate. As the Minister responsible for the Gardai and the courts he was entitled to know this.

In the Dáil in May 1975 (the first anniversary of the bombings) the question of 'names' and the Garda investigation was raised by the opposition Fianna Fáil TD Noel Davern. In response to an article in the London *Times* by the journalist Robert Fisk that three people interned in Northern Ireland 'had claimed they were responsible for the Dublin and Monaghan bombings in May 1974', Mr Davern asked the Minister for Justice, Mr Cooney, if he was aware of this. In a reply read out by the Minister for Lands, Tom Fitzpatrick (Mr Cooney was unable to attend the Dáil that day), Mr Cooney said, 'Nobody has been made amenable for the crimes'. Mr Fitzpatrick then said he had no more information on this matter than the Deputy had. He could say, however, that the Garda Siochána had no evidence as to the identity of the culprits. Mr Davern asked was it not the case that the Under Secretary of State for Northern Ireland had said that these three were in their custody at one stage. Mr Fitzpatrick said he understood that was so but as far as the Garda Siochána was concerned they had no information as to the identification of the culprits. Mr Davern asked was the information not passed on to the Garda Siochána. Mr Fitzpatrick replied that if these people were interned, the internment would have been because there was no evidence to sustain a conviction. If, in fact, these were the persons who carried out offences committed here they could not be held responsible unless the reciprocal legislation which was now being sponsored here and in Britain was passed. Otherwise it would not be possible to bring those people to justice in Northern Ireland for crimes committed here.

Whilst Mr Fitzpatrick and Mr Cooney acted quite honourably and told the truth, as far as they knew it, the information given to them and to the Dáil - and consequently the public - was a monstrous and bare-faced lie, and typified the kind of misinformation the public is subjected to by the State. Not only, as I have repeatedly stated throughout this book, did the Gardai know the 'identity of the culprits', but they knew how the operation was carried out from beginning to end.

In interviews with the *Sunday Independent* in July 1993, following the Yorkshire Television documentary on the bombings, four former government Ministers said they were never told that the Gardai had names. Justin Keating, who was Minister for Industry and Commerce in Liam Cosgrave's coalition government, said:

> Firstly that [that the Gardai had names] was never brought to government and secondly I feel let down as a member of government for not knowing that, because I would have taken an extremely serious view of it. I would also have taken an extremely serious view of the RUC having sat on the investigation. But it is perfectly possible that it went to the Cabinet Security Committee. It might have been a political decision of theirs not to inform their Cabinet colleagues.

The Cabinet Committee on Security consisted of the Taoiseach, Liam Cosgrave; the Minister for Defence, Patrick Donegan; the Minister for Justice, Patrick Cooney; the Minister for Posts and Telegraphs, Conor Cruise O'Brien and the Minister for Local Government, James Tully.

Patrick Donegan told the paper:

> Not only had the list of Garda suspects, and the problems with the RUC, not been brought to a full cabinet meeting but neither were they brought before the Security Committee.

Dr Conor Cruise O'Brien said:

> It did not come before the Cabinet and I was a member of the Security Committee and it did not come before the Security Committee either. If the Gardai had reported any lack of RUC cooperation, then Garret Fitzgerald, who was Minister for Foreign Affairs at the time, would have raised the matter with Merlyn Rees, Secretary of State for Northern Ireland, who said on the programme (YTV) that he had not been made aware of the identity of suspects and the alleged lack of cooperation from the RUC.

Mr Cooney told the paper:

> The Gardai and the RUC may well have been discussing names, but nothing came before me.

CHAPTER 6

THE MONAGHAN BOMB

Eighty-eight minutes after the Dublin explosions, a fourth no warning car-bomb exploded in the border town of Monaghan, six miles inside the Republic.

The bomb, which is estimated to have contained 150 pounds of home-made explosives with a gelignite booster, was packed into a beer-keg and was operated by a clockwork detonating mechanism. The bomb also contained a number of items of farm-machinery including heavy-gauge aluminium and brass cog wheels, designed to inflict maximum death and injury. It was placed in the boot of a 1966 Hillman Minx, which exploded outside Protestant-owned Greacon's bar in the Diamond, in the centre of Monaghan town at 6.58 p.m. Six people were killed instantly (a seventh died later), five male and one female, and fifteen were injured. Three of those died inside the pub and three outside, thirty-one vehicles were damaged and the total malicious injury claims (in 1974) came to £172,391.00.

While the Monaghan bomb was part of the overall strike at the Republic, the two operations were carried out separately by separate teams. The Monaghan attack was carried out exclusively by Armagh loyalists working under the direction of Billy Hanna in Lurgan and included UVF and UDA men - chosen more for their familiarity with each other and the geography of the territory they were about to traverse, than paramilitary loyalty. Despite this the bombers failed to research their mission properly, fouling up the operation and scoring an own goal by planting the bomb outside a Protestant pub, killing four Protestants.

The Monaghan operation began on Friday afternoon at West Street car park in Portadown, Co. Armagh. This is the main shopping precinct of the town and includes a large car park where shoppers park their cars. On Friday afternoon, Dermot Crossey, a Catholic from the neighbouring town of Craigavon, went shopping in Portadown with his wife. At 3.30 p.m. he parked his eight-year-old green Hillman Minx, registration number 6583 OZ, in the car park. When he returned at 4.25 p.m. it was missing. He reported it immediately to Portadown RUC, but by this time it was well on its way to County Monaghan.

Crossey's Hillman was stolen (Gardai estimate it was taken around 4 p.m.) by a group of men representing the UVF and UDA from a nearby Protestant housing estate, who were familiar with the car park as well as the roads leading out of Portadown towards Monaghan. They drove the car south through Armagh city towards the border (a distance of about forty miles), where they collected the 150-pound bomb at a farmhouse just north of the Monaghan/Armagh border. The bomb had been made up and left there for collection a number of days earlier.

Following the bombing a number of witnesses came forward to tell the police, both in Armagh and Monaghan, that they had seen the suspects and the bomb-car that afternoon. Rev. Brian Johnson, who was a clergyman in Portadown at the time, told the RUC he saw a number of men acting suspiciously in West Street car park at 2 p.m. that afternoon. One man, known as Cha Gilmore, whom Johnson identified from police photographs, was trying to force down the window of a car. Nearby was a bronze-coloured car with a leading UDA man, known as 'Nicko' Jackson, sitting in the driver's seat, whom Johnson also identified from photographs. Standing beside him, outside the car, was a UVF commander for Portadown, Stewart Young, whom we met earlier.

While Johnson saw the men at 2 p.m. it can safely be assumed that it took some time, including a number of failed attempts, to acquire a car unnoticed. It's also possible that the bombers watched Crossey parking his car and stole it immediately after he parked it.

The second witness to see the bombers was Mai Flanagan who was on a shopping trip from the Republic to Portadown with her husband that afternoon. She told Gardaí she was a passenger in the front seat of her husband's car while travelling from Portadown to Monaghan. They left Portadown at 5.00 p.m. and on the Armagh side of Middleton in the vicinity of

Long Nancy's Pub (ten miles north of the border) an 'old green coloured' car overtook them travelling at 70 mph. Its left, front mudguard was dented and rusty. In a later interview with police she identified the area she saw the Hillman in as Milford, Co. Armagh. She also identified a piece of the bomb-car as being of the same colour as the car that passed them at Milford. Her husband Peter Flanagan told police he had a recollection of 'tailing this car' to a point about four miles on the Armagh side of Middleton, in the vicinity of Long Nancy's pub. When they reached Tyholland Custom's Post (on the border) he remembered seeing a 'new off-white Thames 30 100-weight van' and a 'big lorry' stopped for customs checking 'but no green Hillman Minx'!

The bombers, of course, did not travel through customs, but, like the Dublin gang, crossed the border by an unapproved road, at a well-known local landmark known as Ward's Cross. This area forms part of the border territory in County Armagh which became internationally famous in the mid-1970s when dubbed 'Bandit Country' by a British Secretary of State for Northern Ireland. It's an area of Northern Ireland which is predominantly nationalist and where the Provisional IRA received its greatest support throughout the 1970s and 1980s. Since the mid-1970s the security forces have rarely travelled these areas by road due to the use of land mines and 'culvert bombs' by the IRA, choosing instead the use of helicopters in intelligence gathering and house searches. It could also be argued that the venture by the loyalist bombers into Monaghan on May 17 carried its own risks, but given that the operation was carried out in strict secrecy, during daylight hours, that risk was substantially reduced.

The next witness to notice the Hillman was Thomas Rushe, who lived near the border at Ward's Cross. He was standing with his bicycle at Ward's Cross at 6.25 p.m. 'or later' when he saw 'a dirty old green car', which he thought was a Hillman, come up the Knockbane Road and cross into the State (local term for Irish free State) at Ward's Cross. This is what he told Gardai:

This car was being driven very slowly and there were two men in the car. The driver was 40 to 45 years old, had grey hair, fairly long, which seemed to blow about and fall down to his forehead, not over his ears. He had long thin sidelocks and a thin, long face, with face bones, hard-looking, a long neck, broad shoulders and was wearing a grey jacket. The passenger was smaller, about 40, dark hair, thin face and was wearing a dark jacket. When the car came towards Ward's Cross it turned right and drove in the direction of the Old Armagh Road towards Killyneil Cross.

Ward's Cross is a particularly difficult border crossing, which forms a rugged humpback hill and emerges on the southern side of the border in a fork with a sharp turn towards the Old Armagh Road. One can understand why an eight-year-old car, containing two people, 150 pounds of explosives, a beer-keg and pieces of farm-machinery was being driven very slowly.

A short distance further on at Killyneil Cross, the bomb-car was observed again, this time by Thomas Treanor, who lived 150 yards on the Monaghan side of Killyneil Cross. At 6.45 p.m. he was standing outside his front door when he heard a car 'from Killyneil Cross direction'.

It stopped about 25 yards away on the Killyneil side of my house. I saw a man get out of the car on the passenger side and I was under the impression that this man was moving from the back to the front seat. I heard two people speaking at the car. One I thought was a young male and the other was an older male voice. I could not get a proper look at the man at the rear as the hedge was too high. I saw the top of the man's head - he had brown and bushy hair. I could not be sure if this man wore a cap. I was under the impression that the occupants in the car were in a hurry. I heard the car door close softly.

When this car drove past Treanor's gate towards Monaghan, I noticed it was dark green and didn't look very clean. About 15 minutes later I heard the fire sirens in Monaghan.

Closer still to its target the bomb-car was seen again on the outskirts of Monaghan town. Matt Waters, a custom's officer, was driving from the town centre towards the Dublin Road (in the direction the bombers were coming from) accompanied by a friend, when he met it. This is what he told Gardai:

> At 6.40pm I was travelling from Old Cross Sq. towards the Mall Road accompanied by Alan Farnam, when I saw an old type Minx, dirty green colour, coming from the direction of the cathedral, travelling towards Dublin Street. I stopped to let it pass before I turned right into Mall Road. I took particular notice of this car as I had a friend in Northern Ireland who has a similar car. The reg. (of the bomb car) contained four figures, followed by OZ or DZ. I noticed a wing was dented. There were two occupants in the front - one was about 25 years. I think there may have been one in the back.

Gardai in Monaghan estimate the bomb-car was parked outside Greacon's bar between 6.45 p.m. and 6.50 p.m., just over ten minutes before it exploded. Despite being planted in one of the busiest streets in Monaghan, no witnesses came forward to say they saw the car being parked. But a number of people saw it being driven into the town centre, and parked in position outside the pub before it exploded. Seamus Murphy, a local man, was sitting in his car accompanied by his wife, Mary 'at the monument' (a short distance from Greacon's pub) at 6.45 p.m., when he saw it being driven through the Diamond. This is what he told Gardai:

> My car was facing towards the North Road (towards Greacon's pub). I remember seeing an old

green Hillman Minx coming from the direction of the Diamond. The driver was about 40, he had dirty blonde hair, thinning and combed straight back. I saw a passenger in this car. The green Hillman was followed by a blue car of the 1100 type. I took particular notice of the Hillman car as I was afraid that I being double parked at the monument would cause an obstruction. I am unable to say where these two cars went to. I can say they drove past me and drove northwards. I then drove my car past Greacon's to the County Hospital. I didn't notice any cars parked outside the windows or doors of Greacon's but it is highly probably that they did park outside Greacon's.

Seamus Murphy's wife Mary corroborates her husband's story and says the second car, a blue vehicle, was driving 'very close to the Hillman'.

The driver [of the Hillman] was 35-40 years, with ginger to fair hair, thinning and combed back. The passenger was 40 years, with dark hair, a thin face and was wearing a hat. I can give little detail about the occupants of the second car but I thought there was a woman passenger in the front.

Two local women shopping in the town, Annie Martin and Veronica McGuigan, saw the bomb-car parked outside Greacon's pub as they left the local post office at eight minutes to seven. The distance from the post office to the pub was 46 yards. Thomas Hagan, another local man, was sitting in his car outside Greacon's bar from 6.30 p.m. He drove away at 6.45 p.m. and told Gardai the Hillman was not there when he left. Patrick Callan, a local bus driver, parked his bus a short distance from Greacon's to buy cigarettes in another pub in the street. He left the bus at 6.55 p.m. and as he entered the pub he heard the explosion. He told Gardaí he distinctly remembered a 'dirty green old type car', which he thought was a Hillman parked outside Greacon's. His eight-year-old son, Ronan, who was with him in the bus, had drawn his attention to it because it was 'badly parked' outside the pub.

Intelligence received by Gardai at Monaghan from across the border during their investigation established that the bombers collected the bomb around 5 p.m. at the farmhouse a short distance across the border. Because the Monaghan attack was organised separate from Dublin, it was considered imperative by the bombers that the explosives be stored as near to Monaghan as possible. This was due in part to the risk of running into an RUC checkpoint in the North but more so the risk of being stopped by IRA men, who frequently mounted checkpoints in south Armagh in the 1970s. Following initial difficulty in finding a Protestant farmer willing to store the bomb (most Protestants in this area had not previously engaged in terrorism due to the overwhelming presence of nationalists), a local Protestant smuggler, operating on behalf of the Portadown gang, persuaded a neighbouring farmer to accept it. (Also crucial to this part of the operation was the former UDR man Ross Hearst. Fifty years old at the time and a native of the Middleton area of south Armagh - just north of the border - Hearst provided vital knowledge of the local border area and its surrounds to the bombers, which enabled them to plan their entry unimpeded into the town, and, more importantly, their escape. Hearst was murdered by the Provos in 1980 but his killers were not aware of his involvement in the worst attack ever to take place in a border county. His daughter - a UDR 'Finch' - was also brutally murdered by the same gang.)

The bomb was assembled a day or two before delivery and stored under bales of hay in the farmer's haggart. Gardaí believe the bombers already had their cargo on board when they overtook Peter Flanagan and his wife, Mai, 'at 70mph' in the vicinity of Long Nancy's pub. They believe the bombers were 'running behind time', due mainly to the delay in 'acquiring' a car at West Street car park in Portadown.

The bombers ran into further difficulty when they reached Monaghan town. The perceived objective of the Monaghan attack, as I mentioned earlier, was to pull Gardai away from that stretch of border where the Dublin bombers intended to cross. A subsidiary but also important objective of that attack was to kill and injure as many people as possible. To achieve that aim the bombers chose - during earlier reconnoitring of the town - to plant their bomb in the Diamond, the main shopping area of the town, where they expected the highest concentration of shoppers on a Friday afternoon. (It has been mistakenly believed for a number of years around County Monaghan that the bombers' target was the home of the O'Hanlon family, staunch Sinn Féin supporters and a resting-place for IRA men (and women) on the run in the 1970s, in Park Street in Monaghan town. Monaghan detectives say that was never the case. The ultimate objective was to bomb the town centre, inflicting the maximum death and injury.)

When the bombers arrived with their bomb they found no room to park in the Diamond. Also part of the original masterplan, according to the Gardai, was that the Monaghan bomb explode at 7 p.m. sharp, an hour and a half following the Dublin explosions and the time the Dublin bombers expected to reach the border. If the Portadown gang were to fulfil their part of the deal, and avert aborting the mission, they had fifteen minutes to do so and escape. The next best option was to 'dump' the deadly cargo in the nearest available parking space. North Road, where the bomb exploded, is one of the widest streets in the town. Oblivious to the fact that Monaghan, like most border towns, had a large Protestant population, many of them involved in business, the bombers took advantage of the space and parked the car at right angles to Greacon's pub. The two occupants then transferred to the blue car that was following, and headed towards the border.

The two terrorists who transported the bomb into Monaghan were Stewart Young and Nicko Jackson, both of whom Rev. Brian Johnson had seen trying to steal a car in West Street car park earlier in the day. At the time Young, who drove the bomb-car, was around thirty-five, blond-haired, wore his hair long and was going bald. Today he is totally bald. He was one of the leading killers in mid-Ulster between 1972 and 1977 and was head of the UVF's second battalion in mid-Ulster. He is reliably believed to have been involved in up to fifty murders (including the murder of his former boss Billy Hanna in 1975) during that time. He was born in the countryside a short distance outside Portadown and married a local woman and has a number of children. Robin Jackson once described him as the 'best operator' he had ever seen: 'He could bring his squad out on any operation anywhere, no matter how big the operation, and get them all home safely.' In 1975 (a year after the Monaghan bomb) Young and his squad took part in the slaughter of the Miami Showband, an operation which Jackson led. Earlier in 1972 he took part in the 'mattress' murder of Felix Hughes, whose body was tied to a mattress and dumped in the river Bann in Portadown. During the murder, Hughes' ear was cut off and later passed around in a loyalist pub in Tandragee as a souvenir. In 1974, Young was present in a house in Portadown when a sixteen-year-old schoolboy, Anthony Duffy, had his throat cut by a gang which included Harris Boyle and 'Cha' Gilmore, whom Reverend Johnson saw attempting to steal a car in West Street car park. During the murder, which was carried out by another UVF man whom we shall meet later called Sammy McCoo, Young's brother, Ivor Dean had sex with a seventeen-year-old girl in another room. In 1975 Young took part in the murder of seventeen-year-old Francis Rice who was stabbed twelve times with a dagger by Robin Jackson and Harris Boyle in Castlewellan, Co. Down (see chapter 10). In 1976 Young planted a car-bomb outside the Step Inn bar in Keady which killed the owner's wife and injured her four-year-old child. According to the former RUC man, John Weir, who operated with Young, the army in Keady, when they discovered that Young planted the bomb, told him to 'fuck off back to Portadown, we don't want you down here'. They did not consider it appropriate, however, to arrest him for the crime.

In 1977, the INLA tried to murder Young in a gun attack on his home in Portadown. Shortly afterwards, believing his days were numbered, he fled to Scotland with his family and has lived there ever since. In 1987, while working for RTE, I tracked him down to the small west-coast town of Troon. For three hours in his comfortable drawing room he denied again and again ever being involved in terrorism.

Young's accomplice on the Monaghan bomb, Nicko Jackson, was a much less important figure. He was in his late thirties at the time and was a UDA commander in Portadown but was not involved on the same scale as Young. Today he is 'retired' from terrorism and lives in a council flat in Portadown spending much of his time in the local pubs. When Thomas Treanor thought he saw a man 'moving from the back to the front seat' of the car when it stopped outside his house near Killyneil Cross, it was Jackson moving from the front to the back seat to prime the bomb and have it ready to kill as many of the citizens of Monaghan town as possible. The third man, 'Cha' Gilmore, observed by Rev. Johnson attempting to steal a car in West Street car park, was a local street thug who spent much of his time beating up people who got in his way. He was peripherally involved in a number of terrorist operations but was not a serious player on the paramilitary scene. Other loyalists involved in the bombing were Ross Hearst (already mentioned), from south Armagh, Sammy Whitten, from Portadown and Nelson Young, Stewart's brother.

The owner and driver of the Monaghan getaway car, a blue Hillman, observed by Seamus and Mary Murphy following closely behind the bomb-car, was Billy Fulton, who earlier had organised the explosives for the Dublin bombs. At 5.45 p.m. that afternoon (and over an hour before the bombing) a customs officer, Joseph Rochford, who was manning the Tyholland Customs Post, noticed a blue car pass through his customs post and enter the Republic from the North. He later described the car to Gardaí as a 'Morris or Austin 1100', which had two men in it. (He was obviously mistaken in the make as Gardaí later established it was a Hillman.)

Five minutes before Rochford heard the explosion he saw the same car, this time with 'three men' in it pass through his customs post returning North. However, as it is almost certain there were four people in the car at this stage, the possibility is that either Rochford only managed to observe three, or the fourth person was concealed in the car - possibly to confuse Rochford as a possible future witness. Immediately after Fulton drove through the customs post he left the main road and entered Armagh via an unapproved road to avoid the permanent British army checkpoint which was positioned a half mile further north.

In 1992, during research for this book, I interviewed a number of Gardai who had worked on the Monaghan bomb investigation at the time. They provided me with the names of Young, Nicko and Cha as the three principle suspects who had been involved in stealing the car and planting the bomb. They also provided me with the name of the farmer who had organised the farm haggart in which to store the bomb as well as the owner of the haggart and they named Billy Fulton as the owner and driver of the getaway car. They received part of their intelligence from senior RUC officers in Portadown (the remaining intelligence they received from local loyalist informers on the border) with whom they had been liaising on such matters over a long number of years. They were 100 per cent satisfied their information was correct.

The Gardai also provided me with the name of the principle RUC officer who supplied the intelligence. When I contacted this officer he was reluctant to meet me but finally agreed. However, he requested that I give him a week to look up his notes as the bombing occurred 'a long time ago'! When I finally met him he was extremely nervous and his hands and lips were trembling. He said he had read his notes but the issue was 'far too sensitive' to talk about and he could not help me. After much persuasion, however, he finally agreed to talk. Reading directly from his notes he said Young and Nicko had planted the bomb and Charlie had helped steal the car. A number of days before the bombing, Billy Hanna had visited a pub in Portadown to put the final touches to the operation. The bomb had been assembled by members of the British Army in a vacant house in a housing estate in the Edgarstown area of Portadown. The house had later been pulled down to make way for new housing. The British soldiers did not travel down to Monaghan and had nothing further to do with the bombing after they made the bomb, the RUC officer said. When I asked him if any of the suspects had been arrested and interviewed about the bombing at the time, or if the Gardai had requested this, he said he could not recall - 'It was too long ago.' When I asked the Gardai the same question they could not recall either.

From exhaustive research I carried out in the Portadown area since 1992, I established that none of the Monaghan suspects were ever interviewed about the bombing. For a number of years during the 1970s, Stewart Young worked as an agent for the RUC - even while active as a killer terrorist - and was controlled by senior RUC officers within the county Armagh area.

For the Gardai the Monaghan investigation on the ground was led by Detective Sgt. Colm Browne, who almost single-handedly broke the entire story. He personally interviewed almost all of the witnesses, including the loyalist informers who provided him with the vital information which allowed him to piece together almost the entire picture. He also visited and interviewed RUC officers in the North but he was not aware at that stage of the British army's involvement. Nor was he aware that the RUC were withholding crucial pieces of the jigsaw for their own personal reasons.

At the end of the investigation it was Browne who wrote the comprehensive report on the Monaghan attack, which was passed by his boss Chief Supt John Paul McMahon to Garda H.Q. in Dublin. When I spoke to Browne during research for this book he refused to cooperate. He is not a lover of the media.

CHAPTER 7

1972/73 BOMBINGS

At 7.58 p.m. on Friday night, 1 December 1972, a car-bomb exploded outside the Liffey Bar close to Liberty Hall, the headquarters of the Irish Transport and General Workers Union (ITGWU) as it then was in Eden Quay along the river Liffey in the centre of Dublin, injuring thirty people and causing extensive damage to the pub and the skyscraper building. Fortunately, no one was killed. Eighteen minutes later a second bomb exploded some 500 yards away in Sackville Place, a tiny side-street off O'Connell Street, on the eastern side, killing two busmen and injuring ninety others. The Liffey Bar bomb, which contained around 20 pounds of explosives, was placed in a false petrol-tank attached to a blue Avenger car which was hired in Northern Ireland the previous day. The second bomb, which was roughly similar in size to the first, was also placed in a false petrol tank attached to a silver grey Ford Escort car, registration number 9551VZ, which was also hired the previous day.

Two minutes before the first explosion an anonymous telephone caller to the Protestant-owned *Belfast Newsletter* in Belfast warned that two bombs would explode in Dublin at five minutes past eight. One was at Liberty Hall and the other behind Clery's in Sackville Place, the caller said and then rang off. Staff at the newspaper then contacted the RUC, who immediately relayed the message to the Gardai but by then the first bomb had already exploded. A number of Gardai who had dashed to the scene at Liberty Hall after hearing the explosion immediately returned to Sackville Place after receiving the warning over their car radio and were frantically attempting to clear the area when the second bomb exploded. One young Garda who raced along the street risking his life checking parked cars missed death (or at least serious injury) by seconds as he entered the local Coras Iompar Eireann (CIE) social club, which was situated in a laneway off Sackville Place, to warn patrons of the bomb and to evacuate the premises. In a statement prepared for the Dublin City Coroner's inquest, which to this day has never been held, Garda Michael Bolton told of his brush with death.

> At about 8 p.m. on 1 December 1972 I left Store Street Station to go to the scene of an explosion at Liberty Hall. Somebody there directed me to direct traffic at Butt Bridge. I was there for a while when Sergeant Galligan called me to go to the rear of Clerys. I went in a patrol car with Sergeant Galligan and Gardai McElligott, Gordon, and Forde. Due to traffic jams we had to get out of the patrol car at the junction of Gardiner Street and Talbot Street. When we got to the junction of Marlboro Street Sergeant Galligan directed me to go to Earl Place via Sackville Place. When I got into Sackville Place, I checked all cars I saw on the street. One of the first cars I saw was a silver grey Ford Escort, Regd. No. 9551.VZ. which was parked about three car lengths from the junction of Marlboro Street on the left hand side. I looked into this car but could see nothing unusual. I continued up Sackville Place still checking the cars. Having checked all the cars in Sackville Place as far as its junction with Earl Place, I then went into Earl Place. I saw three or four cars on the left hand side. There was [sic] an awful lot of people coming out of the C.I.E. Club in Earl Place and people seemed to be walking in all directions. I heard members of the Gardai, including Sergeant Galligan and Garda McElligott, shouting at people to clear the area.

The men killed were George Bradshaw, a thirty-year-old father of two children who lived in Sutton in north County Dublin and 24-year-old Thomas Duffy, a father of one, who lived in Artane, also on Dublin's northside. Duffy's wife Monica was expecting their second child at the time. Both men worked for CIE - Bradshaw as a bus driver, Duffy as a conductor - and both were killed as they dashed from the CIE club following the Garda warning and ran straight into the bomb-car.

The late and misleading bomb warning was almost certainly deliberate and was not intended to avoid casualties but was in all probability intended to have the opposite effect. The Gardai in their efforts to evacuate the named bomb area (the area behind Clery's) inadvertently allowed people to spill out of the CIE club on to the street and proceed in exactly the wrong direction. One bus conductor, Joe Harte, who was in the club at the time told me during research for this book that he believes the Gardai made a mess of things: '90 per cent of the casualties that evening were people who left the CIE club after the Gardai came in. People just dashed from the club and headed in all directions. If people had been told to head for O'Connell Street, away from Sackville Place, which after all had been mentioned in the warning, casualties would probably have been a lot less.' Shortly after the bombing Harte, who worked the same bus as George Bradshaw and who escaped without injury, gave the following statement to the city coroner:

> At 3.40 p.m. on the 1 December 1972 I commenced work on a route No. 31 bus which operates from Abbey Street, to Howth. George Bradshaw, Offington Avenue, was the driver of this bus. At 7.45 p.m. on the same date we completed our first half tour of duty in Abbey Street. George Bradshaw drove the bus to Summerhill Garage. I did not accompany him but went for my refreshments to the C.I.E. club, Earl Place. I had my refreshments at a table in the club with Thomas Duffy, a conductor and some others. As I finished my meal, George Bradshaw joined us. He was accompanied by Leo Wilson, bus driver, and Paddy White also a bus driver. At this stage I went to the snooker hall in the club and George Bradshaw said he would join me there later. I had just started a game of snooker when somebody mentioned that there was a bomb scare. The fellows in the snooker hall and I waited for about a half a minute, suddenly a shower of glass fell around us and at the same time

there was an explosion. I with others left the premises and I did not see George Bradshaw or Thomas Duffy. On 2 December at approximately 2.30 p.m. I went to the City Morgue, Store Street. There I was shown articles of clothing to wit a jumper and an overcoat and a pair of shoes by Garda Dermot Duggan. I positively identified these items of clothing and footwear as those worn by George Bradshaw, my bus driver, when I last saw him at about 8.15 p.m. on 1 December 1972, a short time before the explosion at Sackville Place. Also at the City Morgue I identified to Garda Michael Murphy, Store Street, the body of Thomas Duffy, bus conductor, who was sitting at the same table with the deceased, George Bradshaw and others when I left to have a game of snooker in the C.I.E. snooker hall, Earl Place. In addition I wish to add that on 2 December 1972 I saw a body in the City Morgue. I was not able to identify it due to the multiple injuries, it was beyond recognition. The body that I saw was of the same build and height as that of the deceased George Bradshaw.

A post-mortem examination carried out on the body of Bradshaw by the then State Pathologist, Professor Maurice Hickey, the day after the bombings describes the horrific injuries the deceased man sustained from both the force of the blast and subsequent flames which engulfed the bomb-car:

> The clothing on the body was very extensively torn. A black band, presumably the band of a wristlet watch, was present on the left wrist. The head, neck and front of the chest had been totally destroyed. Fragments of the bones of the skull remained attached to the body by the skin of the scalp and back of the neck. The destruction of the front of the chest extended across both shoulders and the bones of both arms were fractured immediately below the shoulder joints. The hair of the head and the hair on the legs and thighs was singed. Multiple puncture wounds, some caused by

fragments of glass, some by fragments of metal, were present on the front of the chest and abdomen and on the fronts of both legs and thighs. Extensive lacerations were present on the backs of both hands. The upper ribs were fractured on both sides of the chest and both bones of the right leg were fractured above the ankle. Internally blood was present in both sides of the chest cavity, in the abdominal cavity and in the pericardium. The left lung had been punctured. The stomach and intestines had been punctured at a number of points and the liver was ruptured.

A similar post-mortem carried out by Professor Hickey on the body of Thomas Duffy describes his injuries:

The hair of the head and the hair on the fronts of the legs was singed. Very numerous puncture wounds, some caused by fragments of glass and some by fragments of metal, were present on the face, the front of the neck, the front of the chest and abdomen, the fronts of the thighs and legs and on the back of both hands. The back of the right hand was severely burned (third degree). The skull was not fractured and the brain was uninjured. A massive haemorrhage had occurred into both sides of the chest cavity and clotted blood was present in the pericardia cavity. One of the puncture wounds in the right side of the front of the chest had penetrated across the aorta or main blood vessel of the body at its origin from the heart. The aorta was completely cut across at this point. In the abdomen, the intestines had been punctured in a number of places and the liver had also been punctured in a number of places.

The scenes of devastation in the areas surrounding both blasts were considerable. Inspector Herlihy of Store Street Garda Station was on duty in his office when he heard the first explosion and rushed to the scene at Liberty Hall. But like a number of his colleagues he returned hastily to Sackville Place after receiving word of the bomb warning there. In a statement to the Coroner's Court he described the chaos:

> Shortly before 8 p.m. on Friday 1 December 1972 I was at Store Street Station when I heard an explosion in the Butt Bridge area. With a number of Gardai I went to Beresford Place/Eden Quay junction. I saw a large quantity of broken glass strewn over a wide area. There were a number of cars on fire in Eden Quay in front of Liberty Hall. I saw a number of injured people sitting and lying on the footway, at the Quay wall and on Butt Bridge. I immediately set about diverting traffic, clearing the area of pedestrians and vehicles and cordoning off the area. The fire fighting units of Dublin Fire Brigade and Ambulances arrived at about the same time as I did. When I was at Eden Quay for about ten minutes, Superintendent Robinson informed me that a call had been relayed to Garda Patrol cars in the area to the effect that another bomb had been placed at the rear of Clery's, O'Connell Street.

The destruction and chaos along the river Liffey at Eden Quay following the Liffey Bar explosion was described in *The Irish Times* the following morning:

> All along Eden Quay window panes were shattered and facades stripped from frontages as well as on Burgh Quay across the Liffey. People lay groaning, screaming and sobbing on the pavement while others ran around in a dazed and shocked condition. Many were covered in blood, others were knocked unconscious. There were pools of blood on Butt Bridge and Eden Quay where the injured had been lying. Ambulances arrived within minutes at the scene and began ferrying the more seriously injured to hospitals. Police, too, were promptly on the scene and made a passage through the hundreds of onlookers who began to converge on the

scene. Michael Keating, manager of the Silver Swan bar across the river in Burgh Quay, said that he was in the empty upstairs lounge when he heard and saw the bomb explode. 'I heard an ear-shattering bang', he said 'and at the same time I saw a wall of red flames shoot up from across the river. I shouted "hit the deck" as there were about 50 people in the bar downstairs. All the front windows of the building caved in.'

As the bombings were the first to claim fatalities in the Republic from the start of the conflict, the funerals of the two dead men were highly emotional occasions and were attended by dignitaries of both Church and State. On December 5 the *Irish Press* reported the scene at the Catholic church in Merchant's Quay in the centre of Dublin as Mass was concelebrated for the two victims:

> C.I.E. busmen yesterday mourned their two colleagues killed in Friday's bomb blast in Sackville Place, Dublin. Flags flew at half-mast at C.I.E. depots throughout the country and Requiem Masses for the two men were celebrated at the Franciscan Church, Merchants' Quay. Hundreds of colleagues of the two men attended the removal of the remains to churches in the city. Members of the C.I.E. Board, workers from all Dublin city garages, and representatives of the company's individual services attended the 10 o'clock Mass for the two victims. The Garda Deputy Commissioner, Patrick Malone, officer in charge of Dublin Metropolitan area, accompanied by Chief Supt. M.P. Kennedy and Chief Supt. E.C. Crowley, representing headquarters officers, attended the removal of the remains and will attend the Mass and burial of Mr. Duffy this morning.

Shortly before the bombings a Sinn Féin rally, to be addressed by its then president Ruairi O'Bradaigh, was assembling outside the GPO in O'Connell Street. At O'Bradaigh's request the meeting was abandoned for fear of further bombs and to allow the Gardai to clear part of O'Connell Street. Liberty Hall, the tallest building in Ireland, had frequently been used by Sinn Féin for party meetings over the previous twelve months and its Árd Fheis (annual conference) had been held there only a few weeks earlier. The Liffey Bar was a regular haunt of Sinn Féin members and a number of them were actually there when the first bomb exploded. It has long been believed the Liffey Bar bomb was intended to kill or maim Sinn Féin people or at least send a warning of things to come.

The 1972 bombings coincided with a period of great political turmoil in the Republic and many people feared the situation was getting out of hand. Seven weeks earlier, on 12 October, the biggest bank robbery in the history of the State up to then took place at the Grafton Street branch of Allied Irish Banks. Part of a six-man gang of Official IRA men led by two English brothers working undercover for the British Secret Intelligence Service MI6 held the wife, sister-in-law and two children of the bank manager, Noel Curran, hostage in their home while the remainder of the gang forced Mr Curran to travel to the bank and hand over £67,000 from the safe. Kenneth Littlejohn, a former paratrooper in the British Army, and his brother Keith had infiltrated the Official IRA in the Rostrevor/Warrenpoint area of south Down on behalf of MI6 in London in conjunction with the Ministry of Defence. Part of their brief was to encourage the Officials to carry out bank robberies in the South with the intention of raising the political temperature and forcing the Dublin government into introducing internment. Their activities were being coordinated by the head of MI6 in Northern Ireland, Craig Smellie.

Following the raid the Littlejohns fled to England but were later extradited to Dublin to stand trial for the robbery. During the trial Kenneth Littlejohn, who had a previous criminal record in England, announced to the court that he had been recruited by MI6 in London and asked to infiltrate the Official IRA in Ireland. He had met the Under-Secretary for the army at the Ministry of Defence, Geoffrey Johnson-Smith, as well as the Defence Secretary, Lord Carrington, he said. Both men later admitted meeting Littlejohn and confirmed he had worked for the 'services'. It also emerged during the trial that the brothers and their gang had been involved in petrol-bomb attacks on Garda stations in the villages of Louth and Castlebellingham in County Louth close to the border. Kenneth Littlejohn was sentenced to twenty years penal servitude in Mountjoy prison; Keith received fifteen years. Within two years of being sentenced, however, Kenneth escaped from Mountjoy and returned to England. He was last heard of in the Birmingham area in the mid-1980s.

Towards the end of November political tension rose to fever pitch when three armed men, disguised as doctors, attempted to rescue the Chief of Staff of the Provisional IRA from the Mater Hospital in Dublin. Sean MacStiofáin, who was one of the founders of the Provisionals in 1970, had been moved there a short time earlier from nearby Mountjoy prison where he was on hunger strike in protest at his imprisonment for membership of an illegal organisation. During the raid an armed detective on guard outside MacStiofáin's ward fired a shot accidentally wounding a ban-garda colleague in the hand. The rescue attempt failed, however, and the men were arrested and later jailed. A short time earlier the government sacked the RTE authority over the broadcast of an interview with MacStiofáin in breach of the broadcasting act. The interviewer, Kevin O'Kelly, was also jailed when he refused to divulge details of MacStiofáin's whereabouts. A short time later MacStiofáin gave up his hunger strike and was transferred to the Curragh military prison in County Kildare to serve out the remainder of his six-month sentence.

By the end of November a political hurricane was raging in Dáil Éireann over the proposed introduction of tough new legislation by the Fianna Fáil government to tackle the threat more effectively from terrorists and gangsters such as the Grafton Street bank robbers, but more particularly the threat that many people saw being posed to the authority of the State by both wings of the IRA. The previous May the Official IRA announced a ceasefire (which continues to the present day), but a number of its units, particularly in Northern Ireland, refused

135

to recognize it and continued with military operations, particularly bank robberies. Six months prior to the publication of the legislation, the government established a Special Criminal (non-jury) Court to try suspects charged with such subversive activity in the Republic (it was that court which sentenced MacStiofáin).

Article 38.3 of the 1937 constitution allows for the establishment of special courts in cases where the ordinary courts are inadequate 'to secure the effective administration of justice and the preservation of public peace and order'. The first Special Criminal Court was established in Ireland in 1939 under the Offences against the State Act of that year to deal with the IRA, who were waging a massive bombing campaign on the British mainland, which was organised from the Republic, mainly from Dublin. The court, which was composed of military officers instead of judges and sat in an army barracks, remained in existence 'legally' until October 1962 but it did not sit between the years 1946 and 1961, during which time the government deemed it safe to return to the ordinary courts and trial by jury. It was re-activated again in November 1961 following a resumption of the IRA campaign in the late 1950s, this time against targets in Northern Ireland.

However, by 1972 and three years into the Troubles, the ferocity of the Provisionals' campaign in the North and more particularly events such as the MacStiofáin episode, along with the murders of a number of Gardai in the South, convinced the government that the ordinary courts, where jurors were being threatened and intimidated, were inadequate to deal with the problem. After six months of the Special Criminal Court's operation, the government found that a substantial number of suspects charged were being acquitted due to a lack of evidence against them. It proposed therefore to strengthen the law considerably by introducing a Bill called The Offences against the State (Amendment) Act. This new act, proposed *inter alia* that 'where an officer of the Garda Siochána, not below the rank of Chief Superintendent, in giving evidence in proceedings relating to an offence... states that he believes that the accused was at a material time a member of an unlawful organisation, the statement shall be evidence that he was then such a member'. In other words a person could be convicted and sent to prison for being a member of an unlawful organisation if a Garda Chief Superintendent believed he (or she) to be such a member. The new Act also added a number of new offences under which a person could be charged before the court.

The Bill, when first published towards the end of November by the then Minister for Justice, the irascible but redoubtable Des O'Malley, caused uproar amongst civil liberties groups, the Labour Party and sections of the media. Intellectual liberals such as Dr David Thornley, a Labour Party backbencher, and Professor Mary Robinson (as she then was) denounced the Bill and Dr Thornley later visited MacStiofáin in hospital and in a very public display of solidarity with his cause called on the government to release him.

But it was Fine Gael, of all parties, that experienced the greatest internal convulsions over the Bill. Its leader, Liam Cosgrave, an arch conservative who held strong right-wing views on just about everything including Northern Ireland, had instinctively wanted to support the Bill. Over the previous months a number of Fianna Fáil TDs (including the former Dublin Gaelic football star Des Foley) had had the whip removed over their refusal to vote with the government on Northern Ireland issues. It was likely they would vote against the new Bill and Cosgrave, fearing the legislation - which he desperately wished to see used against those he believed to be out to undermine the State - would be lost, urged his party either to abstain or vote with the Bill. But the majority of the party, including Garrett Fitzgerald, whose ambition was to topple Cosgrave and take over the party, saw things differently. Fitzgerald and other so-called liberals believed the legislation went too far and was in danger of making unjustifiable inroads into the right of trial by jury. Others such as Tom O'Higgins and Mark Clinton, who belonged to the right wing of the party, saw it first and foremost as an opportunity to defeat the government, opening the way to a general election and the return of a Fine Gael/Labour Coalition government.

By Friday December 1, after five days of internal wrangling over the Bill, the party was in disarray and close to self-destruction. In his book *The Cosgrave Legacy*, the Dublin political journalist Stephen Collins describes the scene in the Dáil and Cosgrave's dilemma as the vote on the Bill loomed.

> Shortly before 10 p.m. on the evening of 1 December 1972 the lights were burning late in the Dail and Liam Cosgrave's enemies in Fine Gael had him cornered. He was almost completely isolated with only Paddy Donegan ready to stand by him whatever the consequences. Virtually all his TDs and senators were in the process of walking out of the Fine Gael party room in disgust at their leader's determination to vote with Fianna Fail in support of emergency legislation. Suddenly a loud thud was heard and the windows of Leinster House vibrated. The first (sic) Loyalist bombs had gone off in Dublin. They killed two people and saved Cosgrave's political life.

The bombings dramatically changed the course of the Dáil crisis. In a little over an hour after the second bomb exploded, Patrick Cooney, Fine Gael's spokesman on justice, announced to the Dáil that his party was withdrawing an amendment it had tabled to the legislation. The Bill was then passed by a majority of 69 votes to 22 and became law 36 hours later when passed by the Senate and signed by the President, Eamon de Valera. The move was a complete *volte face* by the largest Opposition party, which, up to the bombings, had threatened to vote against the Bill and plunge the country into a general election. As it turned out the government survived until the following February when, after a bruising four-week election campaign, on 28 February Cosgrave replaced Lynch as Taoiseach and went on to lead a coalition of his own party and Labour which lasted for over four years.

On Saturday 20 January, seven weeks after the December bombings, a further bomb exploded in Dublin city centre killing one man and injuring thirteen others. Unbelievably the location was once again Sackville Place and the bombers were now beginning to thumb their noses at the security forces in the Republic by choosing to bomb the same location twice within seven weeks. The bombing was a serious security breach for the Gardai and a moment of acute embarrassment for the politicians who, in stampeding the emergency legislation through the Dáil, had promised to rid the country of such deeds.

The bomb, which contained 20 pounds of explosives, was planted in a red Vauxhall Viva car, registration number EOl 1129, which was hijacked in Agnes Street off the Shankill Road in Belfast that morning. Agnes Street is adjacent to Woburn Street where William Henry, the owner of the car that exploded in South Leinster Street in 1974, was first attacked and 'bundled onto the floor of his car'. The car was owned by a Belfast car-hire company and the driver was taken from the vehicle and detained till after 3 p.m., around the time the bomb exploded. The *modus operandi* was identical to that used in the South Leinster Street and Parnell Street bombings of 1974. The attack coincided with an international rugby match in Lansdowne Road in south Dublin (which was attended by a large contingent of fans from Northern Ireland) and would probably have caused much greater death and injury had it exploded two to three hours later when the city was thronged with rugby fans.

Ten minutes before the blast an anonymous telephone caller to the central telephone exchange in Dublin warned that a bomb was about to explode on O'Connell Bridge. Like the previous two bombings the misleading call was a diversionary tactic in which the bombers hoped the crowds of pedestrians on O'Connell Bridge would be herded by Gardai into O'Connell Street where some of them were almost certain to make their way into Sackville Place. As it happened things did not work out that way and luckily Sackville Place was not overcrowded when the bomb went off.

The man who died was 29-year-old Scottish born Thomas Douglas, who lived in Clontarf on Dublin's north side and who quite extraordinarily was also a bus conductor. Douglas, a Catholic, who arrived in Ireland the previous August to take up a job as an electrician but could not find one, took a job on the buses instead. His girlfriend Moira James arrived in Dublin in October to be with her boyfriend and the couple lived together in rented accommodation on the Malahide Road. In a statement to the Coroner's Court she told of their devotion to each other.

> I have known Thomas Douglas since 1969, when I started going out steady with him. We both lived in Stirling then. We became engaged at Christmas 1971. Thomas left Stirling last August and came to Dublin. He used to phone me approx. every week. He was about three weeks in Dublin before he got a job. He had been trained as an electrician but could not get a job there as one, as the system was different. He then rang me and said he had a job got with C.I.E. as a bus conductor. In September he asked me to come to Dublin and I went there one month later i.e. October 25 I saw Thomas every day during my stay. I never knew him to become involved in any organisation other than the football club with C.I.E. and spent most of his time working or at home in his flat at 76, Malahide Road. I last saw him on the 20 January 1973 as he left the flat at 2.30 p.m. to work at 3 p.m. He was then in his usual good health. Later that day the police informed me of his death. I went to the Mater Hospital on Sunday the 21 January 1973 and saw Thomas's body in the presence of Sergeant Duggan.

Douglas's work colleague Martin Lahey who drove the bus Douglas conducted parted him seconds before the blast. In a statement he said:

> On the 20 January 1973 I was working from 3 p.m. driving a 29A bus from Abbey Street to Raheny. My conductor was Thomas Douglas. We left Clontarf Garage at 3.05 p.m. and arrived at Marlborough Street

terminus at about 3.15 p.m. I pulled in right opposite Sackville Place in Marlborough Street. Thomas said he would go to Easons to buy a paper. He left the bus and I saw him go up Sackville Place. He was walking along the left hand footpath as I looked up Sackville Place from Marlborough Street. I last saw him walking on the footpath opposite the entrance to Earl Place. I looked away for an instant and there was an explosion. I could only see smoke when I looked up the street again. I tried to move up to the scene but a Garda Sergeant stopped me. I did not see Thomas Douglas again. One hour later I was told at the garage that he was dead.

Like George Bradshaw, seven weeks earlier, Douglas's body was severely mutilated by the force of the blast. Professor Hickey, who again carried out the post-mortem, described his injuries in a statement prepared for the coroner's court.

There were multiple minor superficial cuts on the front of the face. The hair of the front of the head and of a moustache was singed. Three fingers of the right hand had been blown away and there were multiple fractures in the bones of the right arm to forearm. A minor cut was present on the knuckle of the index finger of the left hand. The greater part of the right hip and right thigh had been blown away leaving the lower portion of the right leg attached to the body by some skin and flesh of the inner side of the thigh only. The shaft of the right femur and the bones of the right side of the pelvis were shattered. Minor lacerations were present on the right instep and the left heel. The hair on the fronts of both legs and thighs was singed. The right side of the diaphragm was ruptured and the liver had herniated into the right pleural cavity. Only very minor haemorrhage had occurred into the right pleural cavity and into the cavity of the abdomen. Multiple small haemorrhagic zones were present in the lower lobes of both lungs.

One of the injured, 22-year-old John Garvey, from Naas in County Kildare, lost a leg in the explosion. A short time earlier he spoke to a stranger, Michael Kelly from Cork, who was visiting Dublin for the day. Kelly described their conversation:

> I went backing horses and I went to check the results. I had £2 win on 'Late night Extra' in Marlborough Place, in Kilmartin's betting office. I left there and went to Kilmartin's in Sackville Place. That was around 3.15 p.m. I met a fellow whose name was John. We talked about horses and jockeys. I asked him to have a drink and he mentioned that it was the 'Holy Hour'. Just as I walked out the door I saw what I thought was smoke coming out of the back of the car. I stepped back into Kilmartin's as I knew that it was a bomb. After coming out of the door John turned right. About five seconds after I turned back in the door there was a blast. I felt my legs being lifted. I fell and my left shoulder hit against the wall. I got up and came outside and I saw a man lying face downwards on the ground. He was ripped from his thigh to his ankle. He asked me to contact his sister. He said he was from Sallins Road, Naas, and worked in Clery's. He said his name was John Garvey. He was the man I had been talking to a few minutes previously.

Like the 1974 attacks, the 1972/73 bombings were never claimed by the organisation which carried them out, but no one was in any doubt that loyalists from Northern Ireland were involved. The loyalist campaign against Dublin first began on 25 November, a week before the Liberty Hall/Sackville Place bombings, when a parcel bomb exploded in an alleyway outside the film centre at Carlisle Building on Burgh Quay close to O'Connell Bridge in the centre of Dublin in the early hours of Sunday morning. The bomb, which contained less than 10 pounds of explosives, injured twenty-five people who had been attending a late-night showing in the film centre. One of those injured lost a leg. The explosion took place while Sean MacStiofáin was on hunger strike in Mountjoy Jail.

The Liberty Hall/Sackville Place bombings caused the first deaths of citizens in the Republic in the loyalist campaign and sent a message to the South that loyalists were serious about the attacks and that the Provisional's bombing campaign of the previous two-and-a-half years would not go unheeded. But there were other reasons for the attacks as well. The IRA's bombing campaign in Britain began in February 1972, a month after (and in retaliation for) Bloody Sunday, when a bomb planted by the Official IRA exploded outside the officer's mess at the headquarters of the Parachute Regiment at Aldershot, killing seven people. It was a clear signal by republicans that the campaign up to now confined to the streets of Northern Ireland, was being widened with a vengeance to mainland Britain. The loyalists and their controllers in British intelligence, on the other hand, were determined to demonstrate by the bombs in Dublin that they, too, could widen their campaign.

But the campaign was not by any means confined to Dublin, as the 1974 bomb in Monaghan clearly demonstrated. In March 1972 a car containing six republicans returning from a Sinn Féin demonstration in Emyvale in north Monaghan was machine-gunned by men in an Austin Cambridge car. Bullets passed through the car but no one was injured. The attack was led by the man who two years later organised the storage of the Monaghan bomb on a loyalist's farm just north of the border in County Armagh. A week later a petrol bomb attack on the Red Star Inn pub in Emyvale followed by a gun attack on a group of people in a nearby housing estate left one woman injured in the leg. In October 1972 a no-warning bomb explosion in Clones, Co. Monaghan, injured one man.

In December 1972 a car-bomb in Belturbet, Co. Cavan, killed two young people and injured a number of others. The bomb, which was planted in Butler Street in the town center, caused widespread damage to a number of premises including the Ulster Bank. Around the same time a car-bomb destroyed a pub in the village of Pettigo in south Donegal close to the border with County Fermanagh.

In January 1973 a courting couple was stabbed to death in their car near Bridgend in Donegal. The couple, Oliver Boyce and Brigid Porter from nearby Burnfoot, were the victims of a random sectarian attack by loyalists from Derry. Later a Derry man, Robert William Taylor, was charged at the Special Criminal Court in Dublin with the murders but was acquitted for lack of evidence. The murders were in fact organised and carried out by the head of the UDA in Derry, a loyalist called Andy Robinson, who later fled the North to live and work on the oil rigs in Saudia Arabia. An electrical engineer by trade, Robinson worked for army intelligence based in Eglinton barracks in Derry city. Today he lives in the scenic village of Portpatrick in the county of Galloway near Stranraer on the west coast of Scotland. During the 1970s he was close to the loyalist hard chaw Glen Barr, who ran the Ulster Workers' Council strike in 1974. He was also close to the Unionist politician Willie Ross, who of course was not involved in paramilitary activity.

In September 1973 a second car-bomb exploded in Pettigo. Three years later an Enniskillen UDR man, George Farrell, was sentenced to fifteen years at the Special Criminal Court in Dublin for the attack. At his trial Farrell said the attack was planned at the home of the head of the UVF in Fermanagh, Robert Bridge. Nine months later the conviction was quashed on appeal on a technicality and Farrell was released. In 1975 Bridge was sentenced to life in Belfast for the murder of a lorry driver in Fermanagh.

On 15 May 1974 (two days before the big Dublin bombs), a pub belonging to Mr Patrick O'Reilly outside Clones, Co. Monaghan, was demolished by a bomb. At 12.15 a.m., Mr O'Reilly and his family were ordered from the premises by three armed and masked men who placed a bomb in the bar. In June 1974 a proxy bomb was driven into the centre of Clones town but was defused before it exploded by a local man. The same month a bomb exploded in a dance-hall in Carrickode in Donegal causing considerable damage to the building. Four months after his release George Farrell pleaded guilty to the Carrickode attack at the Special Criminal Court in Dublin and again said the bombing was planned by Robert Bridge and that he drove Bridge 'and another man' to the scene. In this instance Farrell's Counsel, Paddy McEntee, told the court Bridge had been dealt with 'on another matter' in Northern Ireland.

In September 1974 a proxy car-bomb placed outside the Garda station in Blacklion, Co. Cavan, was defused before it exploded. The following day a parcel bomb exploded in the nearby town of Swanlinbar injuring one person and causing widespread damage to buildings and parked cars. On 10 January 1975 John Francis Green, an IRA commander on the run in County Monaghan from his native Armagh, was gunned down at the farmhouse of a republican sympathizer, Gerry Carville, outside Castleblaney. The attack was led by Robin Jackson, who fired the fatal shots accompanied by his old pals Harris Boyle, John and Wesley Sommerville and a UDR man called Robert McConnell who we shall meet later. Jackson later boasted to the south Armagh farmer James Mitchell, who housed the 1974 bombs, that he himself pulled the trigger. It has long been believed that the murder was set up by the British army undercover operative Capt. Robert Nairac, but no absolute proof of this, one way or another, has ever been found. Another suggestion is that it was set up by RUC Sgt John Weir and an RUC CID man based at Armagh city called John Poland.

In March 1975 a bomb attack off the Greencastle coast of north Donegal near Lough Foyle damaged a number of trawlers in the harbour. The attack was claimed by the UDA and was in fact carried out by Robinson and his unit, which had murdered the courting couple near Bridgend over two years earlier. In November 1975 a bomb attack at Dublin airport left one employee dead and five others injured. The UFF claimed responsibility.

In January 1976 minor bomb attacks on the Shelbourne Hotel in Dublin as well as a number of stores around the city caused considerable damage but no deaths or injuries. Six months later a further series of minor bomb attacks took place in hotels in Rosslare, Co. Wexford; Killarney, Co. Kerry; Salthill, Co. Galway and Limerick. In all, four people were injured and again the UFF claimed responsibility.

In September 1976 a group of UDA men from Derry burned down a pub in the border village of Castlefin in Donegal after robbing staff of the takings. In 1977 a number of Dublin stores were again hit in a series of incendiary attacks. Amongst them were Dunnes Stores, the Jean Junction and Mr. Gear. Three months later a UDA man from the Shankill area of Belfast, Freddie Paterson, was convicted on three counts of arson and sentenced to nine years. He was arrested in Dublin after an incendiary device exploded in his pocket but he refused to name his collaborators. He was released in early 1982 after serving four and a half years.

Apart from the murders of the courting couple in January 1973, attacks by the UDA in the South did not begin in earnest until 1975. This was due in large part to the fact that the organisation was only formed in 1972 and lacked experience as far as the South was concerned. The UVF, on the other hand, had been attacking the South from 1969 and it had much more experience for the task. All of the attacks in Dublin, and the majority of those along the border up to 1975, were carried out by the UVF.

Shortly before his death in 1998 I interviewed the veteran republican Cathal Goulding, who had had close contacts with the UVF throughout the early years of the 1970s. Goulding, a self-professed Marxist, had joined the IRA as a teenager and was involved in the border campaign of the 1950s and early 1960s along with other veteran republicans such as Ruari O'Bradaigh and Sean Garland. Following the split in the republican movement in late 1969, Goulding became Chief of Staff of the Official IRA.

Throughout 1972/73 he and a number of his official IRA colleagues held a series of meetings with UVF men, both in Belfast and Dublin, to discuss mutual working-class issues such as poverty, unemployment and bad housing. For a time senior figures in the UVF such as Gusty Spence, Ken Gibson and its leader Jim Hanna (no relation to Billy Hanna) expressed an interest in socialism and they believed they and the Officials had many things in common. In August 1973 a meeting to discuss such issues was held in the West County Hotel outside

Dublin, attended by high-powered delegations from both organisations. The meeting, which was top secret, lasted all day and was held in a conference room in the hotel. The Official IRA delegation was led by the party leader Thomas MacGiolla and included Goulding and Sean Garland. The UVF side was led by Jim Hanna accompanied by Billy Mitchell and other senior figures whose names Goulding could not remember.

At the end of the day-long meeting the delegates repaired to the bar for drinks and some informal discussion. Towards the end of the evening, according to Goulding, Jim Hanna pulled him to one side and told him he wished to speak to him in confidence.

> He asked me if we, the Official IRA, would be willing to carry out bank robberies here in the South and they, the UVF, would claim them. Then, if we wished, they would carry out similar robberies in the North and we could claim them. He said army intelligence officers he was in contact with in the North had asked him to put the proposition to us as they were anxious to bring about a situation in the South where the Dublin government would be forced to introduce internment. When I refused to accept his proposition, as we were already on ceasefire, he put his hand on my shoulder and said, 'Look, there's no problem. You see those car bombs in Dublin over the last year, well we planted those bombs and the army provided us with the cars. There's no problem.' When I asked him how the bombings were carried out, he said the 1972 bombs were planted in false petrol tanks in both cars. He said they travelled down the main road from Belfast to Dublin and were stopped at a Garda checkpoint at Swords [in north County Dublin] but because the cars were not reported stolen and the Gardai found nothing suspicious in them they were allowed to proceed.

Following the Goulding interview, I spoke to former Gardai who served in Swords at the time and they confirmed that a permanent Garda checkpoint was positioned on the Dublin-Belfast road, north of Swords at the time.

Goulding said he was shocked at the proposition but because he had known Hanna and Mitchell for some time and had met them a number of times previously he decided to continue with the meetings in his efforts to bring about working-class solidarity across the two communities. However, when the big bombs exploded in Dublin and Monaghan nine months later, Goulding decided to end the contacts as he believed the UVF was not serious about socialism and that he and his colleagues were being strung along.

During his time as head of the UVF in Northern Ireland and until the organisation declared a ceasefire in November 1973, Jim Hanna oversaw one of the most vicious sectarian campaigns ever conducted against Catholics throughout the course of the Troubles. It was the time when Lennie Murphy formed his Shankill Butchers (an offshoot of the UVF) and slaughtered innocent Catholics walking the streets of north and west Belfast. Writing in *Hibernia* magazine in 1975, the present-day *Irish Times* journalist Kevin Myers - who knew Hanna personally - detailed some of his links to the army. Describing a two-day gunbattle in May 1972 between loyalists and republicans in west Belfast, during which soldiers sided with loyalists, Myers wrote:

> The gunbattle was wild and bloody and lasted two days, and involved gunmen from three sides. The Army did admit this. But according to Jim Hanna, who first made his military mark with the U.V.F. in the gunfight, some peculiar things happened. He told me, for example, that a British Army patrol had assisted him and two other U.V.F. men into Corry's timber yards, which overlook the Catholic Ballymurphy, and were present when one of the three shot a young Catholic. He said that an Army Major discovered what was going on and ordered the soldiers to withdraw but they did so without arresting the U.V.F. men. By 1973, Hanna had

become the senior military commander for the U.V.F. in Northern Ireland.

Throughout this time Hanna, as he himself intimated to Cathal Goulding, was run as an agent by British army intelligence officers attached to 39 Brigade and based at army headquarters in Lisburn close to where Hanna lived.

The soldiers running his campaign were two Captains called Anthony Ling and Anthony Box, a Lieutenant called Alan Homer, as well as an officer called Timothy Golden, who at the time was not listed as a member of the Intelligence Corps but was believed to have been an SAS man seconded to Intelligence. These officers were known as 'counter terrorists'. They not only had the sanction of the security top brass but were specially trained by the army for the job. They were involved in bombings and shootings and other terrorist activity over a number of years, as part of a province-wide system of 'counter terrorism', which involved the army, the RUC, MI5 and MI6 and which continued throughout most of the Troubles. According to highly placed sources within the loyalist community and the security community itself, these counter terrorists have been responsible for hundreds of deaths throughout the course of the Troubles. This, the securocrats believed, was the only way to fight the Provisionals. The fact that they were involved in criminality, including murder, was of little consequence.

Despite his reputation and position within the UVF, Jim Hanna was, as paramilitaries go, a moderate. He was instrumental in initiating the talks with the Official IRA and he was also instrumental in bringing about the UVF ceasefire. Frankie Curry, the leading UVF man shot dead in 1999, described Hanna as a 'big softie'. Cathal Goulding described him as 'not the worst'. Perhaps he had become sickened at what he saw going on around him and like today's paramilitarists was attempting to break out of the ghastly cycle of violence which he found himself trapped in. Perhaps he was a man ahead of his time.

It is believed now, twenty-eight years later, that Jim Hanna argued against the plans to bomb Dublin in 1974 and for that he paid the ultimate price. In the early hours of 1 April 1974 (seven weeks before the Dublin-Monaghan bombings) he was gunned down as he sat in a car with a woman with whom he was having an extra marital affair. The following day *The Irish Times* described his murder:

The assassination of a 27-year-old Lisburn, Co. Antrim Protestant in the Shankill Road area of Belfast early yesterday morning is reported to have been part of a power struggle within the illegal Ulster Volunteer Force. Mr. James Andrew, Francis Hanna, a self-employed heating and plumbing engineer, was found shot dead in his car in Mansfield Street off the Shankill Road, just after midnight. He had been hit eight times in the head by shots from an automatic pistol fired from close range. Mr. Hanna is reported to have been a member of a U.V.F. delegation which went to Dublin in January for secret discussions with members of the Official Republican movement. He is thought to have been an explosives expert. There has been pressure within the U.V.F. recently to end the cease-fire which the organisation declared last November. Mr. Hanna is thought to have favoured continuing attempts to obtain a détente with Republicans, and his death may signify a 'Right-wing' take-over attempt by more militant U.V.F. men. The assassination had all the marks of an execution. Mr. Hanna was in a militant Protestant area. A 19-year-old girl from Mossley, Co. Antrim, who was in the car with him, was shot in both legs during the attack. She was taken into a nearby loyalist club by local people to wait for an ambulance but Mr. Hanna was left in the car. The victim's £5,000 house in Lisburn was empty yesterday with a 'for sale' notice pinned to the front door. Mr. Hanna had been living there for about a year with his wife and child. The UVF last night denied that it was responsible for the murder. A statement from brigade staff said that they were as appalled and shocked as anyone else about the incident and that they would 'use all the resources at our disposal to bring the killers to justice'.

Despite their protestations no one who knew the UVF was in any doubt that Hanna was shot by his former comrades. Not only that, but many believed then - and still do - that his murder was inspired by the army, who believed Hanna had 'gone soft' and had outlived his usefulness. Perhaps his revelations to Cathal Goulding in the West County Hotel sealed his fate. Following his murder the RUC took away what was believed at the time to have been incriminating evidence from Hanna's home, including group photographs of Homer and Golden taken earlier by Hanna at Hanna's house. One such photograph which shows Homer jokingly pointing a gun at Hanna while Golden looks on, is still in this author's posssession but cannot, unfortunately, be published in this book due to the age and poor quality of the print.

In 1977, three years after Hanna's death, his right-hand man, Billy Mitchell, was sentenced to life imprisonment at Crumlin Road courthouse in Belfast for the double murder of two UDA men in a loyalist feud in 1975. Following a 77-day trial - the longest at the time in Northern Ireland's criminal history - Mitchell was convicted along with seven other UVF men on charges of executing two men and burying their bodies in a shallow grave on a windswept hillside in Islandmagee in east Antrim. The trial, during which a total of twenty-eight men in all were given fifty-eight jail terms ranging from murder to possession of weapons to armed robbery, by and large ended a six-year reign of terror by the east Antrim UVF. On the morning of their arrests two years earlier, the town of Carrickfergus, where the majority of the men lived, was sealed off by the police and army to prevent them making their escape. One man, George Anthony, a close friend of Billy Mitchell's who held the lofty title of East Antrim UVF Brigadier, attempted to break out of the encirclement by driving his car at high speed round the town in search of a back road which he hoped the security forces had neglected to cover. When he failed to find one Anthony drove his car onto the Carrickfergus beach with the intention of swimming 'to safety'. But in a scene reminiscent of the wild west, Anthony, after his car became bogged down in the sand, emerged with his hands in the air and surrendered to police who were following in hot pursuit. Mitchell on the other hand surrendered without a fight.

During the trial the judge, Justice McDermott, a Catholic, described Billy Mitchell as a 'highly intelligent man' and said he believed the chief prosecution witness that 'the accused' was a 'high-ranking officer '(in the UVF).

From 1969, when he first got involved with paramilitaries, until his arrest, Mitchell had been one of the most influential members of that organisation. Born in 1940 into a Protestant home and brought up in a staunch evangelical tradition, he became one of the prime strategists behind the loyalist campaign. He once told colleagues that his 'initial reasons' for paramilitary involvement 'stemmed from a genuine, albeit misguided, and very naïve sense of patriotism': 'I did not, in the early years at least (1969-1973) feel any real sense of moral guilt or shame in my association with, and participation in, violence. Quite the contrary; as I went up and down the country representing the UVF Brigade Staff I met all sorts of people from all walks of life who fully supported the idea that Protestants were justified in using violence against 'the enemy'.

'By the time I did come to entertain serious doubts about the role and purpose of the loyalist paramilitaries, as they degenerated into gangsterism, I had become hardened to the violence and the suffering, and was indifferent to the mounting catalogue of crime and human misery for which my own organisation was responsible.'

From mid-1974, almost five years into the Troubles, Mitchell says he was 'simply carried along by the momentum of the violence. When you stop thinking of people in human terms, you stop thinking of things like suffering and guilt. If you don't feel guilty you cannot be guilty.' Political terminology, Mitchell says, such as 'Ulster is right and Ulster will fight', 'Put your trust in God and keep your powder dry', together with paramilitary slang such as 'target', 'operation', 'enemy agent', 'republican activist', 'traitor', 'informer' and 'execution' tended to decriminalise the violence and depersonalise the whole conflict. The UVF did not 'shoot people', it 'liquidated enemy agents'; it did not blow up public buildings; it 'destroyed legitimate targets'.

In 1979, and three years into his prison sentence, William Irvine Mitchell finally renounced violence and became a Born Again Christian. And, unlike many of his paramilitary contemporaries, on both sides, who used religion as a flag of convenience to achieve early release, his was a genuine conversion.

Later, in correspondence from his prison cell, Mitchell told colleagues of his 'commitment to Christ' and talked about how he had 'grown in his faith' over the years. He warned young people about the dangers of 'drifting into association with paramilitaries', to help them avoid the mistakes he had made, and he spoke about his growing interest in the rehabilitation of prisoners: 'There must be more that can be done on both counts,' he once said.

During research for this book I interviewed Mitchell about his days in the UVF and about his friend Jim Hanna, with whom he operated for over four years. He refused to discuss the 1972/73 Dublin bombings, which he, along with Jim Hanna, masterminded, or the 1974 bombings, which Billy Hanna masterminded. He confirmed, however, that Jim Hanna was run by the army officers Box, Ling, Golden and Homer.

Describing the culture of violence that existed within paramilitary organisations in those years and how he and his comrades looked upon their victims, Mitchell repeated much of his earlier musings: 'The target became a thing, not a person. This was how we depersonalised the war. Then there was the guy known as the "mindless bomber". The guy who said he was "sent out" to do it. I don't believe in mindless bombers - there is no such thing. Every guy knows what he is going out to do.

Mitchell then explained how the UVF would do a 'hit':

> We would sit around discussing an up-coming attack and someone would say, 'Here's a taig we want to hit and here's the army photograph of him and this is the info on him.' The person to be killed was always 'a target'. However, if someone said 'the guy we are going to kill is John so-in-so who lives in No. 20 such a road. He's the guy with the wife and three kids who works in such a place' then that would raise a few hackles. No one wanted to hear that the guy was a human being with a wife and children as that might prick someone's conscience. So long as he remained a 'target', 'a taig' or 'an enemy' everything was fine.

According to Mitchell, the UVF put out 'disinformation' about information they had on Catholics.

> It was part of the game; all lies. Of course the Brits tried to use prods for their own ends and were trying to infiltrate the organisation. But they were not out to do anyone any favours.

And how well did he actually know Jim Hanna?

> Yes, I knew big Jim Hanna well. He was a big soft guy, but he did know Tony Ling, Tony Box, Alan Homer and Tim Golden well. He also knew two guys called Billy and Pat. He was meeting with all these guys as he lived in Lisburn where they were operating. Billy and Pat were the guys who turned up years later when the SAS were called in to deal with the hijacking of a ship somewhere in the Mediterranean.

The incident Mitchell was talking about was the hijacking in 1985 of the Italian cruise liner the *Achille Lauro* by Palestinian gunmen in the eastern Miditerranean. The hijackers were

154

demanding the release of fifty Arab prisoners held in Israeli jails. British special forces (SAS) were called in and put on stand-by but in the end were not required to intervene.

Mitchell then talked about how his career in the UVF started and how the wives of some men tried to get them out.

> I was based on the Shankill Road from 1970 onwards and travelled in and out from Carrickfergus each day. I was then appointed to the Bde. Staff. But the violence was terrible. For years wives of UVF men tried to get them out of the organisation. Hanna's wife, for instance, was trying to get Jim away to America but he wouldn't go and look what happened him in the end. I don't know if Hanna's wife went herself afterwards.

Despite his willingness to discuss other people, Mitchell steadfastly refused to discuss operations he himself was involved in.

> Why are you always wanting to discuss the past? Why not look forward and discuss the future. Let's look forward not back.

With a record like Mitchell's one can understand why he was reluctant to discuss the past.

Mitchell, who was thirty-two when he bombed Dublin the first time and thirty-four when he bombed it the second time and whose wife Mena and two children (a boy and a girl) stood by him during his time in prison, was released in November 1989 after serving thirteen years. Today he is a member of David Ervine's Progressive Unionist Party (PUP), the fringe loyalist party that speaks on behalf of the UVF. He is a staunch supporter of the loyalist ceasefires and the peace process. Apart from his political activity he spends much of his time working with young people in the community around his native Carrickfergus.

Despite his atrocious past I found him an extremely pleasant and courteous man. He is profoundly remorseful for the suffering he caused others and fully accepts now that what he did was wrong.

Brian Faulkner and Gerry Fitt, Stormont - 1973.
Courtesy of Pacemaker Limited, Belfast.

U.W.C. Strike - 1974.
Courtesy of Victor Patterson Archives/Linnen Hall Library.

Jack Rooney (left) and Hugh Watters (right) both killed in the Dundalk explosion.

Family man: Jim Hanna bombed
Dublin 1972/73.
Courtesy of Victor Patterson Archives/Linnen Hall Library.

Billy Mitchell bombed Dublin three times,
now living in Co. Antrim.
Courtesy of RTE © RTE.

Billy Hanna - led the Dublin bombings gang.

"Major" Harris Boyle - leading role in the Dublin Bombings.

Wesley Summerville - leading part in the Dublin bombings
Courtesy of Pacemaker Limited, Belfast.

William "Frenchie" Marchant - part of the Dublin bombing gang
Courtesy of Pacemaker Limited, Belfast.

Merlyn Rees talking to Pte.Eddie McQuade of the 1st Battalion Queen's Own Highlanders at Mulhouse Base - 1974.
Courtesy of Pacemaker Limited, Belfast.

Stan Orme, Brian Faulkner and Merlyn Rees in May 1974, 13 days after the Dublin bombings.
Courtesy of Pacemaker Limited, Belfast.

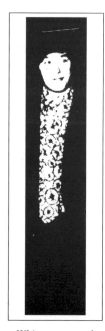

Sammy Whitten - named as one of the Monaghan bombing team, now living in Armagh.

Seamus Ludlow - murdered by drunken Loyalists in 1976

Samuel "Mambo" Carroll who shot Seamus Ludlow in 1976 and now hiding in England.

Merlyn Rees meets Dr Edward Daly, Bishop of Derry, during a visit to Derry when he also met leaders of the Loyalist Community

Courtesy of Pacemaker Limited, Belfast.

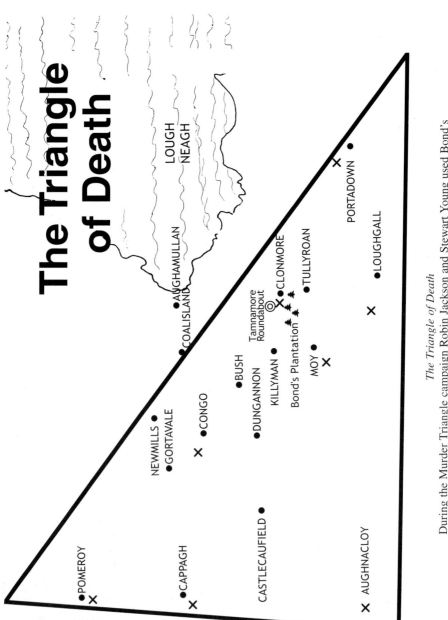

The Triangle of Death

During the Murder Triangle campaign Robin Jackson and Stewart Young used Bond's Plantation (above) to hide and burn cars on their way home after their units carried out murders across counties Armagh and Tyrone.

Courtesy of Fr. Denis Faul and Fr. Raymond Murray.

Robin "The Jackal" Jackson. Died of Cancer in 1988. 21C on Dublin Bombs. thought to have killed up to 100 people.

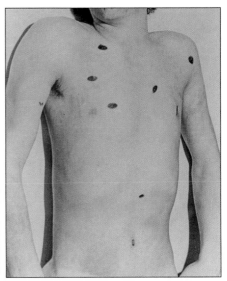

Robin Jackson's handiwork. Some of the stab wounds on the body of Frankie Rice

The body of 16 year-old Frankie Rice

Robert McConnell - leading Triangle assassin

Ross Hearst implicated in the
Monaghan bombing.
Courtesy of Pacemaker Limited, Belfast.

The body of Ross Hearst on the border at
Ward's Cross, murdered by the Provos in 1977.
Courtesy of Pacemaker Limited, Belfast.

John Bingham - Loyalist assassin.
Courtesy of Pacemaker Limited, Belfast.

Ken Gibson - senior UVF man - East Belfast
Courtesy of Victor Patterson Archives/Linnen Hall Library.

CHAPTER 8

THE MAKING OF A KILLER SQUAD

Before his involvement in the Dublin Bombings, Robin Jackson had already established a reputation as a cunning and ruthless terrorist. Nicknamed the Jackal by the media - due to his propensity for roaming the countryside with his squad at night-time seeking out Catholics and murdering them with rapid gunfire either inside their homes or on their doorsteps - Jackson became the great enigma of the Northern conflict.

Members of the Northern Ireland security forces, as well as senior loyalist sources who operated with him over a long number of years, agree that Jackson probably killed more people than any other terrorist throughout the course of the conflict. High-profile killers of the 1970s and 1980s such as Lennie Murphy, the Shankill Butcher, John McMichael, father to Gary, former leader of the now defunct UDP, and Billy 'King Rat' Wright rank among the most notorious in the public mind. But for sheer numbers of victims killed, Jackson's tally probably outstrips all three put together. Some security sources put the figure as high as 100 but there is simply no way of checking the number of people Jackson killed, because of the great secrecy which surrounded his life. For a time during the 1970s and during the worst period of loyalist assassinations, it is estimated Jackson was killing at least one person per week, usually, but not invariably, on a Saturday night. Throughout his long and bloodthirsty career in which he used guns, bombs, iron bars, knives and daggers to murder and mutilate his victims, Jackson's name scarcely became known to the public.

Unlike his fellow terrorist and one-time understudy, Billy Wright, who wallowed in media attention, Jackson shunned publicity and was never once interviewed or photographed by the media. But throughout mid-Ulster where he lived and operated his reign of terror, mainly against innocent, uninvolved Catholics, often in isolated farmhouses, Jackson instilled a fear into the Catholic community paralleled only by that felt by Catholics living on Belfast's peace-line during the reign of the Shankill Butchers. One retired member of the security forces who knew Jackson well described him as Britain's most 'unwanted serial killer'. He was never once charged with murder and his trail of slaughter was largely ignored by the authorities. Not only that but there is incontrovertible evidence, which will be amply demonstrated throughout this book, that Jackson, for a period during the 1970s, was a British agent operating on behalf of the security forces, mainly the British Army. According to William McCaughey, a fellow terrorist and ex-RUC man convicted of the murder of a County Antrim shopkeeper, William Strathearn, in 1977 - a murder that Jackson carried out - Jackson repeatedly told him that he (Jackson) was 'looked after' (by the authorities).

Away from the carnage Jackson was (or pretended to be) a family man and returned home to his family - his children (two boys and two girls) were mere toddlers during his most violent years - and slept with his wife after almost every murder. But he was a man totally devoid of human feeling and appreciation of other people's suffering. To his friends and associates he was a bully. On social occasions he rarely concluded a night out without a fist-fight in which he invariably punched a colleague to the ground. He was quick-tempered, bad-mannered and had a capricious personality. He invariably dominated conversations and according to one UVF man from Lurgan, 'created noise' or 'hummed a song' when other people attempted to speak. He incessantly cadged money from his UVF colleagues, which he never repaid, and was constantly broke. He was also a prodigious lecher and had a string of sexual affairs with young women throughout his married life.

The Jackson story begins in the 1940s in the scenic countryside of south County Down. Robert John Jackson was born in the townland of Ringolish in the parish of Donaghmore on 27 September 1948. The townland has a small, scattered village with a dozen or so houses, a school, a church and an orange hall. The village lies two miles east of the Dublin-Belfast dual carriageway, halfway between the border town of Newry and the County Down town of Banbridge. The area nestles amongst the green, undulating hills of south Down and is one of the numerous patches of serene countryside in Northern Ireland which escaped the violence of the last thirty years. In topography and character the area around Donaghmore, where Jackson grew up, is strikingly similar to parts of the Irish Republic, with large rolling fields bounded by heavy overgrown beech and oak trees. South County Down is particularly noted for Gaelic football. In 1994 the Down Gaelic football team won the All Ireland football championship, the Sam Maguire Cup, for the fifth time in the history of the game in Dublin's Croke Park. Over the past twenty-five years Irish folk and traditional music has experienced something of a renaissance on both sides of the border and nowhere is this more noticeable than in and around the town of Newry.

Robin Jackson's world was a million miles from Gaelic football or Irish music, however. He grew up in a staunchly loyalist home, and village, where the union flag perpetually fluttered from the top of a nearby electricity pole. Jackson's father, a staunch loyalist, worked locally as a farm labourer and the family grew up in poor circumstances in a labourer's cottage in the village. Jackson was ten days old when he was baptised and christened Robert John. Later he became known as Robin to his friends. He attended the local primary school in Ringolish and later attended secondary school in Newry where one of his schoolmates was Jim Hegan, another celebrated name in the annals of the Northern Ireland Troubles, who was wrongfully convicted of the murder of Armagh Catholic Adrian Carroll, in the controversial case known as the UDR Four.

From an early age Jackson hated the sight of Catholics, believing all Catholics to be republicans and therefore intent on overthrowing the State. In later years he told UVF colleagues that the only solution to the Northern Ireland Troubles was to 'wipe out all Catholics', including the three million who live in the Republic. 'If a civil war starts here it's not just the IRA we'll be fighting but the entire Catholic community, so we might as well shoot them now. I don't see the point in just targeting republicans.'

In the mid-1960s Jackson began to hang around the predominantly Protestant town of Banbridge and took a job in the town's shoe-box factory, which had a mixed workforce of Catholics and Protestants. He regularly attended dances in the town's castle ballroom where showbands from all over Ireland performed. He was a keen dancer and, while small in stature, his sturdy frame and striking good looks as well as his swashbuckling, self-confident manner made him attractive to women. It was in the castle ballroom he met his wife Anne Maxwell, a local Banbridge girl, whom he married in the late 1960s. One woman who remembers him from the castle ballroom put it like this: 'Jackson was good-looking and a lot of women, including myself, fancied him. Once Anne Maxwell got her hands on him none of us could get near him.'

By the end of 1968 tension was rising between the two communities in Northern Ireland. The Northern Ireland Civil Rights Association (NICRA) was beginning to hold marches and demonstrations around the province, demanding better housing and jobs for Catholics, and a reform of the electoral system. In the village of Caledon in County Armagh, Austin Curry, who later became a leading light in the SDLP, and other civil rights activists, occupied a house which had been allocated by the council to a Protestant in preference to a Catholic. At Burntollet in Derry a civil rights march on its way from Belfast to Derry city was violently attacked by baton-wielding members of the RUC and its reserve force, the 'B. specials'. A young student from Tyrone, Bernadette Devlin, was making headlines at Queen's university with her fiery speeches attacking the unionist government's discriminatory policy towards Catholics.

Robin Jackson was just twenty years of age, newly married and with a steady job. He was a keen sportsman and was beginning to show some potential as a footballer. Most weekends were spent playing football or 'messing about' with boats at the sea on the east coast of County Down. He was also interested in dogs and regularly went badger-baiting to the

Republic. Despite his personal animosity towards Catholics, the simmering turmoil around the province concerned him little and he viewed it as a problem happening elsewhere. In the late 1960s he availed of an opportunity to develop his football career in Australia and he left Northern Ireland just as the province was about to enter its worst period of inter-communal strife since partition.

By the autumn of 1969 violence had erupted on a massive scale in two of Northern Ireland's best known ghettos - the Bogside in Derry and the Falls and Shankill areas of west Belfast. In the Bogside hundreds of stone-throwing demonstrators emerged on to the streets burning cars and buses and erecting barricades in response to police brutality against civil rights marchers. In response, the Stormont government sent in massive reinforcements of baton-wielding police with riot shields, backed up by the hated B. Specials, who charged the crowds with baton rounds and water cannon. The 'Battle of the Bogside', as it became known the world over, lasted for days with scores of injuries on both sides and hundreds of people forced to leave their homes. In west Belfast rampaging loyalist mobs from the Shankill marched on to the Lower Falls attacking people in their homes and burning scores of houses. The Catholics replied with equal violence and set up vigilante groups who erected barricades from burning cars and buses, preventing police or outsiders from entering the area. Later many members of the vigilante groups acquired guns and joined the Provisional IRA. In Dublin the Irish government became alarmed at the ferocity of the violence and demanded the intervention of the United Nations. In August the British government responded to the crisis by sending in a number of battalions of the British army, who were welcomed on to the streets with open arms by the catholic population of Belfast and Derry.

By early 1970 violence had spread to towns and villages throughout Northern Ireland. Each decade since the State was set up, communal strife had been a feature of Northern Ireland life, but what was happening now was much more serious, and many people feared an outbreak of full-scale civil war.

The initial euphoria with which Catholics had welcomed British troops had turned to open hostility following a number of ugly confrontations between soldiers and civilians. The Provisionals were now viewing the troops as occupiers and were starting to shoot at them. The Irish government and nationalist politicians were demanding the disbandment of the B. Specials, accusing them of naked sectarianism against Catholics, following their role in the battle of the Bogside and the Falls and other similar incidents. The foreign secretary, James Callaghan, who had sent in the troops, was pressing the Stormont government to speed up reforms and forced it to disband the Specials and replace them with the Ulster Defence Regiment (UDR). Unlike the Specials, which was a reserve force to the RUC, the UDR was a regiment of the British army. Thousands of young men (and some women), mostly Protestant, joined, viewing the regiment as the saviour of Ulster from a united Ireland.

Jackson's ephemeral flirt with football came to an end in the early 1970s and he returned to Northern Ireland just as the Troubles were getting under way in earnest. Society was being convulsed by the daily round of rioting, bombings, shootings, death and destruction. Jackson became alarmed at the ferocity of the violence, particularly the Provisionals' bombing campaign. In the pubs around Banbridge and Lurgan the talk amongst most young men of Jackson's age was of joining the UVF, the only Protestant paramilitary organisation in existence in mid-Ulster at the time, to defend the province against what they saw as the final push for a united Ireland by republicans. Jackson decided to join and for the first time met Billy Hanna, who became his military commander. Hanna, who during these early days became an important influence in Jackson's life, encouraged him to also join the UDR as a means of gaining access to guns and intelligence on Catholics and republicans. At Hanna's suggestion Jackson also moved home with his wife to number 12 Ben Crum, a comfortable council house in a small housing complex within the Grey estate in Lurgan and adjacent to the Mourneview estate where Hanna himself lived. The grey estate had been recently built by the housing executive as a result of the sectarian re-housing that was taking place all over Northern Ireland. These two estates largely formed the Protestant side of the town of Lurgan, where the vast majority of Protestants still live. As a further part of the ghettoisation, which would help swell the ranks of the nascent UVF in the town, Hanna encouraged Jackson to bring his friends in to live in the area. A short time later Jackson's brother-in-law, Roy Metcalf, moved in two doors away from Jackson with his wife Mary, who was Jackson's sister. Metcalf later became a top terrorist in Jackson's squad and was himself assassinated by the Provos in 1988. Later William Fulton Neill, a Banbridge factory worker and member of Ian Paisley's Presbyterian church who had known Jackson from his teenage days, moved with his wife to Mourneview and joined Jackson, Hanna and Metcalf in the UVF. Unlike Hanna, who rarely moved outside the Mourneview ghetto while socialising, Jackson began to move around a number of Protestant towns, including Portadown, Tandragee and Lisburn, fraternising with other rising stars in the UVF. Jackson was young, fit and decidedly mobile and was acquiring an insatiable appetite for adventure.

Outside Belfast, the principal area of Protestant paramilitary power has always been mid-Ulster. In paramilitary (though not necessarily geographical) terms this broadly encompasses the towns of Lurgan, Portadown, Tandragee and to a lesser extent the city of Armagh, as well as a number of outlying villages such as Annaghmore, Donaghcloney and Glenanne. Portadown, with its 90 per cent Protestant majority, is considered the most militant of these. To its south-eastern flank, in the heart of the apple country, lies the militant stronghold known as the Diamond, where the Orange Order was founded, and where the Rev. Ian Paisley held a number of political meetings in the late 1960s. The area has a number of well-heeled farmers, with remote farmhouses, who make their living from growing apples and vegetables. Some of these remote farms were later to play a crucial role in the loyalist terror campaign of the 1970s, when guns and explosives were stored on them. Portadown itself is a long, narrow town with a number of sprawling housing estates running off the town's dual carriageway, which runs through the town centre. On either side of the main street are rows of bustling shops intermingled with a number of banks and a large post office. The river Bann runs through the eastern side of the town, which is straddled by a wide bridge linking the town's ring road with the militant loyalist ghetto of Killycomaine. In the north-western corner lies the only Catholic area in the town and includes famous street names such as Obins Street, Garvaghy Road and the over-crowded ghetto of Churchill Park.

Following the army's arrival in Lurgan, a battalion of soldiers moved into a newly constructed complex on Mahon Road, on the southern side of Portadown. Later the base became known to police and soldiers as well as civilians who were interrogated there as 'The Mahon'. Before the Troubles Portadown had one police station off the town's main street, but with the introduction of 'Ulsterisation' in the late 1970s and the partial removal of 3 Brigade from the province, the RUC moved into 'The Mahon', which had been vacated by the army, and established a second police station there. In the town there were two pubs which became the main haunts of loyalist paramilitaries - the Queens in Thomas Street in the town centre and the Golden Hinde in Edgarstown, a hardline loyalist housing estate to the west of the town. The 'Hinde' was the main haunt of the UVF and members of the first and second battalions could be seen there regularly.

Around 1972 Robin Jackson began frequenting the Hinde, where he surrounded himself with a number of the young men he had already met through Billy Hanna and whom he knew he could trust and who would one day join him in forming his own killer squad independent of Hanna. Jackson was hungry for action and was anxious to form a squad on similar lines to that of Lennie Murphy's Shankill Butchers in Belfast - a squad that would take the war to the 'enemy' and instil terror into the nationalist community. Hanna, on the other hand, belonged to the old UVF school of Gusty Spence and was more moderate in outlook than Jackson. Despite his terrorist instincts, Hanna believed that dialogue with republicans could one day form part of loyalist strategy. Jackson had no interest whatever in politics and believed solely and exclusively in the power of the gun. It was inevitable that sooner or later he would become disillusioned with Hanna's style of leadership. But because Hanna was the UVF-appointed Brigadier for the area and controlled all weapons, Jackson would have to wait a further three years before realising his dream of removing Hanna and taking over the unit.

Meanwhile, he was prepared to operate under Hanna's leadership - and alongside the young men Hanna had already sworn into the organisation - while at the same time making many of the decisions affecting the unit and taking responsibility for many of its operations. In effect, Jackson was running a unit within a unit.

Among the young men Jackson chose as part of his inner circle were Harris Boyle and the Sommerville brothers, John and Wesley. Boyle, who at this time was a member of the UDA but later transferred to the UVF, was similar in age to Jackson and was one of Portadown's rising thugs. He lived in the town's Killycomaine estate and, unlike Jackson and the Sommervilles, was single and lived with his parents and brother Billy. One former associate from the UDA described Boyle in the following terms: 'Harris was like Jackson - he ruled by fear and rose to prominence through bullying and intimidation.'

Boyle's brother Billy got involved in terrorism in the early 1970s and served a lengthy prison sentence but renounced violence at the request of his parents following Harris's death at the Miami Showband explosion in 1975. Like Jackson, the Sommervilles were outsiders to Portadown, from a loyalist village called Moygashel on the outskirts of the Catholic town of Dungannon in east Tyrone. They were both a number of years older than Jackson. They worked in the village's linen factory, where a number of other terrorists from the area also worked. They made contact with the Lurgan/Portadown UVF through the UDR, a convenient recruiting ground for loyalist paramilitary organisations. Though less brash and street-wise than Jackson or Boyle, they later became Jackson's leading hit-men in the Tyrone area of mid-Ulster.

Other young men (already in Hanna's squad) chosen by Jackson to form the embryo of his own unit were his brother-in-law, Roy Metcalf, and two young men Sammy McCoo and Philip 'Shilly' Silcock. McCoo, from Portadown, was a cold, astute and ruthless character who became a top gunman in the unit under both Hanna's and Jackson's leadership. He is believed to have murdered over twenty Catholics, including a mother of a large family, Mrs Traynor, who was shot in the head on a park bench in Portadown while out on an evening's stroll with her husband. During the attack McCoo held the woman's head with one hand and fired a bullet through it with the other. During research for this book I interviewed McCoo in Portadown. In a cold, calculating show of defiance, he frankly owned up to his career as a terrorist and showed no remorse whatever for the suffering he inflicted on others. He readily admitted his involvement with Robin Jackson and the security forces and boasted of operating on both sides of the border. When I asked him about his notorious reputation and if he wasn't scared of working as an army agent, he put it like this:

> During the latter years of my involvement in terrorism my name began to crop up everywhere. It was McCoo this, McCoo that, everywhere I went. So I made a conscious decision to get out before I got caught. Yes I worked for the army, of course; documents and all; across the border; the lot.

Was he ever scared that these same army people might one day turn against him and have him killed?

> I was very conscious of it all the time. These are ruthless people but when you're involved in this business your adrenaline is pumping and you don't care about your own life. But I was very careful. When I sit in a pub with a pint in my hand, even to this day I always face the door so no-one will creep up on me from behind. When I did a hit I got away from the scene fast. Once I got 300 yards down the road that

was it. I knew I was clear. There was no evidence and nothing could be pinned on me.

Silcock was the youngest member of the squad and lived in Lurgan near Jackson and Hanna. Like Jackson he remained active up to the early 1990s and was one of the notorious warlords operating in the background behind Billy 'King-Rat' Wright during Wright's campaign of the late 1980s and 1990s. Others who joined Jackson's inner circle from time to time were William McCaughey, John Weir and Robert McConnell, a UDR sergeant and leading loyalist terrorist from Newtownhamilton. Stewart Young, who carried out the Monaghan bombing, ran his own UVF unit in the Triangle with his brother Avor (Ivor), but he did join Jackson's unit on specific hits from time to time.

Other rising paramilitary figures frequenting the Golden Hinde around this time were the Whitten brothers, Jackie and Sammy, whose family was involved in the building trade, Billy Fulton, Robert 'R.J.' Kerr, a petty criminal and street bully who got involved in terrorism for what he could get out of it, 'Big' Davy Mulholland, the Parnell Street bomber, Billy 'Duffy' Cooper, a big man with broad shoulders who later turned to religion, and the Jameson brothers, Jackie and Stewartie, whose family ran their own licensed premises (the Queens) in Portadown. Along with Hanna and Jackson, these were the men who formed the core of loyalist paramilitary power in mid-Ulster in the early 1970s.

Like Belfast, Derry and other towns in the province, Portadown was a hive of activity throughout the early years of the 1970s with marches, demonstrations and political meetings on a daily basis. Many young men, who in normal circumstances would be concerned with holding down a job, getting married and getting on with life, were drawing the dole, getting involved in petty crime and joining paramilitary organisations. Apart from the stated objective of saving Ulster from republicanism, they were getting carried away on the overblown hype, which they had never experienced before. But despite the hyperbole and the violence there was also camaraderie manning the barricades which were a feature of daily life at the entrances to all residential areas. There were opportunities to meet new friends in the pubs and drinking clubs which were springing up in the town and an opportunity to show off in the company of other hard men.

The Provisional IRA was formed in 1970. During that year the organisation exploded 150 bombs, mostly in commercial areas, across Northern Ireland, but mainly in Belfast and Derry. The campaign was intended to force the army to withdraw large numbers of soldiers from the Catholic ghettos in order to protect the industrial life of the province, thus lifting the siege of those ghettos where the army was now installed in force.

In August 1971 the Stormont government (with the blessing of the British government) introduced one-sided internment, mainly in response to the Provos' campaign, sweeping up hundreds of men from within the Catholic community across the North. The government believed (on the erroneous advice of the army) that the violence was Marxist-inspired and was confined to a minority of hard-core terrorists from within the Catholic ghettos. The military hawks within the army, particularly the Intelligence Corps, believed a military victory was attainable.

Five months after the introduction of internment, on 30 January 1972, British paratroopers shot dead thirteen unarmed civilians (a fourteenth died later) during a civil rights march in Derry in what became known as Bloody Sunday. Whilst the army maintained that its soldiers returned fire in response to IRA snipers who, it claimed, had fired up to '60 shots' at them first from within the crowd, history has shown this not to have been the case. All fourteen victims were innocent, unarmed civilians.

The fact is that during those early days of the conflict the security and political establishment both in Belfast and London believed that tough security policies, including internment, would solve the problem, just as they did during the IRA's 1956-1963 campaign. (Indeed it has recently come to light that a very senior Tory government politician, who cannot be named here for legal reasons, asked army generals to assassinate the entire IRA leadership in the early 1970s.) They believed that despite the Irish government's refusal to introduce internment in the South the previous August to coincide with its introduction in the North, it was only a matter of time before it would. But history has shown that the Irish government's decision was the correct one. It is widely accepted now, and has been for some years, that Bloody Sunday was a deliberate act of mass murder by the British army, whose senior officers believed that such incidents would deter future illegal (as it was) marches by the Civil Rights Movement and that the widespread unrest which accompanied and followed such demonstrations would eventually fizzle out and that the wider problem across the province would cease to exist.

A top secret army memo released to the current Saville inquiry into Bloody Sunday by the British Ministry of Defence shows that army officers, in the days leading up to the Bloody Sunday march, countenanced the possibility of shooting unarmed civilians, to 'quell trouble'. The memo was written by Lt Col Harry Dalzell-Payne on 27 January 1972 - three days before the march - who said that if the ban on marches that was in place was to be upheld, 'then we must take stronger military measures which will inevitably lead to further accusations of brutality and ill-treatment of non-violent demonstrators'. Dalzell-Payne continues:

> The only additional measure left for physical control is the use of firearms, ie, 'Disperse or we fire'. Inevitably, it would not be the gunmen who would be killed but 'innocent members of the crowd'. This would be a harsh and final step, tantamount to saying 'all else has failed', and for this reason must be rejected except in extremes. It cannot, however, be ruled out. We must await the outcome of the events planned for the week-end of 29/30 January '72'.

The fall-out from Bloody Sunday reverberated around the world and the Irish government withdrew its ambassador from

London and called for the intervention of the United Nations. In an emotional public attack on the British government, the then Taoiscach Jack Lynch said the events of Bloody Sunday might in time be forgiven but would never be forgotten. In Dublin a rampaging mob led by members of Sinn Féin burned the British Embassy in Merrion Square with petrol bombs, under the noses of the Gardai, who refused to intervene, following a mass demonstration to the building.

According to the Derry journalist Eamonn McCann, who himself was a prominent member of the Civil Rights Movement in Derry in the late 1960s, the torching of the embassy was the realisation of anti British anger in the wake of the massacre. Writing in the *Sunday Tribune* on 12 September 1999, following the release to the Saville inquiry of a taped conversation between Ted Heath and Jack Lynch that took place within hours of the massacre, McCann wrote:

> On 2 February a huge crowd - the biggest demonstration seen in the Republic for a generation, according to *The Irish Times* - made it into Dublin city centre despite a complete absence of public transport for a march to the British Embassy in Merrion Square organised by Dublin Trades Council. The marchers carried 13 coffins, hundreds of black flags and a forest of placards demanding a British withdrawal from the North. For more than an hour, the building was subjected to a fusillade of stones and bottles before resort was made to petrol bombs and the embassy burned down. Republicans were prominently involved. Elsewhere, a British Airways office, shipping offices and branches of British-owned chain stores were attacked. Over the three days between the killings and the funerals, no British planes were permitted to land at Dublin, Cork or Shannon airports. According to one observer the work-stoppage on the day of the funerals was, proportionately, the biggest political strike in history, anywhere, ever. *The Irish*

Times reported that *all* workplaces in the Republic came to a standstill.

But it is the contents of the Heath-Lynch conversation itself - 'obviously recorded', according to McCann, by the British - which make for the most interesting reading. McCann writes:

> What is most striking about these exchanges is the evident imbalance in the relationship between the two men. Heath is brusque and belligerent throughout. Lynch anxious and plaintive.
>
> Far from Heath feeling called to account for the killings, he appears irritable to the point of rudeness in refusing to concede that any blame might attach to British policy or to the British Army. Insofar as he allocates fault, he points towards the Bloody Sunday marchers for having defied a ban on parades and to Lynch's own government for not having tackled nationalist law-breaking in a more robust fashion.
>
> If Lynch had denounced the Derry march in advance, he suggests at one point, the killings might never have happened.
>
> At a number of points in the conversation, it seems that it is Lynch, not Heath, who is under reprimand.
>
> At no stage in the conversation, which must have lasted more than 15 minutes, does Heath express personal regret for the deaths, much less offer an apology.
>
> The tone is set at the start, Lynch apologising for ringing 'at this hour'. He then speaks virtually uninterrupted for, it would seem, up to two minutes, before Heath interjects, to say 'Yes', and then, in his first substantive contribution, to assert that he 'obviously' cannot accept 'any accusations'.
>
> Lynch contributes around 70% of the conversation, and almost all of the direct observations and suggestions. Heath initiates no line of discourse, other than, emphatically and repeatedly, to imply or directly

to ascribe culpability to nationalists and civil rights organisers. This is the only substantive point made by Heath throughout - that those who organised and took part in the march brought the disaster on their own heads by breaking the law.

The release of the tape and its mind-bending revelations went virtually unnoticed in this country, which tells us much about the mealy-mouthed attitude of Irish people towards big brother across the water. Here's a man, the Prime Minister of Britain, whose army has just massacred thirteen innocent civilians on an Irish street, being
'brusque', 'belligerent' and 'irritable to the point of rudeness'.
My God!
Thirteen people are dead and this silver-haired buffoon is refusing to accept 'any responsibility' whatsoever and is insulting our Taoiseach down the phone at 1 o'clock in the morning. In other words, the marchers deserved what they got. If they hadn't gone on the march they wouldn't be dead. Typical of a pig-headed British politician who believed that the bog-oak Irish were still living somewhere back in the 1840s on a diet of potatoes. If they step out of line shoot them. It is not difficult to imagine what Heath and his government would have done if the shoe had been on the other foot and Irish soldiers had shot thirteen Protestants in a border incident in south Armagh or south Down, for example. British tanks would probably be at Drogheda within two hours. While it is true that the Provos had spent the previous two years blasting everything that moved across Northern Ireland, neither Mr Lynch - the gentleman of Irish politics all lhis life - nor the civil rights movement were responsible for the Provos.
No. What was required that night was a strong Irish Taoiseach - a kind of Robert Mugabe without the fascism - who would stand up to Heath's bullying and make him account for what Bernadette Devlin (as she then was) described on the night as Ireland's 'Sharpville'. Unfortunately - and sadly - Lynch had neither the balls nor the stomach for such a fight. Indeed - unfortunately and sadly - Irish Taoisigh down through

the years have never had the guts to stand up to bullying British politicians, preferring instead to kowtow with cap in hand, regardless of the humiliation.

And the taping of the conversation. Who was responsible for this? Again, no questions asked. An Irish Taoiseach telephones a British Prime Minister in the middle of the night and his conversation is secretly taped. Who do these people think they are? Or better still, who do they think we are?

Mr. Heath knew better than anyone that Jack Lynch was a decent, upstanding politician - unlike some of today's gangsters - who had probably saved the country from civil war less than two years earlier. He should have afforded him the respect he deserved.

With a massive upsurge in violence following internment and Bloody Sunday, as well as world condemnation of the massacre, it was becoming clear to the British government that overt military repression by the British army against Catholics would not work. Two months after Bloody Sunday, Heath abolished the Stormont parliament, blaming the Prime Minister, Brian Faulkner, for bouncing him into supporting internment, which he was now beginning to have doubts about. From that moment hence, British military policy in Northern Ireland took a dramatic turn. No longer would the army shoot at peaceful marchers in the street. No longer would British guns be seen to point at Catholic areas only.

The Smart Brains in the British army, assisted by the Secret Intelligence Service (SIS) MI6 (and later MI5), decided that in order to defeat the Provisional IRA, the Southern government, the Southern security forces and the Southern public must be brought on side. It must be clearly demonstrated to the South, through the media and whatever other means possible, that PIRA was a common enemy - loyalist guns after all were for shooting Catholics and did not threaten the State. Therefore, cooperation in future with the South, not confrontation.

As a substitute for open military repression, the Smart Brains were devising a new policy (which would remain top secret from just about everyone except those involved) called counter terrorism. This is a process whereby army officers, with years of experience fighting guerrilla movements around the world, secretly train and arm one side (the 'friendly' side) in an ethnic, inter-communal war against the other. In Ireland the friendly side was of course the loyalists, and counter terror was about to be used against republicans, nationalists and, if necessary, uninvolved Catholics. Death squads of loyalists would be trained, armed and supplied with names, addresses and photographs of 'targets' to be 'taken out' within the Catholic community. Such a policy, the Smart Brains believed, would instil terror in the Catholic community and force it to withdraw its support from the IRA. If you destroy the water the fish swim in you destroy the fish. In some cases hitmen, or 'agents' as they became known, were taken away and secretly trained in other countries for such missions. In one case Anthony Doherty, a republican activist from the north Antrim village of Portglenone, who in the early 1970s switched sides and began working as an agent for the RUC special branch and military intelligence, was taken to a secret army base in Wales. There he underwent intensive training in the art of survival and assassination techniques. On one occasion he was sent alone into the mountains on an endurance test and was forced to survive by eating worms and frogs and drinking cows' blood. He was also trained in the use of guns and was shown how to murder people with knives and daggers by 'getting the blade well in under the ribs'. In the end Doherty told his handlers he was not prepared to become an assassin for the British army against his own people and left.

Billy Mitchell, the UVF man from Carrickfergus, told me during his interview (see chapter 7) that during his time attending planning meetings with the UVF to murder Catholics, the UVF commander from the area where the 'target' was to be 'hit' would invariably present the meeting with 'an army photograph' of the target, which would then be given to the gunman designated to do the hit. When I pressed Mitchell on the question of the army photograph and if he was not exaggerating the matter he said almost 'every single murder' carried out by the UVF in the Shankill area during his time was done with the help of either an army or police photograph.

It was so common amongst loyalists in the early to mid-70s that after the first year or two no-one even noticed any more - it was just normal, par for the course.

Counter terrorism, the security establishment now believed, was a much more workable policy than shooting people in the street. In that way nothing could be proved. The loyalists would not talk out of fear of reprisals (they were invariably threatened by their handlers that 'talking' meant instant death for themselves or members of their families), and allegations of collusion by nationalists could easily be discounted as Provo propaganda. The Irish government would be likely to give the benefit of the doubt to the British version of any future controversial events (in the absence of proof) and could easily be kept on board.

Such was the security environment Robin Jackson found himself in when he embarked on his career as a terrorist and later as a leading counter-terrorist agent on behalf of army intelligence in the early months of 1972. His first encounter with army intelligence officers was during visits to Billy Hanna's home in Lurgan and on visits to the Legion clubs at weekends. Later, army officers visited his home regularly in Ben Crum and Jackson's wife Ann made tea for them.

Jackson's first known involvement in terrorism was his part in a midnight raid on a territorial army base in Lurgan in October 1972 in which eighty rifles, twenty sterling sub-machine guns and thousands of rounds of ammunition were stolen. The raid, which was carried out with the help of UDR men working at the base, was led by Hanna and Jackson with a number of other local UVF men in support. While making their escape in a Land Rover the terrorists ran out of petrol and were forced to abandon the vehicle and hurriedly transfer part of the haul to a UVF man's car. The following morning police found the Land Rover with guns and ammunition inside and others 'strewn around the road'. It later emerged that the landrover had a 'spare' tank of petrol, operated by a switch under the dash, but which the gang was not aware of.

Despite Hanna's reputation he and his unit were the unlikely makings of a paramilitary squad which, seventeen months later, would successfully carry out the biggest bombing operation ever perpetrated in Ireland or Britain since the conflict began. If proof were ever needed that the mid-Ulster Brigade of the UVF received help from the British army in bombing Dublin and Monaghan in 1974 the raid on the territorial army base is it.

CHAPTER 9

THE MURDER TRIANGLE

1972 was the worst year for violence in Northern Ireland since the Troubles began in 1968. In that year 467 people died compared to 174 for 1971 and 250 for 1973. The decision to abolish Stormont, the bastion of unionist power and the linchpin of the union, dealt a catastrophic blow to the Protestant community and sent alarm bells ringing throughout the wider Tory establishment in Britain, which had close historical links to the monied and landed classes in Northern Ireland, that the union itself was now under threat. Hardline elements within the intelligence community of MI6, MI5 and the intelligence wing of the British army, all of whom were intertwined with the British aristocracy, including the Monarchy, believed the Heath government was weak and would cave in to republican demands. The unionist community itself was outraged and tens of thousands of people marched through Belfast to City Hall demanding the return of Stormont. William Craig, who had earlier been sacked by the then Prime Minister, Terence O'Neill, for his hardline stance against reforms, set up an extreme breakaway unionist party called Vanguard, which he hoped would eventually replace the official unionist party which he saw as discredited. A number of new paramilitary organisations sprung up around the province around this time, most notable of which was the Ulster Defence Association (UDA), which was established under the auspices of the British army. In an interview in his Belfast office in 1987, Craig told me the UDA was set up at the behest of army intelligence officers who believed the Ulster Volunteer Force (UVF) alone was too small to counter the new threat from the reinvigorated Republican Movement.

Other smaller paramilitary groupings established around this time, or slightly earlier, were the Red Hand Commando, set up by a homosexual shopkeeper from Portrush in County Antrim, John McKeague, and TARA, also set up by a homosexual housefather, William McGrath. McKeague had been one of the leading organisers of the 1969 Falls Road pogrom, and the sole aim of his new organisation was the assassination of Catholics. McGrath, who was later convicted of buggering young boys in what became known as the Kincora Boys Home Scandal outside Belfast in the mid-1970s, was a mysterious figure and the role of his organisation never became clear, although it was heavily infiltrated by British intelligence and was involved in gun-running for a time. One of its most active members at the time is today a leading journalist.

But by far the largest paramilitary organisation to appear on the scene was the UDA. It described itself as a political organisation and claimed that its primary aim was the mobilisation of Ulster Protestant working-class people to defend the province against Dublin rule. Its first chairman was a British army deserter, Dave Foegul, who lasted less than a year in the job. It opened headquarters in Gawn Street in east Belfast and drew its membership mainly from the defence committees which had sprung up in Belfast and other towns around Northern Ireland during the disturbances of 1969/70. But far from being a political party, the UDA developed into a vicious terrorist organisation responsible for some of the worst atrocities ever committed in Northern Ireland. It imported guns from abroad to murder Catholics and established a string of torture chambers around the province known as 'Romper Rooms'. These were usually disused basements or underground flats where Catholics, and occasionally disloyal Protestants, were tortured, beaten and very often shot to death. Catholics were usually strung upside down from a ceiling and beaten unconscious by a chanting mob. Protestants who stepped out of line had their legs or arms broken by placing them in a vice-grip or by dropping cement blocks on them. One of the most prominent leaders of the romper-room culture was John McMichael, who was assassinated by the Provos in late 1988.

But by far the best known and most notorious of the early leaders of the UDA was Charles Harding Smith, who became its chairman after Foegul's departure, when the organisation was engaged in one of its most vicious campaigns ever against

Catholics. Smith was an army agent and (like Billy Hanna in Lurgan) took his orders from army officers who visited his home in Belfast regularly. In 1972 police in London arrested Smith and four others and found British army documents on them which gave the names and ranks of alleged junior IRA men in Belfast. The four were later put on trial, accused of attempting to import £100,000 worth of arms into Northern Ireland for loyalists. Among the four arrested with Smith was John White, the former senior spokesman for the Ulster Democratic Party (UDP), the one time political wing of the UDA led by Gary McMichael. White later served a life sentence for the gruesome double killing (by multiple stabbing) in 1973 of Paddy Wilson - Gerry Fitt's election agent - and his girlfriend. Following two assassination attempts on his life in the mid-1970s Smith fled the North with his family and settled in Halifax in the North of England where he died of cancer in 1991. In an interview in her Halifax home during research for this book, Smith's widow told me of her late husband's involvement with the army. She said army officers came to her house regularly over a two to three year period dressed in civilian clothes.

> The moment they arrived Harding took them into the sitting room and closed the door. Apart from bringing them tea I had no part in the discussions and I had no idea what they discussed. They often visited as regularly as once a week and discussions often went on for hours.

The soldiers, who were directing Smith's campaign of murder, ensured that at all times meetings and discussions with a leading loyalist terrorist were conducted in strict secrecy away from prying eyes. For years before his death in Halifax, Smith talked to his family about the possibility of writing a book on the conflict.

He always talked about how the public was being conned about what was happening in Northern Ireland. He wanted to write a book and let the public know the truth but in the end he never did. Deep down I suppose he was too scared to reveal it but even on his death-bed he regretted not having done it.

Protestant terror gangs have never publicly acknowledged that innocent Catholics were fair game for attack but privately many of their leaders, including Robin Jackson, made no secret of the fact that they saw all Catholics as 'the enemy to be wiped out'. In Protestant west Belfast, 1972 also saw the emergence of a notorious sectarian murder gang (already referred to in chapter 7), which became known as the Shankill Butchers, the sobriquet given to it by the media following the discovery of a number of its victims' bodies, who had been mutilated, before or while they were dying, with butcher's knives. The Butchers were a splinter group of psychopathic killers who broke away from the UVF, though many of their murders had the tacit, if not active, support of the organisation. The gang was set up by a twenty-year-old petty criminal called Lennie Murphy, who developed into a blood-thirsty monster and who once declared that the only way to kill a man was to 'cut his throat'. Between 1972 and 1977 the Butchers inflicted a reign of terror against innocent Catholics walking the streets of west Belfast, usually late at night. In most cases they tortured their victims by cutting strips of flesh off their bodies. They then cut their throats from ear to ear and dumped their bodies on waste ground. Some had their teeth pulled out with a pliers while still alive. According to former RUC Sergeant John Weir, Robin Jackson, for a time in the mid-1970s, operated with the Butchers in Belfast and took part in a number of the grisly throat cuttings. Jackson was highly admired throughout the loyalist terrorist community and there is little doubt that his expertise, particularly in kidnapping and planning escape routes, would be invaluable to the Butchers and they would have learned much from him. Weir himself was part of Jackson's inner circle and was present when Jackson shot dead William Strathearn in 1977. He would have been privy to many of the dark secrets in Jackson's life.

Extremists such as Murphy and Jackson, backed by fanatics in the army and the intelligence service, were determined to send a message back to the government that they would not be pushed down the road towards Dublin. They believed the IRA bombing campaign of 1970/71 had paid off, resulting in the fall of Stormont. The government sat up and listened and they would now listen to Protestants. Thus the long dark years from 1972 to 1977, when a total of 1,589 people were killed by both loyalists and republicans, got under way in earnest.

As the counter-terror plan for Belfast, drawn up by the intelligence community in the early months of 1972, got under way throughout the summer, a complementary, but different style of campaign, was getting under way in mid-Ulster, led by Hanna and Jackson, but also directed by the intelligence community. Not to be outdone by their brothers in the Big City, Hanna and Jackson were determined to prove that countrymen can fight wars too. Their campaign was different, however, in that it was conducted in rural countryside across three counties in an area that became known as the Murder Triangle. The area comprised and the name derived from a triangle of countryside which stretched from Banbridge in south Down to Aughnacloy in south Tyrone and Pomeroy in mid-Tyrone, in which victims of the campaign were murdered. Most victims were killed either in their homes, on their doorsteps or travelling to or from work. The Shankill Butchers on the other hand - whom Jackson continually strove to emulate - operated in north and west Belfast - an area no greater than five square miles. The majority of their victims were abducted, tortured - many of them over several hours - then murdered and their bodies dumped in parks or on waste ground.

Until his assassination in 1975, Hanna remained in charge of the unit (though his influence and control were inexorably declining), but apart from the Dublin bombings rarely went on hits but directed operations and supplied most of the weapons. While Jackson and Boyle, in later years, did carry out a number of grisly stabbings and throat cuttings, the unit in the early years largely specialised in hit-and-run type murders in which victims were gunned down with speed and aggression by high-powered automatic weapons. On several occasions up to three members of one family were massacred, with Jackson doing most of the shooting. The unit travelled fast and far in high-powered cars, often covering up to 150 miles of a round trip on one hit. Apart from the Dublin and Monaghan bombings, the unit was also involved in a number of spectacular operations in the Republic, more of which we shall see later in this book.

Whilst a number of murders in the early years were planned at the Hanna-Jackson base in Lurgan, much of the slaughter carried out throughout the Murder Triangle was planned at James Mitchell's farmhouse in south Armagh, from where a separate loyalist unit, made up mainly of members of the security forces, was already operating.

Mitchell himself, apart from helping to make bombs, was not a habitual active terrorist nor was he a particularly malevolent person but he believed Protestants were engaged in a war against Catholics and in wars people get killed. It was a warped view of the conflict and one that was held by many people on both sides.

For a number of years during the 1970s the farmhouse was protected by a UVF unit from Portadown under the command of Portadown builder Jackie Whitten, who also carried out renovations to the house. The UVF men carried weapons and patrolled the grounds of the farmhouse during night hours. This, it's believed, may have been the reason the house was never attacked by republicans, who were aware of its existence. But Mitchell did receive a number of anonymous threatening letters during these years.

After Jackson the leading assassin operating out of the farmhouse was Robert McConnell (see chapter 8), the leader of the security forces unit, who was a close personal friend of Mitchell's and who spent much of his time at the farmhouse throughout the period 1973 to 1976. During the worst period of the Triangle - 1975 and early 1976 - McConnell was to the forefront of many of the attacks against Catholics in south

Armagh, north Monaghan and north Louth. His initial introduction to terrorism was through a chance encounter with other seasoned terrorists who worked at a potato crisp factory in Tandragee (where McConnell held down a full-time job) and who were already in paramilitary organisations. Later his friendship with Mitchell, whom he met through the security forces, brought him into mainstream terrorism and transformed him into a leading doorstep hitman.

As well as the Queens and the Golden Hinde pubs in Portadown much of the social drinking took place in the pubs around Tandragee. One introduction led to another and McConnell eventually met up with Jackson and Hanna and other members of Jackson's squad, all of whom began visiting the farmhouse. By mid-1973 much of the UVF and UDA in mid-Ulster, as well as the Security Forces Unit (SFU), were meeting regularly at the farmhouse to plan and carry out hits in the Murder Triangle. Later many senior UVF and UDA men from Belfast also visited the farmhouse, which was fast becoming a kind of kindergarten for loyalist paramilitaries. John Weir and William McCaughey, who at this time were both members of the RUC's Special Patrol Group based at Armagh city, were part of the SFU at the farmhouse. In fact, Weir was promoted sergeant while at the height of his terrorist career at the farmhouse. At the time he was the youngest constable ever promoted sergeant in the history of the RUC and later served as sergeant-in-charge at both Newtownhamilton and Crossmaglen stations.

The SFU did not join paramilitary organisations on the advice of the paramilitaries themselves, who suggested that as members of the security forces they could acquire and move guns around and 'clear' roads for paramilitary operations without fear of detection and in that way could serve the 'cause' better than joining their organisations. But the SFU, it was agreed, would carry out hits in its own right and would not be confined to providing 'cover' for the paramilitaries. With the SFU in place at the farmhouse and the Hanna-Jackson unit up and running in Lurgan, Catholics throughout mid-Ulster were about to feel the heat as the Troubles entered the mid-1970s.

At the farmhouse McConnell was in charge of his unit's operations. He was a ruthless psychopath who detested Catholics and, like Jackson, believed they could be 'shot' into submission. At home he was gentle and caring. He lived on the top of a windswept hillside overlooking the border in a run-down farmhouse without bathroom or toilet where he cared for his aged parents and invalid sister, whom he helped to church each Sunday. At weekends he tended his small farm, working his tractor over the drumlin hills that form much of the border terrain between the two parts of Ireland. In the UDR he perfected his skills as a marksman and spent much of his spare-time target practising at the regiment's firing ranges.

At the farmhouse he formed a close 'working relationship' with a full-time RUC reservist, Lawrence McClure, who was a key member of the SFU unit, and for over three years neither did a hit without the other. At the joint police/army base at Newtownhamilton, where he checked on duty most nights, McConnell became friendly with members of the Intelligence Corps who were based at battalion HQ in nearby Bessbrook. (Another frequent visitor to the base, says John Weir, and with whom McConnell became friendly, was RUC Superintendent Harry Breen who was based at Armagh city. Whilst not personally involved in terrorism himself, Breen continuously encouraged McConnell, and indeed Weir, to 'keep the attacks going'. Breen, who along with a colleague, Supt Bob Buchannon, was murdered by the Provos in an ambush north of Dundalk in 1989, was a frequent visitor to Garda stations along the border during these years. It was returning from such a visit to Dundalk Garda station that he and Buchannon drove into the Provo trap. The Gardai, with whom Breen continuously consulted on cross-border security matters, were being duped and were not aware of his terrorist links).

Unlike Jackson, who was sharp and streetwise and had a healthy suspicion of the British, McConnell was naïve and had a malleable personality. He trusted the British, who manipulated him and used his skills as a killer to terrorise the

Catholic population of south Armagh. During his short terrorist career it is reliably believed that McConnell murdered up to thirty Catholics (most of them uninvolved) across the Murder Triangle. According to Weir, who was present at the farmhouse on numerous occasions when planning details for 'hits' were worked out, with up to fifteen men (and some women) present, most of them members of either the RUC or the UDR, McConnell, before setting out, invariably made a last-minute 'phone call to his contacts in the army or the police to check that the roads were 'clear'.

> McConnell was the chief planner and leading operative at the farmhouse. He was the one always pushing for hits and coming up with new ideas. Before we set out on an operation McConnell always went to the hallway and made a call to his contacts, mainly in the army, to ensure the roads were clear. He would hang up the phone and return to the meeting and signal the 'all clear'. We would then set out safe in the knowledge that no matter how the operation went we would not be arrested.

Such was McConnell's arrogance and self-confidence that on one occasion during a gun and bomb attack on a pub in Crossmaglen he placed the bomb on a window-sill and then approached the door to open fire. As he raised his gun he suddenly dropped it again and returned to the window and calmly moved the bomb nearer the centre of the window where he could see customers drinking inside. He then strolled up to the door and opened fire before making off in a waiting getaway car.

Another key player in McConnell's unit was UDR captain John 'Jack' Irvine (already referred to in chapter 4) who played a crucial role in the murder triangle campaign. Irvine worked as an undercover agent for the SAS and sustained a serious eye injury during training exercises at their base in Castledillon, near Portadown, and was invalided out of the UDR as a result.

Irvine was the main supplier of bomb-making material to the farmhouse during the Triangle years. For each bomb, Mitchell, who bankrolled the campaign from his huge farm, paid him £1,000. In the early 1980s Irvine resigned from the UDR and, with his wife Shirley, fled Armagh following the wrongful arrest and subsequent imprisonment of four members of the UDR on a charge of murdering Armagh Catholic Adrian Carroll, in the controversial case known as the UDR Four. According to Loyalist sources Irvine had been blamed with 'setting up' the four men and, believing his life was in danger, decided to move. In 1992 I caught up with him and his wife in their elegant home in Hollywood, Co. Down. They refused to discuss the past and said the Official Secrets Act forbade them from doing so. Irvine now spends his retirement 'dabbling' - as he put it - in the antiques business. Robbing gelignite from quarries is probably not as lucrative as it used to be.

Bomb-making material was also transported to the farm during those years by RUC constable Jimmy Hunter, who was based at Armagh city. Hunter was later promoted sergeant and transferred to Warrenpoint in County Down, where he was murdered by the IRA in the 1980s.

Another celebrated name associated with the farmhouse during this period was the misguided and ill-fated undercover British army operative Capt. Robert Nairac, who was also murdered by the Provos in 1977. Like his undercover allies at Lisburn, who ran Jackson and Hanna, Nairac kept his distance and did not fraternise openly with paramilitary figures at the farmhouse. He was close to Jackson and Boyle (to whom he provided weapons, names, addresses and photographs of Catholics and republicans throughout the Triangle) and other members of the unit and visited Jackson's house in Lurgan regularly where Ann Jackson made him tea on numerous occasions. On one occasion he was photographed standing with Jackson in Jackson's house for a family album. Nairac was not aware of it but it was Jackson's way of securing his insurance policy should the day arrive when the authorities wished to talk to him about his terrorist activities.

Nairac was also close to McConnell and other members of the SFU during his exploits in south Armagh. On Saturday afternoons he played rugby with the RUC in Armagh city where John Weir remembers playing against him a number of times.

CHAPTER 10

MURDER MOST FOUL

Saturday night was action night for Robin Jackson. It was the night when he and his UVF comrades did most of their 'Taig (derogatory term for Catholic) bashing'.

Saturday night was the night when most young men under the age of thirty went on the town. It was the night when young people let their hair down, and very often found themselves walking home alone, separated from the herd. Such late-night stragglers often became easy prey for hunters and killers of Catholics such as Jackson and his squad who often stalked their victims for hours before springing the trap.

On Saturday night, 17 May 1975, seventeen-year-old Francis Anthony Rice, his brother Damien and two friends, Martin Morgan and Dominic Burns, walked the one and a half miles from Rice's home in Burrenreagh Park outside the town of Castlewellan in south County Down to the town centre, arriving there around 9 p.m. It was arranged beforehand that on reaching the town Damien, Martin and Dominic would hitch a lift to a dance in the nearby town of Newcastle, and Frankie - as he was known locally - would remain in Castlewellan where he was due to meet up with other friends.

It was the first month of summer and already holidaymakers were beginning to visit south Down, an area of great scenic beauty. Each summer families - many with teenage sons and daughters - from many parts of Ireland visited the area and parked their caravans on a designated holiday campsite called the Demesne on the outskirts of Castlewellan. Frankie Rice had his eye on the teenage girls.

Frankie was the oldest of eleven children (seven boys and four girls), all of whom still lived with their parents, Francis and Teresa Rice, at Burrenreagh Park. Frankie was a keen sportsman and spent much of his spare time playing football with the local Bryansford Gaelic football club. He worked in Thomas Kelly's paint store in nearby Ballynahinch and travelled by bus daily to and from work.

Castlewellan is a mixed community of Protestants and Catholics with Catholics marginally in the majority. It nestles under the scenic Mourne Mountains in the southeast corner of Northern Ireland twenty miles from the border. Like many other rural towns in the province it escaped the worst of the Troubles, but sectarian tension in the early years, followed by the murder of a number of soldiers and policemen, led to sharp polarisation between the communities.

Also at weekends Frankie and his friends regularly frequented the Oak Grill bar in Castlewellan town centre. Unlike most young men of their age they rarely drank alcohol but usually hung around the premises' snack bar or 'messed about' on the pavement outside on the lookout for girls.

As the four young men reached the town centre they split up. Frankie continued walking towards the opposite end of the town (towards the Demesne), whilst Damien, Martin and Dominic crossed to the Newcastle Road where they hitched a lift to Newcastle. Later that night they returned to Castlewellan on the 11.15 p.m. bus and spent some time in the Oak Grill drinking tea. Around 11.40 p.m. Damien Morgan, Martin Morgan's brother offered them a lift home, which they gladly accepted.

As they drove down the town, unknown to them, Frankie Rice, having returned from his adventures, crossed the main street to the Oak Grill. He spoke to a local man, James Fitzpatrick, who was standing outside eating chips. Fitzpatrick later recalled their brief conversation:

> Frankie came over towards me and asked where the rest of the boys were. I told him they were away out the road in the car. Frankie went to walk away and he said: 'I'm away on out the road'.

It was approximately 11.50 p.m. when Frankie set out on his own - something he did occasionally at weekends. Shortly before Frankie set out, his parents, Francis and Teresa, left a local hotel bar in the town (which they visited occasionally on Saturday nights) and also walked home. They were not aware of Frankie's whereabouts (they assumed he was with friends), nor he theirs, but they did notice Damien Morgan's car passing them on the road with their other son Damien inside.

As Francis and Teresa proceeded down the main street, they noticed a red (what they thought was a 'Ford Sierra') car with its windows 'blacked out' acting suspiciously ahead of them. As they drew near, the car pulled out to the centre of the road and remained there with its engine running. It proceeded to follow them part of the way but then suddenly disappeared.

A mile further on, as Francis and Teresa turned left off the main road on to Burrenreagh Road, a neighbour pulled up to give them a lift. The remaining distance to their home was less than half a mile. As they boarded the vehicle the red car they had seen earlier careered round the corner from behind, almost 'sweeping' them off their feet. It continued down Burrenreagh Road at high speed and disappeared into the distance.

A half-mile out of Castlewellan the road forks. The right fork leads to Banbridge and the left to the village of Kilcoo, which leads to the town of Rathfriland and eventually to Newry. Frankie Rice's home was off the Rathfriland Road. As Frankie neared the fork he was observed by a local man Francis Ward, who was driving in the opposite direction towards Castlewellan with his wife Mary and a friend, Jennifer Rice - no relation to Francis - in the car. Ward saw two men walking behind Frankie at a distance of 'a couple of hundred yards'. He also noticed a car ('like a sports car') with 'only its side-lights on' parked along the road ahead of Frankie on the same side - close to the fork. Ward thought the car was 'dark coloured' and could see 'only one person' inside.

Frankie Rice did not arrive home as expected and at 4 a.m. his father reported him missing to Castlewellan police. What exactly happened to Frankie immediately after Ward saw him has never been fully established, but at 9.20 a.m. the next morning his mutilated body was found dumped in a laneway off a back road seven miles away in an area called Cabra near Rathfriland. Arthur Barry, a local man, was returning from church with his wife and two daughters when his wife noticed 'somebody lying in the lane'. When Barry investigated, he found Frankie's body 'lying parallel to the run of the lane with the head towards the road and the feet towards the gate in the field'. He later told police the body was 'lying face downwards at full stretch, legs straight and the arms ... clasped under his body'.

Barry rushed home and alerted Newry police who contacted their colleagues at Rathfriland - in whose area the body was found - and at 9.35 a.m. Sgt. Gordon Nesbitt and Constable Orr arrived on the scene. At 12.15 p.m. Francis Rice identified the dead youth as his son Frankie and the body was removed to Daisy Hill Hospital, Newry.

A post-mortem examination by State Pathologist Thomas Marshall the next day found that Frankie had been stabbed twelve times - five times in the chest, once in the shoulder, once in the stomach, once in the back, once in the hip, once in the knee, once in the forearm and once in the left hand. There were abrasions on the right eye, left cheek, chin, left hip, left arm, right upper arm and right wrist. There was also a 'cluster of abrasions' on the left shin and two cigarette burns on the right upper arm. There was also dirt in the 'sacks' of the eyes, suggesting the dead man had been dragged along the ground, probably after death.

The weapon used, which was found at the scene, was a double-edged 9¼ inch dagger - of the type used by the army and UDR (as they then were) in Northern Ireland - and some of the chest wounds penetrated 'back to the shoulder blades'. A 'puncture' wound to the back of the right forearm and a 'wavy incision' on the back of the web between the left thumb and forefinger suggested Rice attempted to ward off the dagger blows and protect himself with his hands and arms. The number of abrasions on the body also suggested the dead youth was badly beaten, most likely by fists and boots, and was turned over on his stomach ('stabbed once in the back') whilst being murdered during what was almost certainly a lengthy and brutal ordeal.

A forensic examination of the scene by Scenes of Crime Officer James O'Neill from Newry police found that there were 'three bloodstains on the Convent road' (the main road perpendicular to the lane where the body was found) opposite the entrance to the lane. The largest bloodstain was four feet four inches from the nearside of the road. O'Neill also established that there were 'no trail-marks in the dirt' and found 'an absence of bloodstains down the entrance'. He also found that there were 'no signs of a struggle near the point where the body was found'.

O'Neill's report appeared to establish that Rice was murdered elsewhere and his body transported - most likely during the early hours of Sunday morning - to the laneway. Bloodstains, near or on the middle of the road ('four feet four inches from the near side') indicated the body was removed with great haste from a vehicle - believed to be a van - which almost certainly pulled up on the middle of the road for nothing more than a number of seconds - the driver having made no attempt to park or pull in to the grass margin.

Throughout Sunday, news bulletins in Britain and Ireland carried the grim, familiar news of another murder in Northern Ireland. The body of a seventeen-year-old Catholic youth 'shot in the chest, hand and knee' has been found in a laneway in Castlewellan, Co. Down, trumpeted most of them. Monday's papers followed hard with similar details but added that a man claiming to represent a loyalist group calling itself the 'Young Militants' had phoned a Belfast newspaper to say they had killed 'Mr Rice', who was a 'Provo', in retaliation for the murder the previous weekend in Derry of RUC Constable Paul Gray. Constable Gray had been murdered by an IRA sniper concealed in a shoe shop the previous Saturday afternoon while on foot patrol near the city walls. However, the claim that Frankie Rice had been murdered in retaliation was likely to have been used as an excuse in an attempt to mollify public opinion - in the wake of the barbarity meted out to Rice. The two murders were unlikely to have been connected as the planning for the Rice murder probably started several weeks beforehand.

The Young Militants had been heard of once or twice previously - the name was used to claim responsibility for the Dublin and Monaghan bombings a year earlier - but no such organisation ever existed. The name was used as a cover by certain UVF gangs following acts of unusual barbarity which they feared might stoke up public anger and provoke a backlash against them should they use the organisation's real name.

On Tuesday a second caller to a Belfast newspaper said the murder had been carried out by the Protestant Action Force (PAF), the name normally used by the UVF in mid-Ulster to claim responsibility for acts of terrorism from the early 1970s. The caller said Rice was one of three Official IRA men in the Castlewellan-Rathfriland area. 'The other two will be dealt with in due cause' (sic). The killing had nothing to do with the Young Militants, the caller said. Asked by the recipient of the phone call to provide proof of the killing, the caller replied:

> If the security forces are asked they would show that Rice died of stab wounds, whereas Young Militants claim to have shot him. Rice had been interrogated before being killed and made a lengthy statement. During interrogation he attempted to escape and was stabbed in the leg. His dying words were 'Jesus Christ I'm fucked'.

A short time later a statement issued by the Command Staff of the south-Down, south-Armagh Brigade of the Official IRA said: 'At no time has this man had any connection with the Official IRA.'

Frankie Rice had tenuous links to the junior wing of the Provisional IRA but at seventeen was not a serious player on the paramilitary scene. Separate claims of responsibility by callers purporting to represent two different organisations, together with the claim that Rice was in the Official IRA, showed a degree of confusion and apprehension within the UVF - the organisation actually responsible - over the barbarity of the murder.

The initial garbled claim that the Young Militants were involved and that Rice was a 'Provo' and had been shot was probably made in the heat of the moment by the gang that killed him. However, the likelihood is that the UVF leadership in Belfast discussed the matter over a 48-hour period - in the wake of widespread public revulsion - and decided that the PAF would claim the murder but to avert the risk of retaliation by the Provisionals on Protestants in isolated border areas Rice would be branded an Official IRA man. The Officials were on ceasefire and were unlikely to retaliate.

Throat-cutting and mutilation of young innocent Catholics walking the streets of North and West Belfast could be - and to a certain degree was - carried out with virtual impunity, due largely to the topographical protection and cover a city ghetto provides. The open rural countryside of south Down and south Armagh, close to the border, where many Protestants lived in fear and where the Provisionals operated almost at will, was a different matter. The bad-mouthing of Rice, claiming he used obscene and blasphemous language before or while he was dying was a further attempt by his killers to justify his murder.

Shortly after the gruesome discovery of Rice's body, local police began a murder enquiry, concentrating their efforts on what could be described as loyalist sympathisers in and around Castlewellan.

By 10.30 a.m. on Sunday morning officers were knocking on doors in Upper Square, the Protestant side of the town. Around 11 a.m. an officer called to the home of Eric Cullen, a lorry driver in his late forties who was also a part-time UDR soldier. Cullen was married with grown-up children, including four sons. The officer was interested in speaking to the two eldest sons, Eric junior and Cyril. Eric junior, who was nineteen, was washing his car outside when the officer arrived and asked him to account for his movements the previous night. Cullen said he'd been out with his girlfriend, Anne Priestly, in a pub in Ballynahinch and had arrived home around 1 a.m. The policeman then spoke to Eric senior who confirmed his son's story. He then asked to speak to Cyril, who was eighteen, but was told he had not returned home the previous night and had probably stayed over with his girlfriend in the nearby village of

Dundrum. The officer left, satisfied he had received a plausible account of the young mens' movements the previous night. A number of other local men were also interviewed but all provided satisfactory alibis.

Police investigations continued for a number of months but, as frequently happened in similar cases throughout the course of the Troubles, the culprits were never found and the investigation was abandoned.

The dead man's family, as well as nationalists in general in the area, were angered at the failure of the police to track down the killers and accused them of bias against Rice due to his republican links.

Four weeks after the murder an incident occurred in Castlewellan which local people - mistakenly - believed was linked to the tragedy. At 8 a.m. on Saturday morning June 14, 27-year-old George Kirkpatrick, a Protestant and a single man, who lived with his parents at Dundrine Road, Castlewellan, crossed the yard of his home to his car to go to work. He was employed as a lorry driver with a local quarrying firm called F.S. Herron. His mother, whom he was particularly devoted to, walked with him to his car. As he turned the key in the ignition, a four-pound bomb, attached to the chassis near the right front wheel, exploded. Kirkpatrick sustained serious injuries to his right foot - and is still partially disabled - while his mother sustained fractures to her right leg but made a full recovery.

No organisation claimed responsibility and no one was ever charged. As expected, local people of both communities automatically blamed republicans, believing the attack was in retaliation for the Rice murder and that Kirkpatrick had been involved in killing Rice.

During the police investigation of the bombing, however, officers told Kirkpatrick the attack was not sectarian but was the work of loyalists and was linked to a dispute over Kirkpatrick's girlfriend, Winifred Gibson. The timing was sheer co-incidence. The previous December, Gibson, who later became Kirkpatrick's wife, broke off the relationship to go out with an Armagh man, who, unknown to her, had paramilitary connections. The relationship turned sour, however, and shortly before the bombing she threatened to leave him and return to marry Kirkpatrick. The man then threatened her that 'her life would be made difficult' if she did. After the bombing she received anonymous phone calls warning her not to visit Kirkpatrick in hospital.

Meanwhile the controversy over the Rice killing continued. The barbarity of the attack frightened local people, as nothing so savage had ever occurred in the community before. The Rice family was devastated that Frankie had suffered such cruelty before and while he was dying and no one had been brought to book.

Over the following three years Francis and Teresa Rice conducted a robust campaign to have the killers caught. They lobbied police, clergy and as many politicians as were willing to listen, and Teresa wrote letters to the newspapers. Each time a letter appeared the family was visited and harassed by members of the security forces - mainly the UDR - and officers 'tore out presses', 'ripped up floorboards' and 'read private letters'. A second son Donard was arrested and taken to Gough Barracks, Armagh, where he was threatened and beaten. He was shown pictures of his brother's mutilated body and was told he would 'end up like that' if his family persisted with the campaign.

Then one day the Rice family's luck changed. In February 1979 eleven members of the Shankill Butchers were each sentenced to life imprisonment for their parts in the murders of nineteen Catholics over the previous seven years. An RUC Inspector, Jimmy Nesbitt (now retired), reckoned to have been one of the best investigators in the business, led the team which trapped and put away the Butchers. The trial received widespread publicity in Ireland and Britain.

Teresa Rice read the gory details and saw a familiar parallel between the barbarity meted out to the Butchers' victims and that of her own son. She read about Jimmy Nesbitt's 'wonderful' work in bringing the perpetrators to justice. Shortly after the trial she contacted Nesbitt and explained the details surrounding her son's death stating that no one had been prosecuted. Nesbitt promised the case would be looked into.

Within weeks of Nesbitt's response a new police team, drawn from the established Serious Crime Squad at Gough Barracks, Armagh, and RUC Headquarters, Belfast, was assembled to reinvestigate the murder.

One of the first witnesses reinterviewed during the new investigation was Damien Rice, who accompanied Frankie to Castlewellan the night before (Friday) as well as the night of (Saturday) the murder. In a statement he told police he saw a local man he claimed to recognise acting suspiciously with others the night before the murder in the town's square. This is what his statement contained.

> On the night before the murder while standing outside the Oak Grill with Frankie and a friend I noticed a man, George Kirkpatrick... in a dark red car with a black roof, I think it's a Cortina, but it's a large Ford, driving up and down the town... and at times stop and talk to his friends. I seen him do this every night I was in the town. About half an hour later as me and Frankie were hitching a lift to a dance in Newcastle I saw a car coming down the road... the car stopped above the junction with Newcastle Road. I recognised the driver as George Kirkpatrick. He watched us for a while, maybe three or four minutes... at times he would put his head down. Then he drove down into Newcastle Road; round the upper side of Lower Square and on up the town. I didn't see him after this. Shortly after this Frankie and I got a lift to Newcastle.

In the second part of his statement Damien told police what he saw the night Frankie was killed while standing outside the Oak Grill after returning from Newcastle with Martin Morgan and Dominic Burns:

> I saw Kirkpatrick's car at the telephone kiosk across from the Market House. There was a number of men

about it. Eventually I went into the Oak Grill and had a cup of tea. I sat for about ten minutes. I came out and stood outside for about five minutes. The other two were still inside. They came out. The car was parked half way between the Market House and the end of the lower part of Upper Square. We came out home.

A number of other witnesses, with relevant information, were also re-interviewed. After several months of the new investigation police were ready to start making arrests. They had assembled a picture, they believed, of all the events surrounding the murder, which would lead them to the killers.

At 6.20 a.m. on the morning of Tuesday, 29 July 1980, police arrested George and Winifred Kirkpatrick at their home in Newcastle - where they had moved following their marriage - and took them to Gough Barracks, Armagh, for questioning about the murder five years earlier of Frankie Rice. Two days later officers arrested Cyril and Eric Cullen at their respective homes (they, too, had married and settled down) and conveyed them to Armagh. A number of other suspects were also arrested but were subsequently released. Whilst the sudden and unceremonious nature of the arrests, five years on, had a chastening effect on the four young people, all of them believed their arrests were a mistake and they would shortly be released.

Four hours after his arrest George Kirkpatrick was taken to interview room number two, where his first interview began at 10.35 a.m. His wife was taken to an adjoining room where she was interviewed by female officers. Over the following thirty-six hours, with breaks for meals and an overnight break on Tuesday night, Kirkpatrick was interviewed ten times by six officers - two sergeants and four constables. Each day's interviews consisted of three sessions - morning, afternoon and night - with two officers present. Morning sessions lasted 2½ to 3 hours, afternoons 3½ to 4 hours, nights 3½ to 4 hours. Occasionally the sessions were interrupted to allow for a change of interviewing officers. The team consisted of Constables John McAteer, Ken Hassan (who were most familiar with the case), Sergeants Tom Clements and William McKimm and Constables Cecil Wilson and Oliver Philips.

Kirkpatrick's first interview was conducted by McAteer and Hassan, both attached to the Armagh Crime Squad. McAteer introduced himself and Hassan and informed Kirkpatrick they were making enquiries into the murder of Francis Rice. They questioned him about his background, who his friends were and what he was doing the night of the murder. McAteer's notes contained the following account of the interview:

> He stated he was employed by F.S. Herron, Castlewellan, as a lorry driver since 1971. He got married in 1976 and has been living at... Newcastle since 1977. At the time of the Rice murder... he went about with Norman Kelly.. Billy Huston... Eric and Cyril Cullen. At the time of the murder Kirkpatrick had a red Ford Cortina with a black roof. He stated that his girlfriend, Winifred Gibson (now wife), did not drive that car. He states that he took his parents to the 'Old Tom' Public House in Castlewellan on Saturday, 17 May 1975, but does not remember if he collected them or not. Kirkpatrick could not remember much in general about that night. He stated that they parked most nights opposite the Oak Grill in Upper Square... and that they discussed people who were in the IRA who were going in and out of the Oak Grill... He denied that he ever knew Francis Rice or that he (Rice) was ever in his car.

Kirkpatrick denied all knowledge of the murder throughout Tuesday and most of Wednesday according to notes recorded by all six officers. He continued to deny ever knowing Rice and said some other car must have been mistaken for his. In an interview with Clements and Philips recorded at 12.15 p.m. on Tuesday Kirkpatrick said he couldn't understand why he was being accused of the murder. By Wednesday evening, however, according to McAteer's notes, Kirkpatrick was beginning to talk. In his final interview between 7 p.m and 10.35 p.m. he asked what was going to happen to him. McAteer told him he couldn't say until he first heard what he had to say, but if he was involved he would be charged. Kirkpatrick then talked about his house in Newcastle and said he would have to sell it. How would he get money to pay his mortgage... while he was in jail? He was told he and his wife could sort something out between them.

Following robust questioning, during which Kirkpatrick's mouth started to quiver and he began to 'sweat round the head', McAteer succeeded in drawing him into discussing the murder. Kirkpatrick said: 'I can't tell youze, it's too hard,' but then made a full admission implicating himself and the Cullens.

Next morning, at 9.45 a.m., in the presence of the same officers, Kirkpatrick allegedly made the following statement and signed it:

> On Saturday night the 17 May, 1975 I left home in my car, a red Cortina. I brought my father and mother to Castlewellan and took them to the 'Old Tom' Pub. This was about twenty past nine. I then went and I think I had a drink in Ross's Pub and eventually ended up parked in the middle of Castlewellan town, opposite the Oak Grill. I sat for some time on my own before Eric and Cyril Cullen came and got into the car. We drove around the town a few times to see who was about. Eventually we ended up back in the Upper Square sometime between half eleven and twelve. We sat for a while and then we saw a young fella leave the Oak Grill. One of the Cullen's said that he was a fella called Rice and he was a Provo. Some of them suggested picking him up and giving him a bit of a thumping. We waited until he walked out the Kilcoo Road and I drove out after him. The boys bundled him into the car and told me to drive on out the road. I drove on out to Cabra and turned right down a road and stopped beside a gate into a field. We got out and started to give the boy a bit of a thumping. During this a knife appeared and I think it was Eric who had the knife. Rice was stabbed; I am

not sure how often. We panicked and got back into the car and drove back into Castlewellan and I dropped the two boys off. We left Rice lying at the hedge. I went home and went to bed. The next morning I checked the inside of my car and everything was all right. I don't know where the knife went. As far as I am concerned this was an accident.

On Friday morning, 2 August 1980, Kirkpatrick appeared before Newry Magristrates' Court charged with the Rice murder and was remanded in custody to Crumlin Road prison, Belfast, to await trial. His wife, Winifred, was released without charge.

The Cullen brothers were arrested forty-eight hours after Kirkpatrick and taken to cells in the same block. Seventeen officers working in relays were assigned to interview them. Their interrogation began at approximately 10 a.m. on Thursday and followed the same procedure as that of Kirkpatrick - three sessions a day with two detectives continually present. Both men denied the murder and said they couldn't recall what they were doing on a specific night five years earlier, but they 'were probably' with their girlfriends. As the interrogation progressed, Eric remembered being interviewed by a detective the morning after the murder. He gave that detective an account of his movements, which he accepted. He had nothing to do with the murder.

By the end of the first day, however, both men were allegedly beginning to talk. Notes recorded by Det. Sgt Henry Cooke reveal that Eric was beginning to change his story. He allegedly admitted being in Kirkpatrick's car with Cyril in Castlewellan Square after leaving his girlfriend at 9.30 p.m., and seeing Rice 'having an argument' with 'another boy' whom he didn't know. He then left and went home. During a contemporaneous interview, with two other detectives, Cyril allegedly admitted he 'might' have been in the car, and by 10.30 a.m. next morning - at the start of the second day's interrogation - admitted he 'was' in the car.

By 2.30 p.m. on Friday, Detective McAteer, having 'broken' Kirkpatrick on Wednesday, was ready to resume his role as chief interrogator of the Cullen brothers. With Detective Sgt William McKimm he met Eric, whom Kirkpatrick had allegedly 'named' as the killer. According to McAteer's notes Eric continued to deny the killing but allegedly repeated his admission that he'd been in Kirkpatrick's car. He saw Rice walk down from behind the Oak Grill and he told the others he was a Provo. An hour into the interview, however, Eric became ill. The shock of his arrest and the strain of aggressive questioning had taken its toll. The interview was suspended for half an hour and resumed at 4 p.m. Three-quarters of an hour later, he allegedly made a full admission to the killing and agreed to make a statement. This is what it contained:

> On Saturday 17 May 1975 I was out with my girlfriend until about 10.00 p.m. I left her home at that time and I then went up to Upper Square, Castlewellan where I met up with my brother Cyril and George Kirkpatrick at King's Shop. The three of us got into Kirkpatrick's car, which was a red coloured Ford Cortina with a black roof. The car was parked in the car park in the middle of the Square. I sat in the front and Cyril was in the back. We drove around the town a few times and then parked in the Square opposite the Oak Grill. At about 11.30 p.m. I saw a young fellow who I knew to be called Rice coming from the back of the Oak Grill. I told my brother and Kirkpatrick that the talk was that Rice was a Provo. Rice walked down the Main Street and out the road towards Kilcoo. We all decided to follow him and as we caught up with him at the Dublin Road just past the factory Kirkpatrick stopped the car and Cyril and myself got out and walked behind Rice. Kirkpatrick drove down the road towards Kilcoo and stopped about a hundred yards in front of Rice. As we approached the car Cyril and me caught up with Rice. We caught hold of him and forced him into the back seat of the car and got in beside him. We both held Rice and Kirkpatrick

drove on out the road towards Rathfriland. He turned into a side road and stopped at a gateway at the entrance to a field. We took Rice out of the car and all three of us started to punch and kick him. At this time Rice tried to escape and I had a dagger with me which I pulled out to try and scare him. I stabbed at Rice with the knife a number of times and stabbed him in the front of the body. I don't know how many times I stabbed him but I remember he fell down on the ground. We then all jumped into Kirkpatrick's car and drove back to Castlewellan. I cannot remember what I did with the knife. Kirkpatrick dropped Cyril and me off in the Upper Square and we went home. I never meant to kill Rice at any time only to beat him up.

While Eric was confessing to McAteer, Cyril, meanwhile, was allegedly making a similar admission to Detectives Robert McCabe and David Norwood in a nearby cell. Between 2.05 p.m. and 3.10 p.m. Cyril, on being informed of the contents of Kirkpatrick's statement, allegedly replied: 'They are near enough right.' He then 'agreed' to make his own statement. This is what it contained.

On Saturday night the 17 May, 1975, I was in Castlewellan along with a few boys. At around 10.30 p.m. I met Eric my brother. Earlier that night I had been in Dundrum at a pub drinking. Eric had been in a pub in Castlewellan. I saw George Kirkpatrick drive into the square in his car, it's a Ford Cortina, red coloured with a black vinyl roof. Both of us went over and got into the car with George. I am not sure if I sat in the front or back seat. George drove around the town for a while with us with him, he came back and parked in the Upper Square. By this time it was shortly after 11 p.m. We sat in the car and talked for a while. About half an hour later a fellow came out of the Oak Grill, I didn't know him, but one of the other two said that it was Rice and that he was a Provie. We watched him walking down the Main Street and then he walked on towards Kilcoo. The three of us decided to lift him and give him a bit of a beating. We followed him out the road, to the dip in the road, just past the old houses on the left. George stopped the car and Eric and I got out, and started to walk behind Rice. George drove on up the road a bit past Rice. When Rice reached the car, Eric and I bundled him into the back seat and got in beside him. George drove on out the road over the Burren Bridge and along a side road. I didn't know where we were. George stopped the car and we took Rice out, all three of us were beating him. Somebody took out a knife and stabbed repeatedly. The three of us got into the car again and George drove Eric and I home. I want to say now that at no time was it our intention to kill Rice. It was just a bit of horseplay that got out of hand.

The following morning (Saturday) Eric and Cyril Cullen were charged before Downpatrick Magistrates' Court with murdering Rice and were remanded to Crumlin Road prison to await trial.

Following their incarceration in Crumlin Road the three men were visited by their solicitors and immediately protested their innocence and claimed their statements were a 'concoction of the police'. All three claimed they were pressurised so much by the interviewing officers that they would have 'signed anything' to get out of Armagh (Gough barracks). They claimed detectives threatened them, cursed at them, shouted continuously in their ears and kicked furniture around the room to get them to confess. They did not allege physical abuse but said police 'tricked' them into signing sheets of paper onto which confessions were later written.

During the interviews detectives would 'compose' events from the night of 17 May which would put them in 'certain places' at 'certain times' which were 'completely false'. They would flatly deny such 'composition' but detectives would 'insist and insist' until they (the accused) became so confused and disoriented they did not know what they were saying. All three said the statements they signed were virtually blank sheets of paper which did not contain the admissions of involvement in the murder which later appeared on them. These were added later by the police.

On Thursday, 11 June 1981, a year after their arrests, the trial of Kirkpatrick and the Cullen brothers opened at Belfast Crown Court. All three were charged that:

1. On a date unknown between the 16th day of May 1975 and the 19th day of May 1975 in the County Court Division of South Down, they murdered Francis Anthony Rice.

2. That on a date unknown between the 16th day of May 1975 and the 19th day of May 1975 in the County Court Division of South Down, they assaulted Francis Anthony Rice thereby occasioning him actual bodily harm, contrary to Common Law and section 47 of the Offences Against the Person Act 1861.

3. That on a date unknown between the 16th day of May 1975 and the 19th day of May 1975 in the County Court Division of South Down they stole and unlawfully carried away Francis Anthony Rice against his will.

4. That on a date unknown between the 16th day of May 1975 and the 19th day of May 1975 in the County Court Division of South Down they assaulted Francis Anthony Rice and unlawfully and injuriously imprisoned the said Francis Anthony Rice and detained him against his will.

The case was heard before Lord Justice O'Donnell (a Catholic), who also presided over the Shankill Butchers trial, sitting alone without a jury in keeping with Northern Ireland's Diplock Courts' procedure.

The Crown case alleged that the three defendants admitted their parts in the killing in signed statements taken during interviews with detectives at Gough barracks, Armagh, in July/August 1980. Six police witnesses testified that the statements were made without any inducements, threats or promises being made to the accused. Three doctors who examined the defendants during the course of the interviews also gave evidence that they had not received complaints from the men about ill treatment.

All three defendants denied the charges and alleged the statements were a concoction of the police.

In his defence Kirkpatrick said that at the time he took his parents 'every Saturday night' to the 'Old Tom Bar' in Castlewellan. After dropping them off he 'always' drove to a pub in the village of Leitrim some miles away where he drank with friends. He would then collect his parents sometime after 11 p.m. and drive home. This was a routine he kept every Saturday night. The first he knew of the murder was when he heard it talked about in the town the next day. Both Eric and Cyril Cullen said they had been with their girlfriends the night of the murder and like Kirkpatrick had only heard about it in the town the next day.

Eric Cullen's girlfriend, Anne Priestly, and both her parents testified that Eric was in their house on the night of the murder until 1 a.m. - after returning with Anne from the pub - when he left for home.

Cyril Cullen's girlfriend, Sandra McCavery, both her parents and her brother Ronald all testified that Cyril Cullen stayed the night in their house the night of the murder, after he and Sandra returned from a pub in Dundrum shortly after midnight.

The trial lasted four and a half days and on the afternoon of the fifth day Justice O'Donnell began his summation. He said he believed the three had acted in consort to commit the murder and that the defence case had been 'totally discredited'. He was prepared to accept the evidence of the police witnesses regarding statements made by the accused and he found all three guilty.

He sentenced each one to life imprisonment for murder and also to ten years for false imprisonment and kidnapping; the sentences to run consecutively.

After the verdict, Eric Cullen, senior, who by this time had resigned from the UDR, began a campaign to obtain his sons' release and clear their names, claiming they were the victims of a gross miscarriage of justice. Kirkpatrick's Aunt Hilda - his parents were unwell and unable to campaign - began a similar campaign.

The two families lobbied the clergy, the police and as many politicians as were prepared to listen. They petitioned the Northern Ireland Office and the Home Office in London, but to no avail. They refused to go public, however, for fear of reprisals. They were only too aware of the ruthlessness of loyalist paramilitaries and knew that a public campaign in which a finger might be pointed at the real killers could place them in mortal danger. A number of policemen with whom they discussed the matter warned them of the dangers of fingering others.

Shortly after entering Crumlin Road prison in August 1980, to await trial, the Cullen brothers were approached by a prisoner whose identity they did not know but whom they believed to be a senior loyalist paramilitary figure. The man asked the reason for their imprisonment and when told assured them 'everything would be put right'. 'Don't worry I know youze are innocent youze'll be okay'. The man then asked who the police investigating the crime were and when told he again assured them he'd 'fix everything up' when he got out.

The man was Robin Jackson, who was on remand with two other men on a charge of possessing weapons. The Cullens subsequently learned that Jackson was fully aware of their arrest and interrogation before approaching them and that he was concerned that three innocent men of his own political persuasion were being asked to take the rap for something they did not do. Jackson was later sentenced to seven years - but served only three due to remission - on the arms charge. During twelve years in prison the Cullens heard nothing further from Jackson.

Sometime after their encounter with Jackson, the Cullens were approached by a second prisoner who also made empty promises about getting their names cleared. The man was John Sommerville, brother to Wesley and a leading member of Jackson's squad.

Sommerville had been arrested and charged - belatedly - after giving himself up and confessing to his part in the Miami Showband massacre. He was considered a hard terrorist who had cut his teeth in the very early 1970s, with his brother, in the Hanna-Jackson unit. He was involved from a very early stage in the Murder Triangle campaign and was across the border on numerous attacks, including the murder of John Francis Greene in Monaghan in 1975. Following the Miami disaster and the death of his brother during the attack it's believed he took little or no further part in terrorism.

In 1980, with his past weighing heavily on his mind, he approached a clergyman in Dungannon, near where he lived, and asked to be taken to a police station to confess 'all he knew'. The clergyman took him to an RUC station where he was interviewed. Sommerville confessed to his part in the Miami attack because of the guilt he felt over his brother's death. He did not, however, confess to the other crimes in his long paramilitary career.

Like Jackson, Sommerville expressed concern to the two men over their predicament and promised to 'put things right'. 'I know you guys are innocent. I know that for a fact. You guys will beat this charge. There is no way you guys will go down for this.' He also told them the 'knife' which killed Rice was 'still around' and could be 'produced' if that would help to clear them. Sommerville did not 'clear them' and did not produce the knife.

Frankie Rice was, of course, murdered by Robin Jackson and his Flying Squad with Jackson doing the stabbing. As well as Boyle and the Sommervilles he was also accompanied by Stewart Young, who carried out the Monaghan bombing. It is possible a woman was also involved. The two men observed by Francis Ward walking behind Rice at the fork in the road were Jackson and Boyle. In a statement to police, Ward described the men as 'one tall and one short and stocky'. Boyle was over 6ft. and slim; Jackson was approximately 5'7' and stocky.

The murder was set up by a number of local Castlewellan men who cannot be named here for legal reasons, who became aware of Rice's republican links. Jackson and Boyle occasionally visited Castlewellan on Saturday nights to sell UVF mementos and recruit local men into the organisation. Whilst a number of locals did join, they did not constitute an active UVF cell and did not pose a serious terrorist threat - on their own - in the area.

Police never established for certain how Rice was abducted or where he was tortured and murdered. The likelihood is, however, that as Rice drew near the red 'sports' car which Francis Ward saw parked ahead of him, a man (or possibly a woman) in the rear seat opened the door and asked him for directions. As Rice approached the car and leaned forward to respond the person probably engaged him in further conversation about the details of the 'directions' drawing him ever closer towards the inside of the car. At this stage Jackson and Boyle probably arrived on the scene and bundled Rice from behind headlong into the back seat. The abduction was probably over in seconds (Rice never stood a chance) which may explain why no one saw him being abducted.

The 'red car' with blacked out windows which Francis and Teresa Rice saw following them in Castlewellan was almost certainly the same car Ward saw. When it 'careered' round the corner at Burrenreagh Road, almost sweeping them off their feet, it probably contained their eldest son, Francis.

Following his kidnap, Rice was probably taken to a disused house or farm shed in the area where he was interrogated, tortured and killed. At least five people took part in the interrogation, which probably lasted two to three hours, the purpose of which was to extort information from Rice about the IRA. As a fit and agile young man, Rice - almost certainly - fought a hard battle to survive and escape his tormentors. He was probably held down by at least four people while a fifth - Jackson - stabbed him.

In the year prior to the Rice murder there had been an upsurge in IRA activity in the south Down area. In November 1974 a local part-time UDR man, John McCready, was shot dead in Newry by the Provisional IRA. McCready was a large potato grower who supplied potatoes to many people around Castlewellan and his murder caused deep resentment among the Protestant community. It is believed the Rice Murder was in direct retaliation for McCready. Jackson, who at the time was shortly to assume the redoubtable mantle of commanding officer of the UVF in mid-Ulster from Hanna, wanted retaliation.

Kirkpatrick and the Cullen brothers served twelve years in prison - and were released in 1992 - for a murder they did not commit. Theirs is the great forgotten miscarriage of justice. I have researched this case over a period of two years and am totally satisfied they are innocent. Not only were they not present at the scene of the murder but the suggestion - which has been part of a whispering campaign for a number of years in the area - that they 'fingered' Rice for Jackson or disposed of the body after the murder, is totally and utterly false. Neither of the three men knew Jackson before the murder and neither did they know Frankie Rice.

All three hung around the town of Castlewellan - and messed about in cars - during the early to mid-1970s. That is not denied. But so, too, did most of the other young men, of both communities, who lived in the area at the time.

There are a number of basic defects in the Crown case which the Appeal Court in Belfast should now urgently look into. These are:

1. In its submission to the court the prosecution case - which is not published in this book due to pressure on space - alleged that after abducting Rice the three defendants 'then took Rice to an unknown destination where they stabbed him to death and then dumped his body in a laneway in Cabra'.

   However, all three defendants in their alleged statements said that after abducting Rice they took him to the road beside the lane where they beat and stabbed him:

   Kirkpatrick: 'The boys bundled him into the car and told me to drive on out the road. I drove on out to Cabra and turned right down a road and stopped beside a gate in a field. We got out and started to give the boy a bit of a thumping. During this a knife appeared... Rice was stabbed...'

Eric Cullen: 'We both caught hold of him and forced him into the back seat... Kirkpatrick drove on out the road towards Rathfriland. We turned into a side road and stopped at a gateway at an entrance to a field. We took Rice out and all three of us started to punch and kick him... Rice tried to escape and I had a dagger... I stabbed at Rice.. he fell down on the road'.

Cyril Cullen: 'Eric and I bundled him into the back seat... George drove on out the road ... George stopped the car and we took Rice out, all three of us were beating him. Somebody took out a knife and stabbed repeatedly. The three of us got into the car again and George drove Eric and I home.

There is a clear contradiction here between the evidence the Crown presented to the trial about where Rice was killed and the alleged statements of the three accused presented by the police in the book of evidence. This contradiction must be examined by the appeal court.

2. The Scenes of Crime Officer, Detective James O'Neill who carried out a forensic examination of the scene found ' three bloodstains' on the Convent Road - beside the laneway. If Rice was stabbed twelve times with a dagger on the road beside the lane with some of the wounds 'penetrating back to the shoulder blades', then it's highly likely a large pool of blood would have been found on the road. O'Neill also found that there were 'no trail-marks in the dirt', 'an absence of bloodstains down the entrance' and 'no sign of a struggle near the point where the body was found'.

If Rice was 'punched and kicked' by all three men and then stabbed, the roadway, the grass-margin, the gate entrance and almost certainly the laneway to where the body was found would be a complete mess with blood everywhere. It is simply absurd to suggest that the three men could take Rice from the back seat of a car on to a roadway, beat and stab him to death, dump his body in an adjoining laneway, and leave only 'three bloodstains' on the road.

During the years 1972–1975 Kirkpatrick says he was 'always about the town' of Castlewellan driving 'up and down and round about' with friends. They were young and 'a bit wild' and that was how they got their kicks. But he says he never sat in his car and watched anyone. The car Damien Rice saw with the driver 'watching' them and 'putting his head down' from time to time was almost certainly Jackson and his gang following their movements in a car similar to his, Kirkpatrick says.

The claim by the prosecution that Rice was taken to 'an unknown destination', and its inability to provide a single shred of evidence about that destination, clearly demonstrates the weakness in the prosecution case. If the three accused men were prepared to tell police under interrogation in Gough barracks all other details of the murder, why withhold that portion? It seems odd that accused men under intense pressure from interrogating police are weak enough to 'break' on 75 per cent of the evidence but strong enough to 'hold out' on the remaining 25 per cent. I offer one explanation:

The construction of events leading up to and including the abduction of Francis Rice was made reasonably simple by the evidence of two crucial witnesses - James Fitzpatrick, who saw him leave the Oak Grill shortly before midnight, and Francis Ward, who saw him walking out the Newry Road, with two men, one tall and one short, walking behind and a car parked in front.

The nature of Rice's injuries and the discovery of the dagger near the body made the cause of death simple to evaluate. Overall the Crown case defies logic. That seven witnesses, all relatives and partners of the Cullen brothers, lied to the police in the provision of alibis, seems almost incredulous. Furthermore, the prosecution conveniently ignored two very important factors which - in Northern Ireland terms during the conflict - were crucial to the case. None of the three accused men had ever been charged or convicted of a criminal offence before and none of them were or ever had been members of a paramilitary organisation. That men with such unblemished characters would murder a teenager in such a barbaric way also defies logic.

The Cullen brothers, in age and physique, closely resembled Jackson and Boyle and matched neatly the description of the two men Ward saw walking behind Rice. Eric Cullen was nineteen, tall and slim; Cyril was eighteen, short and stocky. Boyle was early twenties, tall and slim, Jackson was mid-twenties, short and stocky.

Eric Cullen was the only one of the three men with a tattoo of a knife on his arm, which he acquired as a kid in the boy scouts long before the conflict began. Yet he was the one who did the stabbing, according to the prosecution. This also fitted neatly into the case for the prosecution.

In fact, Eric Cullen was the quietest and shyest of the three defendants. He was the one least likely of all to commit a murder. Perhaps if he were a tough, hardened terrorist who had mutilated a seventeen-year-old boy, he would not have broken down and become ill under interrogation.

There is one final, uncanny twist to the story, which is also perhaps worth noting. Frankie Rice was murdered on 17 May 1975, the first anniversary of the Dublin and Monaghan bombings (17 May 1974) in which Jackson, Boyle and Wesley Sommerville played leading roles. In their eyes, the bombings were a 'major success' - they tore the hearts out of Dublin city centre as well as Monaghan town and killed thirty-three people, and they (the perpetrators) got away with it. Perhaps they felt they had an event to commemorate or maybe even celebrate.

CHAPTER 11

IN THE WRONG PLACE

Sunday morning, 22 June 1975, was a normal Sunday for 48-year-old Christy Phelan from Whitechurch near Sallins, Co. Kildare. Around 9.15 a.m. he and other members of his family cycled the one and a half miles from their cottage home to 9.30 a.m. Mass in the local church in Ardlough. After Mass Christy went for his customary Sunday morning stroll with his dog towards the nearby railway line which runs through Kildare, linking Dublin with the south-west. Occasionally he brought his fishing rod and fished for trout in the lower reaches of the river Liffey. Other times he dropped into the local graveyard to pray at the tomb of his deceased relatives. But his favourite pastime was chatting to neighbours while he leaned his elbows on the south wall of the hump-backed bridge which straddled the railway line.

Christy was a kind, genial man who knew his neighbours well. He worked locally as a farm labourer and was a devoted husband and father to five children, aged ten to nineteen. Like many citizens of the Republic he viewed the Northern Troubles from a distance but scarcely understood what they were about.

Leaving home he told his wife Molly he'd return for dinner and look after the house while she took the children to a County Sports Day in the nearby village of Kill, where eleven-year-old Martin was participating in an athletics competition. By 1.30 p.m. Christy had not returned and Molly, believing he had gone fishing and decided to extend his stay, put his dinner in the oven and headed to the sportsground with the children. Fifty minutes later a bomb ripped through the railway line on the southern side of Barronrath bridge, blowing away a section of the line and leaving a massive crater in the ground. Martin Phelan, who is now thirty-seven, remembers hearing the explosion as he took part in a race at the sportsground.

As Gardai and railway workers from Coras Iompar Eireann (CIE), the Republic's transport company, rushed to the scene to investigate, a railway employee found the body of Christy

214

Phelan lying on its back in a clump of bushes just inside the bridge wall on the southern side. He had not been killed by the explosion but had been stabbed repeatedly by a 6-inch double-edged dagger almost four hours earlier. The body was so badly mutilated from the stab wounds as well as blows to the head, that a local man, William Cullen, who was asked by Gardai to identify the body, and who knew Christy well, could only say that he thought it was him. His clothes were so badly saturated in blood that he was eventually identified by the belt he was wearing.

Precise details of the events leading to Christy's death have never been fully established - as no one has ever been charged with the murder - but a three-year investigation by a team of detectives from Dublin's Murder Squad, which was then in existence, did, according to officers who worked on it, build up a picture which is 99 per cent accurate.

The story begins in the village of Bodenstown three miles south of Barronrath. Each year during the 1970s around the third week of June, members of Provisional Sinn Féin, Official Sinn Féin (now The Workers Party) and the Fianna Fáil party travelled to Bodenstown to commemorate the birth of the eighteenth-century Irish revolutionary, Theobald Wolfe Tone, the 'Father of Irish Republicanism' in 1763.

A lawyer by profession and educated at Dublin's Trinity College, Wolfe Tone was one of a number of Protestant intellectuals who opposed British rule in Ireland in the eighteenth century. He was one of the founders of the United Irishmen, who in 1798 staged a series of uprisings against British rule throughout the country. In July 1798 Wolfe Tone was part of a 3,000-strong expedition of French grenadiers that sailed from France to Lough Swilly in County Derry to support the rebellion. He was taken prisoner on arrival by the British and the following November committed suicide (some historians believe he was poisoned in prison) by drinking hemlock at the age of thirty-five. He was buried in Bodenstown, the birthplace of his father.

In the 1970s Fianna Fáil, which is the largest political party in the Republic and has been in power for approximately fifty-six of the last seventy years - since it first entered government in 1932, and Official Sinn Féin visited Bodenstown on the same day (always a Sunday), Fianna Fáil in the morning, the Officials in the afternoon. Provisional Sinn Féin usually visited the following Sunday.

The Provisional IRA called its second ceasefire of the Troubles in 1975. That was the year Robin Jackson's flying squad came of age. In that year it killed more people than in any other year of its existence. Many people believe the ceasefire, which came about as a result of the 'Feakle Talks' (when Irish clergymen initiated a peace process of sorts when they met members of the IRA's Army Council in Feakle, Co. Clare), frightened loyalists who believed Harold Wilson's government of the time was about to make major concessions to the Provisionals. The loyalists' response (and that of their controllers in British intelligence) was to increase violence, not reduce it.

Following the 'success' of the Dublin and Monaghan bombings a year earlier, Jackson's strategy (Hanna was still his commander but only in tutelage) was to 'hit the South' at every possible opportunity. Sunday, 22 June, was the turn of Fianna Fáil and the Officials to visit Bodenstown. It was widely known that a large contingent of both Official and Provisional republican groupings (whose members came from all over Ireland, North and South) travelled the last leg of their journey (from Dublin to Kildare) by special chartered train. On June 22 Robin Jackson decided to attack the train ferrying the republicans - believing it was the Provisionals he was targeting. The Official IRA, the military wing of Official Sinn Féin, had called a ceasefire three and a half years earlier - which continues to the present day - and were not considered a threat any longer to the Northern State by loyalists. Not only that but the fact that throughout 1972/73 and part of 1974 senior figures from both the Officials and the UVF had met secretly a number of times to explore the possibility of establishing common ground between them in the areas of poverty, unemployment and social justice in general made it highly unlikely the UVF would deliberately target the Officials.

According to Gardai a loyalist bombing squad, consisting of at least six men, travelled from Armagh to Bodenstown early on Sunday morning to carry out the mission. The squad was led by Jackson and once again included Harris Boyle and Wesley Sommerville. The other three they are not definite about but believe John Sommerville may also have been present. The intention was to bomb the railway line and derail the train.

The gang arrived around 10 a.m. at Barronrath bridge in two vehicles with a made-up bomb, ready for priming. They parked the vehicles close to the bridge that straddled the railway line - passersby reported seeing strange vehicles parked in the area - and 'almost certainly' posted one man at the wheel of each vehicle for a quick getaway. They then positioned at least one, 'but possibly two', men just inside the wall of the bridge on the southern side, concealed in bushes, to act as lookouts in case Gardai or nosy neighbours approached the scene. Two other men, almost certainly Harris Boyle and Wesley Sommerville (as happened in the case of the Miami Showband murders) carried the bomb across a gate on the northern side, down a 12-foot embankment and under the bridge to the southern side.

They then removed gravel from the side of the line, dug a large hole and placed the bomb in it - the intention being to explode the bomb a number of minutes (possibly even seconds) before the train arrived, blowing away a section of the line which would then derail the train at high speed causing serious death and injury. The gang believed that if the time lapse between the explosion and the arrival of the train was limited to minutes, then railway employees (or the Gardai) would not have time to reach the scene, determine what happened and warn the train driver in time to halt the train.

The bomb was fitted with an alarm clock timer and was set to explode at 2.20 p.m. However, the train was due to pass through Barronrath at approximately 1.45 p.m. - 35 minutes ahead of the timing of the explosion.

By 1 p.m. that afternoon over 300 Official republicans had congregated at Dublin's Heuston railway station, to board the train to Sallins, a village two miles north of Bodenstown and the only railway station in the immediate vicinity. There they would join a further 5,000-strong contingent of supporters who were travelling by car from around the country for a colour party parade to the graveyard where Tone is buried, led by seven pipe bands from north and south of the border. The Heuston contingent included sixty Fianna children - from the youth wing of the party - as well as the wife of the party leader, May MacGiolla.

Earlier in the day (and around the time Jackson's squad was planting the bomb), the former Taoiseach, Jack Lynch, who was leader of the Opposition at the time, accompanied by senior party figures and a number of former ministers, laid a wreath at Tone's grave and gave an oration in his honour.

Back at Heuston the specially chartered train pulled out of the station at 1.20 p.m. - a number of minutes behind schedule - and headed for Sallins. It passed through Barronrath at 1.55 p.m. and arrived without a hitch at Sallins a short time later. At 2.20 p.m. the bomb exploded.

Rail experts say upwards of fifty people would have been killed and a further 200 seriously injured had the bomb gone off before the train arrived. The device was planted over 50 yards south of the bridge which meant that if the lead carriages of the train were derailed the middle carriages would buckle in such a way that the hind carriages would have been catapulted into the air and would have struck the north wall of the bridge, causing much greater death and injury than would otherwise have been the case. The experts say the bombers must have been aware of this and planted the bomb accordingly.

I have been unable to establish for certain what went wrong with the operation and why the bomb was incorrectly timed. Today loyalists in County Armagh put it down to what they call a TPFU - a Typical Prod. Fuck Up. Throughout the history of the conflict, loyalists have had by far the greater number of failed operations (particularly in bombings) than republicans, which experts put down to sheer incompetence and inexperience. Indeed, many loyalists speak jealously of the 'much greater success' of republican paramilitaries than that of their own.

Gardai had no way of establishing for certain how Christy Phelan came in contact with his killers, as no member of the gang has ever been apprehended. However, detectives with years of experience investigating serious crime believe the following sequence of events is probably accurate.

Christy Phelan, who had a habit of speaking to just about everyone he encountered on his travels, approached the southern wall of Barronrath bridge, looked over it and saw a number of men 'working' on the railway line below. In his customary affable manner Christy probably spoke to the 'workmen' and used words such as: 'Be dad lads yez are even out working on a Sunday', believing the terrorists were CIE maintenance men carrying out repairs on a Sunday. The lookout, or lookouts, which probably included Jackson himself (who invariably took upon himself the task of supervising operations he was involved in) believing the gang's operation was now compromised, emerged from the bushes, grabbed Christy by the throat and with the help of other gang members dragged him over the wall on the southern side into the bushes, where at least one of them proceeded to stab him with a dagger. It is likely that by this time the gang members planting the bomb had raced to the scene and joined in the brutality, beating and kicking the helpless man.

That afternoon Garda officer John Brennan was driving his patrol car in the nearby town of Naas with colleague Garda Peter McGarry beside him in the front passenger seat. At 2.40 p.m. - twenty minutes after the explosion - he received a message over his car radio that an explosion had been reported on the Dublin-Limerick railway line at a place called Barronrath bridge.

Brennan raced along the narrow, crooked roads from Naas to Barronrath and discovered the body of Christy Phelan lying in the bushes. In a statement to the Kildare county coroner, Dr Bill O'Donnell, a week later this is what Brennan said:

> I am a member of An Garda Siochána stationed at Naas. On the 22/6/75 I was driving the Naas Traffic Car accompanied by Garda Peter McGarry 17515c. At 2.40

p.m. I drove to Barronrath Railway Bridge, Kill, Co. Kildare. I looked over the wall of the bridge and I saw a man lying on his back and his face was heavily stained with what appeared to be blood. There was also marks on his chest and his tie appeared to be pulled tight around his neck. The man appeared to be dead. I immediately contacted my Station by radio. The body was lying on the Straffan side of the bridge and a few feet from a P & T pole. The body was dressed with a trousers held by braces and belt. He also had a blue shirt, the front of the shirt had stains resembling blood stains. One of his shoes was under his left arm. Both his fists were clenched and were resting on his stomach. I took charge of the scene and did not allow anybody interfere with the position of the body. William Cullen, 1510 Boston, Kill, Co. Kildare, identified the body to me as that of Christopher Phelan, Whitechurch, Straffan, Co. Kildare. I later identified the body to Doctor J. Harbinson, State Pathologist. At 8.30 p.m. the body was removed by ambulance to the Morgue at Naas County Hospital. I accompanied the body in the ambulance and I remained with the body at the Morgue.

At 4.55 p.m. State Pathologist Dr John Harbinson arrived at the scene and conducted a preliminary inspection of the body before carrying out a post-mortem at Naas Hospital later in the evening. This is his report:

There were two stab wounds on the front of the body. There was dried blood streaming from the mouth down the left cheek. The tie was knotted tightly, and a small ligature mark was visible on the right side of the neck. The right lower eyelid was swollen. At 7.00 p.m. I recorded the air temperature as 70°F. Rigor mortis [stiffening of the body] at this time was well established. At 10.30 p.m. I commenced my post-mortem examination in the mortuary of the County Hospital, Naas. I proceeded to undress the body. The items comprised a wristlet watch, a necktie, a thick brown leather belt, the one remaining shoe, which had come off the foot en route from the scene, a pair of black and blue golf-pattern socks, a pair of trousers with braces, a pair of underpants, a blue nylon shirt, a white cotton vest. In the pockets of the trousers I found an Irish one pound note, a piece of plug tobacco, and a match box with a few matches in it. The following signs of injury were present on the body: a stab wound on the right side of the front of the neck, a gaping wound seven eighths of an inch long, half an inch below the right collar bone, a stab wound in the middle of the chest, a wound on the thumb side of the right wrist. This wound sloped towards the elbow. It was consistent with a defensive injury. A wound on the palm of the left hand, a wound between the bases of the left middle and ring fingers. A ligature mark on the right side of the front of the neck. A bruise on the right lower eyelid, which was swollen. A group of two abrasions on the right cheek, below the right eye. An area of patterned abrasions on the right side of the upper lip. An abrasion on the right side of the chin. A group of abrasions mainly on the left side of the chin. A vertical abrasion on the right lower lip, extending down on to the chin. A bruise of the upper lip with a long laceration on the inner surface of the upper lip. A group of two abrasions on the front of the neck. An abrasion on the right side of the neck. An abrasion over the top of the left shoulder blade. An abrasion on the right shoulder, with a faint bruise nearer the midline and an abrasion below the right shoulder. A group of abrasions on the back of the left upper arm above the left elbow. There was a further scratch below the elbow. A group of abrasions on the back of the right arm. A group of abrasions on the front of the left shin. Other external features were: bleeding into the lower lid of the right eye and haemorrhages on the lower lid of the left eye. There was early putrefactive change on the front surfaces of both legs in the thigh region. These were manifested as blistering and loosening of the skin and 'marbling' of the veins. This was due to the extreme heat of the day, and the dependant position of the legs as the body lay on the railway bridge embankment. The body was 5'6' in height. The undersurface of the scalp and temporal muscles showed a crop of haemorrhages indicative of asphyxia. There was bruising of the scalp and underlying skull above the right eye socket. There was a bruise over the back of the head. Dissection of the left temporal muscle revealed extensive bleeding into it. Dissection of the skin of the neck revealed bleeding in the fat above the ligature mark on the right side of the neck. There was bleeding on the surface of the salivary gland. Dissection of the strap muscles on the right revealed bruising beneath the ligature mark in the right sterno-hyoid, right sterno-thyroid, and right crico-thyroid muscles. Further dissection revealed a fracture of the right upper horn of the thyroid cartilage and a fracture of the hyoid bone. There was bleeding into the muscles, adjacent to both fractures. Dissection of the left side of the neck revealed bruising in the left sterno-mastoid and sterno-hyoid muscles over the thyroid gland. There was considerable bleeding into the tissues overlying the left ala of the thyroid cartilage. The hyoid bone was fractured with bleeding around the fracture site. There was bleeding over the left end of the hyoid bone. The knife track in the neck, ran backwards, downwards and to the left, transfixing the windpipe. This wound track petered out in the apex of the left lung area. The track beneath wound No. 2 entered the chest in the space between the first and second right ribs. The wound track passed into the upper lobe of the right lung. The depth of this wound track in the lung tissue was six inches. Wound No. 3 was situated over the breastbone. The track extended through the left margin of the breastbone, at the level of the space between the fourth and fifth ribs. It entered the front of the heart through the wall of the right ventricle under the coronary groove. The wound track left the heart through the left ventricle and passed into the lower lobe of the left lung. The total length of the track was 7'. The right lung was collapsed due to puncture by the stab wound. The left lung was deeply congested and water-logged. Apart from its stab wounds, the heart was healthy. There was blood in the right chest cavity, amounting to one litre, from the stab wound in the right lung. There was blood in the sac around the heart and this sac showed two perforating wounds. I examined a knife found near the scene of the crime, and its measurements were as follows: 13' long, with a blade nine and one sixteenth of an inch long. I examined a second knife at 4.50 p.m. on the 27th June 1975 in the Garda Technical Bureau. The knife was a dagger-type of sheath knife, with a fixed blade of stainless steel. The blade was blood-stained, especially around the hilt. The blood had dried. The knife was 10 7/8' long overall, with a double edged blade 6' long. The deceased man died from shock and haemorrhage as a result of stab wounds in the chest. I examined the knife shown to me which was blood stained. The wounds in the body are consistent with infliction by this knife. The 7' track in wound No. 3, though one inch longer than the blade of this knife, can be explained by the compression of the chest during the knife thrust. Wound No. 3 must have necessitated very considerable force to inflict as it passed through the breast-bone. The remaining stab wounds passed through soft tissue, and therefore would have required less force to inflict. The injuries on the neck indicate partial strangulation of the deceased man immediately prior to his death. It would seem probable that the strangling injury was inflicted by the deceased man's own tie, which was pulled tight. From my temperature recordings of the scene of the crime, I am of the opinion that this man died only a few hours prior to my examination, probably late in the morning of the same day, namely Sunday 22nd June. The abrasions on the shoulders, of pressure type, were probably due to the pinioning of the deceased man against a hard and irregular surface while being strangled and/or stabbed.

It is clear from Dr Harbinson's report that the deceased man, apart from the stabbing, was severely beaten before and while he was dying.

As the gang fled the scene they discarded the murder weapon - the six-inch dagger - in a nearby field from where Gardai recovered it during the murder hunt. A 13-inch knife found near the body had apparently not been used and may have been left as a decoy in an attempt to conceal the identity of the real weapon used, and prevent Gardai from finding it and, perhaps, through the RUC, linking it to other murders.

Nothing is known for certain of the route by which the gang escaped but it is believed they followed the road from Barronrath to the main Dublin-Naas dual carriageway and travelled through Dublin city to the border. With over three and a half hours to spare they were almost certainly safely back across the border before the bomb exploded. Given the extent of Christy Phelan's injuries it is almost certain some of the gang were heavily bloodstained. As they were anxious to rid themselves of the dagger, as a precaution against being stopped at a Garda road-check, it is likely they also had an early change of clothing along the way.

Following the murder and the attempted massacre of Official republicans, rumours abounded that the Irish Republican Socialist Party (IRSP) and its military wing the INLA, which a year earlier broke away from the Officials, were involved. The split resulted in a vicious blood feud between the two factions which lasted for a number of years and which led to the assassination of the veteran republican and charismatic leader of the breakaway group, Seamus Costello, by the Official IRA in 1977. Earlier Costello had been behind the attempted murder of a former colleague and fellow veteran of the Official republican group, Sean Garland, who was shot and wounded near his home in Ballymun in north Dublin. From the outset, however, Gardai had no doubt who was behind the Sallins outrage. One Garda officer I spoke to said they never once suspected republicans.

> From the moment we were called to the scene of Christy's murder and saw the damage to the railway line we knew it was loyalists. We knew the cut of their hatchet. We never once suspected republicans despite the fact that a civil war was taking place between the two groups. But we knew that no one group of republicans would dare attempt to murder 300 members of another group. That would be collective suicide. Besides we were always aware of the possibility that at some stage loyalists might try to target Bodenstown. Bodenstown was a sitting duck for loyalists.'

The Garda investigation into the murder of Christy Phelan was led by Dan Murphy, the head of the Murder Squad. Murphy had played a key role in the unsuccessful hunt for the Dublin and Monaghan bombers a year earlier and despite the failure of that investigation he had by this time acquired an intimate knowledge of loyalist paramilitaries and their *modus operandi*. During the investigation Murphy made contact with his old friend, Frank Murray, the Catholic detective who played such a crucial role in the bombing investigation a year earlier. Within days Murray discovered from his contacts that the Hanna-Jackson unit had murdered Christy Phelan and that the murder had been the result of a bungled attempt to bomb the Sallins railway line. Murray came up with four names of 'definite suspects' who his contacts claimed had been to Sallins, which he immediately passed to the Gardai. Among the names were Jackson, Boyle and John and Wesley Sommerville. Following further investigation, Murphy asked Murray to arrange to have the suspects arrested and interrogated with a view to having them extradited to the South. In a repeat of the Dublin-Monaghan debacle, however, Murphy once again found the investigation frustrated by the RUC, who refused to cooperate. Jackson and Boyle were again untouchable. Murphy then, once again, took his case to the Commissioner, Ed Garvey, and asked that contact be made with RUC headquarters in Belfast to have the matter sorted out, but again Garvey refused.

One senior officer who worked on the case but who asked not to be named told me during an interview for this book that he felt so disgusted over the behaviour of his own Commissioner and that of the RUC that he considered resigning from the force.

> We had four definite names of suspects all from the Armagh area. I really felt that if the RUC had to co-operate we would have secured convictions. I was disgusted and I seriously considered resigning from the job.

Having failed in his efforts with the RUC, Dan Murphy then turned his attention to the Phelan family. Anthony Phelan, the eldest of the family, had not gotten on with his father. There were rows and arguments on an ongoing basis between both men but nothing more serious than that which occurred between most fathers and sons. However, Dan Murphy sought to exploit this and attempted to extract a confession from Anthony that he had killed his father. In a series of interviews stretching over a number of days, the young man was quizzed repeatedly about the rows. In a heavy-handed and intimidatory fashion he was forced by Murphy to retrace his steps through surrounding fields where he and his father had argued and he was taken to the blood-soaked scene at the railway line where his father's body was found. All in an attempt to force him to confess to something he had not done. But the young man refused to budge.

But there was further humiliation and disappointment in store for the Phelan family. When asked later by Molly Phelan, Christy's widow, who the culprits were who murdered her husband, Murphy told her it was the IRA - despite knowing that this was a bare-faced lie.

For twenty-seven years the Phelan family have not only seen the killers of their father and husband escape justice, but they have had their suffering compounded by lies and deceit perpetrated by the very people who were supposed to have alleviated that suffering.

This case cries out to high Heaven for justice. Nothing less than a full and open investigation into the events surrounding the murder of Christy Phelan and the subsequent Garda investigation will suffice. But there is a much wider issue at stake here. As mentioned earlier, Jackson, Boyle and Wesley Sommerville were three leading members of the loyalist gang which bombed Dublin thirteen months earlier. Within a month of that bombing and at least a year before Sallins, the Gardai in Dublin were aware of their involvement. They had their names, addresses, photographs and paramilitary affiliation on file.

When the Sallins attacks took place, the Gardai became aware that the very same people were involved again. Yet nothing was done by the then Garda Commissioner Ed Garvey (who after all had the power to force the hand of the RUC) to have them arrested and extradited. It simply wasn't good enough and the truth must now be told.

CHAPTER 12

MURDER IN THE DEAD OF NIGHT

Sunday, 24 August 1975, was a scorching hot day in Ireland. In Dublin's Croke Park, the headquarters of Gaelic football, Derry and Dublin Gaelic football teams were playing in the All Ireland Football Semi-final. Ever since the founding of the Gaelic Athletic Association (GAA) in 1884, the body which runs Gaelic football in Ireland, the people of the nine counties of the province of Ulster - but particularly the Catholics (and some Protestants) of the six counties - have been amongst the most enthusiastic supporters and participants of the game in the country. When in 1960 an Ulster county from within the six counties - Down - won the All Ireland Final (the Sam Maguire Cup) for the first time by beating Kerry, the aristocrats of the game for the previous seven decades, that enthusiasm grew ten-fold.

On Sunday, 24 August, up to 15,000 fans not just from County Derry but from all over the six counties, crossed the border into the South to attend the match. After a hard-fought and highly competitive game, Dublin, the home county, won by a score of 3 goals, 13 points to Derry's 3 goals and 8 points. After the game Gardai in Dublin arrested a number of hooligans for minor offences but the game itself was played in a sporting and friendly atmosphere.

Amongst the contingent of Northern Ireland fans who travelled to the game were two friends and workmates, Sean Farmer a 32-year-old married father of four children from a small village called the Moy, near Dungannon, in County Tyrone, and Colm McCartney, a 22-year-old single man, from Bellaghy in south County Derry. Both men worked for a road construction company called Blackwell, an English firm based in County Antrim, which specialised in widening and re-surfacing roads. Farmer was a digger driver; McCartney a fitter. At the time Blackwell was engaged in a major construction project upgrading large stretches of a twenty-mile route between the city of Armagh and the town of Newry. Both men worked on the project. To be near his work McCartney lived in lodgings in Newry, which lies almost fifty miles south of his home village of Bellaghy. Farmer lived with his wife and family in the Moy. Both men were ardent GAA fans and both played Gaelic football with their respective club teams. Neither had any interest in politics or involvement with any organisation, political or paramilitary.

On Sunday morning McCartney left his parents' home in Bellaghy around 7 a.m. in his Ford Cortina car and travelled to the Moy to collect Farmer. Shortly after 8.30 a.m. both men set out for Dublin in McCartney's car with McCartney at the wheel. The journey south, which took them through Armagh city, Newtownhamilton in south Armagh, Dundalk and Drogheda in County Louth and Balbriggan in north Dublin, was uneventful. They reached Drumcondra, the north Dublin suburb near where Croke Park is situated, around 12 mid-day in time for the first game - the All Ireland minor semi-final, between Kildare and Tyrone. After the games they repaired to a restaurant on the northside of Dublin for refreshments, where they ran into a number of people who had also been to the match. Following a lengthy discussion, in which the ins and outs of the game were thoroughly thrashed out, the two men set out for the border around 7 p.m. They reached Dundalk around 9 p.m. where they stopped off again for further refreshments, and further post-match discussions.

Around 11 p.m. they crossed the border, returning North at a point halfway between Dundalk and Newtownhamilton, the arrangement being that McCartney would drive Farmer to his home in the Moy and return later to his digs in Newry. Around 11.30 p.m. a short distance from Newtownhamilton they noticed a red torch-light - similar to that used by the police and army - being waved in a circular fashion through the air in front of them. This has been the *modus operandi* used by members of the security forces manning checkpoints on the roads of Northern Ireland at night, throughout the thirty years of the Troubles, to alert oncoming motorists to the fact that a checkpoint lies ahead and that they wish the motorist to stop. McCartney and Farmer believed they were being stopped at a routine military checkpoint and McCartney brought his car to a halt. As he did the man waving the torch, who was dressed in military uniform with a blacked-out cap-badge, approached McCartney's window. After a short discussion in which the men were asked their names and addresses and where they were coming from, they were both ordered to stand by the roadside a number of metres apart, with their backs to the road. Within seconds McCartney was shot a number of times and fell dead into the ditch. Farmer was then shot in the side of the head and also fell dead. Before fleeing the scene the men set fire to McCartney's car. Thirty minutes later the mens' bodies were found lying 50 metres apart by three policemen who, thirty minutes before the shooting, had been stopped at the checkpoint themselves. Believing the checkpoint to be suspicious, they sped from the scene and immediately checked with their base at Newtownhamilton station and discovered there were no military patrols in the area that night. By the time they returned to the scene it was too late.

The bogus checkpoint was a carbon copy of a similar operation which three weeks earlier had been used along the Dublin-Belfast dual carriageway to lure three members of the Miami Showband to their deaths. The Newtownhamilton operation was led by Robert McConnell, Jackson and Lawrence McClure from the south Armagh farmhouse with a contingent of UVF men from Portadown in support. It was planned over the previous three weeks at Mitchell's farmhouse and was a revenge attack for the Miami fiasco which, along with the showband members, claimed the lives of two senior UVF men, Harris Boyle and Wesley Sommerville, (both of whom were frequent visitors to the farmhouse) when a bomb they were planting on the showband wagon exploded prematurely as they tried to kick it under the driver's seat. The Newtownhamilton operation was organised on similar lines to that of the Miami, with UVF men who were also in the UDR dressed in military uniform and carrying torches manning the checkpoint. Other similarities were the use of up to fifteen heavily armed UVF men from Portadown lying in ditches and hedges around the scene with their weapons at the ready in case of an IRA ambush and the use of a number of vehicles parked at varying distances along the road and in side-roads, to ferry the men to and from the scene. In the case of the victims, however, the roles were reversed: in this case the victims were travelling north across the border: in the case of the showband attack the musicians were travelling south across the border.

Whilst no evidence has ever emerged to show that the gang were aware of who they were ambushing, there is little doubt that the trap was planned and laid for Derry football supporters returning from Dublin that day. The route chosen by the gang was one of a number of routes normally used by motorists travelling between Derry and Dublin. Sometime after the shooting McClure confided to John Weir, the crooked ex-RUC man, that he and McConnell led the operation. He did not mention Jackson out of fear of retribution.

As McCartney was the driver it appears he was shot first. He was obviously not aware he was about to be shot and did not attempt to escape and took a direct hit in the back as he stood facing the ditch. Farmer, on the other hand, appears to have made a dash to escape when he heard McCartney being shot. Unlike McCartney he was first shot in the side of the head and fell dead 50 metres from McCartney. It is unlikely the two men were separated by that distance when first ordered from the car.

The following day the UVF in Belfast issued another of its indecorous denials of involvement in the murders, followed by a long-winded and rambling diatribe against the Catholic and republican community across the North. In its statement it said it had been informed by the Protestant Action Force (PAF) - which of course was the UVF itself in mid-Ulster - that one of its units 'carried out the double killing'. Resorting to the fatuous language it used following the Miami massacre, the UVF said it had border patrols operating in the south Down, south Armagh and south Fermanagh areas 'on Sunday night', but did not record any incidents. However, the statement then went on to warn that its campaign against the nationalist community would be stepped up and it named thirteen organisations which it said its battalions would henceforth regard as legitimate targets and would take military action against. These were: the Official IRA and Official Sinn Fein, Provisional IRA and Provisional Sinn Féin; the Irish Congress of Trade Unions; the Ancient Order of Hibernians; the Irish Communist Party; the Communist Party of Ireland (Marxist Leninist); the Irish Republican Socialist Party; People's Liberation Army; Irish Freedom Fighters; People's Democracy and the Northern Ireland Civil Rights Association.

At the inquest into the mens' murders in Armagh city the following July, the three policemen who passed through the checkpoint gave evidence of what they saw. The driver of the unmarked police car was uniformed constable Robert Gibson. This is what he said:

I am a constable in the Royal Ulster Constabulary presently stationed in Newtownhamilton in the County of Armagh. On Sunday 24 August, 1975 I was on mobile patrol (driving) accompanied by Sgt. Bartholomew and Const. M. Coleman. Both Sgt. Bartholomew and Const. Coleman were carrying S.M.G.'s. At 10.45 p.m. we were travelling along the main Newtownhamilton/ Castleblaney Road in the direction of the border. We were intending to check the Fane Valley Piggery at Altnamackin, from which pigs had been stolen on previous Sunday nights. We had just passed the junction with the Cortamlet Road and were approximately 600 yards from the border. As I drove round a gradual right hand bend and approached a long straight stretch of the road I saw a red light being shone in the middle of the road. I drove up towards the light putting on the main beam headlights. In the headlights I could see the figure of a man standing in the middle of the road waving a red torch. This man was wearing full combat dress, a combat jacket, army uniform trousers, black boots, and a dark beret with some type of badge in it. I slowed down and stopped beside this man who approached me and asked to see my driving licence. As he did this he changed the colour of the torch beam to orange and shone it into the car. When he did this he saw that both Sgt. Bartholomew and Const. Coleman were pointing S.M.G.'s in his direction. He realised immediately that we were policemen. He stepped back and said 'Oh it's you Police'. At this point I had become suspicious of this V.C.P. [vehicle checkpoint] There were no vehicles in sight and also this man was not a member of the local U.D.R. as I know the members of our local U.D.R. Also the man's hair was too long and his accent was wrong for him to be in the Army. I could see that this man was about 5'7' or 5'8' and of slight build though I could not see his face due to the torch he was carrying. As he spoke I could tell from his accent that he was an Ulsterman though he was not a South Armagh man. As he stepped back, startled, I accelerated away from the V.C.P. I drove away in the direction of the border and returned to Newtownhamilton. As I drove back, Sgt. Bartholomew and Const. Coleman informed our station by radio of this incident and asked the guard to find out if there were any Army or U.D.R. patrols out in that Altnamackin area. The reply came through that there were not patrols out in that area. We had just arrived back at Newtownhamilton Police Station a few minutes when we received a report of a shooting incident in the area we had just left. With Army cover I returned to Altnamackin with other police. On my arrival I saw the body of a male person fully clothed lying face downwards in the roadway. He appeared to be dead. A further 50 metres from that spot I saw a body of another male person fully clothed lying face downwards on the grass verge close to the hedge. I saw what appeared to be bullet holes in his back. I assisted to preserve the scene.

Sergeant Patrick O'Neill, a Scenes of Crime officer at Clogher RUC station, gave evidence of examining the mens' bodies:

On the 25th August, 1975 at 8.30 a.m. I arrived at the scene of a double murder which had occurred on a minor tarmacadam road in the townland of Altnamackin, Newtownhamilton, Co. Armagh. On arrival I established that the scene had been preserved and the bodies were still in the same position as when shot. I had the scene recorded in situ by Sergeant Thompson (Photography Branch, H.Q.) prior to examination. Const. De Voy (Mapping Section, H.Q.) also performed his duties at the scene. My examination commenced by making close observation of the body of a male person who was lying in the 'prone position' with his right arm underneath. This body was lying on the nearside of the road with its head facing the Newtownhamilton/Castleblaney Road and was dressed in a green velvet jacket, brown trousers, green striped shirt and brown shoes. I removed a Driving Licence from his pocket and identified him as Colm McCartney. I established that he had been shot twice in the back once in the left buttock and once in the chest. Close to the body I found two spent cases, of 9 mm ammunition. Underneath the body I found a .45 bullet and a .9 mm bullet. Both were bloodstained. Close to the left side of Colm McCartney's head I found two damaged .9 mm bullets imbedded in the tarmacadam and both bullets indicated that they were fired from close range as the body lay on the ground. The road at this point was 13'9' wide with grass verges of 6'6' each. The road was straight with an undulating surface 66 yards from Colm McCartney in the Cortamlet Church direction. I observed the body of a second male person. This body was lying in the prone position close to the hedge and on the grass verge also on the nearside. On examination of the clothing I found a Driving Licence and I subsequently identified this body as Sean Farmer. He was wearing a blue jacket, maroon trousers and brown boots. I observed that he had been shot once in the left side of the head, four times in the back and once in the scrotum area. On the grass verge beside the body of Sean Farmer I found one spent case of .9 mm and one spent case of .45 ammunition. I also procured one .45 bullet from a pool of blood near the body of Sean Farmer and two .45 bullets from the front of the clothing. These had passed through the body and had lodged in the jacket area. From the bullets and spent cases found at the scene of both shootings there were indications that three weapons were used and were namely a .45 revolver, .45 automatic colt pistol, and a Sterling Sub Machine Gun. At 11.30 a.m. 25 August, 1975 I attended the Post Mortem Examination on Colm McCartney at Daisy Hill Mortuary. The Pathologist was Dr. Press. During the Post Mortem I took possession of a .9 mm bullet from the left leg of Colm McCartney. I also observed that he had been chewing 'gum' at the time of being shot and this was still in his mouth. I also took possession of blood samples for Forensic Examination. At 3 p.m. 25 August, '75 I attended the Post Mortem Examination of Sean Farmer. During the Post Mortem I took possession of a .45 bullet from his right side and two blood samples for Forensic Examination. At 8.15 p.m. 25 August, '75 I returned to the scene of the 'double murder' at Altnamackin, Newtownhamilton. Approximately half a mile from the murder scene in the townland of Armaghbrague I observed a Ford Cortina car Reg. No. COI 8009 parked 20 yards off the Cortamlet Road. This car was owned by Colm McCartney and was completely gutted by fire. The car had been saturated by inflammable liquid and ignited, but nothing of Forensic significance was found in the debris.

It is clear from Constable Gibson's report that the three officers became frightened when stopped at the checkpoint and probably believed, genuinely, that the men manning it were republicans and that their lives were in danger. The fact that they returned to the scene with reinforcements within approximately forty-five minutes also proves, in my opinion, that the officers were not in cahoots with the gang, despite a widely held belief to the contrary amongst nationalists in the twenty-seven years ever since.

However, the fact that McConnell - who was hiding in the bushes during the encounter with the police - kept his unit at the scene, carried out a double murder, drove McCartney's car some 20 yards into a side-road and burned it, all after the police had fled, proves beyond a shadow of a doubt that he had security clearance from his handlers in the army that night. McConnell, more than anyone, was only too aware that the first thing the fleeing officers would do was call in reinforcements.

Needless to say no one was ever charged with the Football Fans' attack and McConnell and Jackson were free, as ever, to repair to the cavernous environment of Mitchell's farmhouse to plan their next onslaught. Over the following weeks, and probably spurred on by the bellicose language of the UVF statement, Jackson (with Hanna now safely out of the way) and McConnell devised a new strategy which would, in the short term at any rate, take the war to the 'enemy' with a ferocity not seen heretofore in the Murder Triangle. Bogus checkpoints would be ended - the public outcry following the Miami and Football Fans attacks brought an uncomfortable level of heat onto the activities of the army and UDR. Instead a campaign of well-organised twin attacks by both units at the farmhouse against the Catholic community on the same day - mainly against homes and pubs - would be launched.

The first of these took place on Friday, 19 December - six days before Christmas and four months after the Football Fans' murders.

Shortly after 6 p.m. sixty-year-old Hugh Waters, who ran a tailoring business in Francis Street in the town of Dundalk, just south of the border, had entered Kay's Tavern public house in Crowe Street to deliver a parcel of clothes he had altered to the owner when a bomb in a car parked outside exploded, knocking him to the floor. He died a short time later. The car, a Ford Sports, with the bomb in the boot had been parked outside the pub less than ten minutes earlier. A second man, Jack Rooney, who was walking past the Town Hall on the opposite side of the street, was struck by a piece of the car and died three days later following an eight-hour operation. Twenty other people, most of whom were also inside the pub, were injured, some seriously. The bomb-car, which was fitted with false Southern registration plates belonging to a lorry, was parked in one of the busiest shopping streets in Dundalk and was designed to inflict the maximum death and injury. The no-warning explosion destroyed two buildings, which caught fire after the impact and caused widespread damage to other premises for a distance of 50 yards on either side of the pub.

The bomb was planted by Jackson and other members of his unit, who escaped back across the border in a blue Hillman Hunter just as the bomb exploded. The Garda investigation into the Dundalk bombing was again led by Detective Superintendent Dan Murphy. During research for this book, retired Detective Sergeant Owen Corrigan, who was stationed in Dundalk at the time, told me that when he and Murphy asked the RUC for help in tracing the Hillman Hunter they refused. 'We knew it was Jackson who planted the bomb but the RUC refused to cooperate in tracing the car so there was nothing we could do about it,' Corrigan said. Needless to say no one was ever charged with the attack.

Three hours after the Dundalk bombing, and in what was the second leg of a coordinated operation, McConnell led his unit in an unusually vicious attack on Donnelly's Bar and Filling Station in the village of Silverbridge close to Newtownhamilton in south Armagh. The attack was designed to kill dozens of people at peak drinking time in the crowded bar but in the end, luckily, fell far short of McConnell's expectations.

As the unit arrived at the pub in two vehicles, the publican's fourteen-year-old son, Michael Donnelly, was serving petrol to a local man, John Taylor, outside. On seeing the two vehicles arrive, the boy, sensing something was wrong, made a dash towards the pub (to raise the alarm, it's believed) but before he could make it McConnell, who had sprung from one of the vehicles, shot him dead with a sub-machine-gun. McConnell then opened fire, at point blank range, on Taylor, shooting him in the head and maiming him for life. Meanwhile a second gunman (believed to be RUC man William McCaughey), who simultaneously sprung from one of the vehicles with McConnell, shot dead a second local man, Patrick Donnelly (no relation to the owner), who was waiting for petrol in the forecourt. With the two victims shot outside, McConnell then burst into the pub and opened fire on a packed bar, shooting dead one man, Trevor Bracknell, and seriously injuring three others. As McConnell withdrew to the street, two other members of the unit carried a 25-pound cylinder bomb into the bar. As the gang fled the scene, back to Mitchell's farmhouse, the bomb exploded, demolishing part of the pub and starting a huge fire. One man lost a foot and a hand in the explosion.

Immediately following the attack but after McConnell's unit was safely out of sight, a contingent of British soldiers landed by helicopter on a hilltop overlooking the village. The operation was being overseen by an Army Major based in south Armagh who was McConnell's handler, but who cannot be named here for legal reasons. Silverbridge was - and still is - a hardline republican area where a number of IRA men lived. It was widely known that many of them drank in Donnelly's. McConnell had sought and received assurances from the Major that in the event of immediate retaliation by the Provos army help would be at hand to sort the situation out.

Others who took part in the attack were: a local woman, Lily Shields, James Mitchell's girlfriend, who, along with Lawrence McClure (the RUC man from the farmhouse), reconnoitered the pub ahead of the gang, decoyed as a courting couple; Sammy McCoo from Portadown and a second UVF man from Portadown. A number of months later charges were brought against McCaughey, McClure and Lily Shields, who were accused of taking part in the attack, but the charges were later dropped by the Crown Prosecution Service. No explanation was ever given as to why, but it is believed the farmer James Mitchell threatened the RUC that if the prosecutions went ahead, he would reveal the entire story of the security forces' involvement in the Murder Triangle.

The two attacks, which were designed to strike terror into the nationalist community on both sides of the border at the same time, were deliberately timed to occur three hours apart. Jackson would have preferred to strike the Dundalk pub much later in the evening when the bar was crowded with customers, but Dundalk, he believed, was hostile republican territory and not a safe place for a loyalist bomber to be late on a Friday night. Silverbridge, as far as McConnell was concerned, was also hostile territory, but he had the protection of the British army and had no doubt his own security and that of his unit was assured.

The gelignite for both bombs was stolen from quarries around Armagh by John Irvine and supplied to Mitchell's farmhouse in a Land Rover. They were assembled in Mitchell's back yard by Mitchell himself, with Irvine supplying the fuse and the timing mechanism.

CHAPTER 13

'THE GUNMEN CAME IN'

Sixteen days after Silverbridge, and with a break for Christmas, the McConnell murder machine was ready for action again. It was as if Silverbridge had never happened. For McConnell and his unit life was becoming something of a terrorist fantasy world. One hit after another - all within a radius of 10 square miles - with a seemingly limitless freedom to attack where and when they wished. And, within twenty-four hours of each orgy of slaughter McConnell - in his glistening UDR uniform - was back on the roads of south Armagh patrolling the countryside and manning check-points to ensure that the community remained free of law-breakers and terrorists.

What a fantasy world *we* all lived in during those years, believing the 'poor old security forces' were caught in the middle of a religious war between two feuding sides. What a load of bullshit!

On Sunday evening, 4 January 1976, John, Brian and Anthony Reavey were watching television in the living room of the family home at Kingsmills Road, Whitecross in south Armagh in the heart of the Murder Triangle. John, who was twenty-five, and Anthony, seventeen, were at either side of the fire and Brian, who was twenty-two, was in the middle. The remainder of the family (there were thirteen in all, including the parents, though some of the older members had already married and set up home elsewhere) had earlier gone visiting and the key was in the front door. At 6.10 p.m. the key turned and the door was pushed in by a 'huge man with big broad shoulders' wearing a mask, a khaki uniform and holding a gun. As the man entered he was followed briskly by two more men also wearing masks, uniforms and carrying guns. The Reavey brothers, on hearing the door open and believing other members of the family had returned, scarcely turned their heads. As the three gunmen entered the living room, the brothers were still unperturbed, believing members of the British army had arrived to search the house - an occurrence not uncommon in Catholic homes around south Armagh at the time - and were wearing masks to conceal their identity.

As the lead gunman drew his weapon, the brothers - sensing something serious was wrong - sprang from their seats and made a dash to the nearby bedrooms. The three terrorists immediately opened fire at point blank range, spraying the living room with bullets and turning the house into something akin to a war zone. Anthony, who was sitting close to one of the bedrooms, escaped the first onslaught and dived under a bed. Brian, who was second in the line of fire, was hit several times and staggered dead into the fireplace of the same room. John, who was furthest from the gunmen as they entered, had only managed to raise himself from his chair when he was struck with several bullets and fell to the floor on his mouth and nose. One of the gunmen then stood over him and pumped several more bullets into his neck, back and shoulders, killing him outright. The gunman who shot Brian immediately chased Anthony into the bedroom, stood on his feet, which protruded from under the bed and fired several rounds down through the bed hitting him a number of times in the thighs and legs.

The gang, believing all three were dead, calmly and meticulously searched each remaining room in the house, shooting the locks off each door as they went, for further members of the family but found none. They then made their escape in a getaway car parked in a side road some distance away, driven by a fourth man, and headed towards the south Armagh farmhouse.

As the gunmen departed, Anthony, who was still alive but seriously injured and unable to walk upright, stumbled and crawled a distance of some 200 yards to the home of his nearest neighbour, Patrick O'Hanlon, who alerted the police and ambulance service. In a deposition to the Coroner's inquest in Armagh three weeks later, O'Hanlon described the scene, when Anthony Reavey reached his house.

> On Sunday, 4 January 1976, at about 6.15 p.m. I was sitting in the front room of my house at 37 Kingsmills Road, Whitecross, Co. Armagh, when I heard someone

slapping the front door and shouting, 'Pat let me in it's Anthony'. My wife, Angela, reached the door first and opened it and as she did so Anthony Reavey put his hand on her shoulder and fell against her. I asked him if he was in a car accident. He replied: 'The gunmen came in, Brian's dead and I'm dying'. He then said something like 'They're all dead'. We then wrapped him in blankets. My wife phoned for help and I went for the priest. I came back and then went to the Reavey house. There was no one there except John Martin Reavey and Brian Reavey. Both of them appeared to be dead. I stayed at the house until Father Hughes of Whitecross and the police arrived.

Anthony was rushed to nearby Daisy Hill Hospital in Newry where casualty staff on duty found his condition on arrival to be 'very poor'. Dr Wahab, a casualty officer, described his condition to the inquest as follows:

> He was very shocked, pale and appeared to have a lost quite an amount of blood. He was suffering from three gunshot wounds of the right thigh and leg and severe gunshot wounds of the left thigh and leg.

A short time later the bodies of John and Brian were removed by ambulance to the same hospital.

Two weeks after his admission, Anthony Reavey was discharged from hospital - his wounds having practically healed - and returned home on crutches. A week later, however, he suffered a brain haemorrhage and was rushed unconscious back to Daisy Hill from where a short time later he was transferred to the Royal Victoria Hospital, where he died on 30 January without regaining consciousness. In his autopsy report to the coroner's inquest, the State Pathologist for Northern Ireland, Professor Thomas Marshall, gave the following outline of the cause of Anthony Reavey's death.

... On Saturday, January 25, he went to a friend's house in Beleeks and stayed the night. His girlfriend also stayed the night. She spoke to him at about 11.15 a.m. the next morning and he seemed in good form; he was in bed eating some breakfast. His girlfriend left for Mass and at 11.40 a.m. his friend who had remained in the house heard him shouting. He found him sitting on the top of the stairs complaining of severe pains in the head. He seemed faint and was trying to vomit. His friend got him into bed and sent for an ambulance. When his girlfriend returned from Mass she found him semi-conscious. He shouted 'no, no' a number of times. The ambulance came and took him to Daisy Hill Hospital. On admission, he was unconscious and a lumbar puncture revealed a clear fluid. On January 27 he was transferred to the Royal Victoria Hospital. He was a bit chesty and this became worse on January 28. He remained unconscious and tests failed to reveal the cause. At 8 a.m. on January 29 his breathing stopped and he was intubated and put on a respirator. He died at 5.20 p.m. on January 30, 5 ½ days after becoming unconscious.

Concluding his report, Dr Marshall made the following observation:

Death was from natural causes. It was due to a massive haemorrhage into the left side of the brain. This was a congenital abnormality and the bursting of one of the blood vessels which precipitated the haemorrhage was a spontaneous event. No other disease was found. He bore scars on the lower limbs as a result of the bullet wounds he had sustained about three weeks before his fatal illness. This episode of wounding played no part in his death.

To the present day, Anthony Reavey's family dispute Dr Marshall's findings, that the shooting 'played no part in his death'. Anthony was a young man in perfect health and had never been ill in his life. He was 5' 7½" in height , of slim, hardy physique, was extremely strong and fit and played Gaelic football regularly. Dr Marshall maintains his brain haemorrhage was caused by the bursting of a blood vessel which arose from a 'congenital abnormality' ; which means an abnormality existed in his brain from birth. This is quite possible and as a result it is likely that Anthony would have suffered a brain haemorrhage at some stage in his life and might not have lived out a full life to old age.

Shortly after the shooting Constable William Poots, a Scenes of Crime Officer attached to Newry RUC station, arrived at the house to carry out a scenes of crime search. In a report to the inquest he gave the following details of what he found in the living room where the three brothers were sitting when the gunmen entered.

1. 33 spent 9 mm cases on floor to right of hall door
2. 1 live round 9 mm on the floor to left of hall door
3. 1 bullet head on floor to left of hall door
4. 4 bullet heads from settee
5. A pool of wet blood on floor in front of settee
6. A bullet head from hallway

Constable Poots then examined the living room for bullet marks and found the following:

1. 6 strikes on door leading to the kitchen and bathroom area
2. 1 strike on wall above settee
3. 1 strike on wall behind china cabinet
4. 1 strike on ceiling
5. Number of strikes, approximately 10, in and around blood in front of settee
6. 1 strike on wooden chair
7. 1 strike on wall to right of fireplace

In the passageway to the bathroom/kitchen area Poots found the following:

1. 2 strikes on doors of hot press
2. 1 strike on bottom of kitchen door
3. 1 strike on skirting board opposite kitchen door

In the bedroom, Constable Poots found the following:

1. 10 spent 9 mm cases from the floor and on the first bed
2. 1 bullet head from floor beside the first bed
3. 1 bullet head from the clothes of the first bed
4. 1 bullet head from beneath the second bed
5. 1 bullet head from floor to right of fireplace in bedroom
6. 1 bullet from wall above the first bed
7. A pool of wet blood from beside the second bed
8. 1 strike on skirting board beside first bed
9. 1 strike on wall at bed level of first bed
10. 4 strikes on wall above first bed
11. 1 strike on leg of wooden chair
12. 2 strikes on seat of second wooden chair
13. 1 strike on chest of drawers

The following day Poots returned to carry out a final examination of the house and found further bullet heads.

1. A bullet head from hallway
2. 1 bullet head from window frame in bedroom
3. 1 bullet head from skirting board behind settee in living room
4. 1 bullet head from back of easy chair in living room
5. 1 bullet head from bottom of kitchen door

It is evident from Constable Poots's report that the three gunmen went berserk firing their weapons inside the house and were determined not only to kill everyone present but to riddle the bodies of their victims with as many bullets as possible.

Between them they fired almost 50 rounds from four different weapons - a 9-mm SMG, a 9-mm pistol, a 9-mm parabellum weapon and a .455 caliber revolver.

John Reavey was shot eighteen times, mainly in the neck and trunk, and according to the autopsy report died instantly - possibly from a bullet strike which fractured the spine of his neck and the base of his skull. Most of the bullets entered his shoulders, back and legs and exited through the front of his body, which indicates he was lying face down during most of the shooting. The report also states that the firing came mainly from his left which further indicates that John, having seen the gunmen and realising the danger, arose from his chair and attempted to run towards a bedroom (a different room from the one his brothers entered) immediately to his right but was cut down before he could make it. According to his family, John Reavey had been out late the previous night and had only gotten out of bed a short time before the attack. It's possible he was in a drowsy state (possibly even dozing in front of the television) when the gunmen struck, reducing his capacity to react quickly.

Brian Reavey was shot at least four times, all bullets entering his body from behind which indicates he had at least reached the doorway of the bedroom and possibly even entered it when the first bullets struck him, fired by a gunman chasing him from behind.

The murders were carried out by McConnell, accompanied by three members of his unit. The three men who entered the house were Robert McConnell, who led the attack and whom Anthony Reavey described as a 'big man with massive broad shoulders' who 'filled the doorway' as he entered. With him were two members of the security forces (a reserve policeman and a UDR man). The getaway car was driven by Lawrence McClure, who himself was also in the RUC. The car, an 1100 saloon, was stolen in Armagh City the previous Friday evening and was set alight a short distance from the scene of the attack.

McConnell, who did most of the shooting and who shot John Reavey, was carrying the SMG and the pistol. The attack was planned at Mitchell's over Christmas and was spearheaded by McConnell, who believed, incorrectly, that the Reavey brothers were involved in terrorism. He would normally have access to accurate security force intelligence on the IRA in his capacity as a part-time UDR man but in this instance (as frequently happened throughout Northern Ireland during the course of the Troubles) he was fed inaccurate information by bent members of the security forces who believed the Catholic community in general should be made to pay for the violence of the IRA.

No member of the Reavey family has ever (before or since the attack) been involved in terrorism. It is believed that some policemen held a grudge against the family as a result of their rise from 'rags to riches', as one member of the family put it. In their youth the Reavey brothers were extremely poor and grew up in a council cottage. By the time the murders took place their circumstances had profoundly changed. Some members of the family had professional jobs and others were involved in the building industry. In the years since, they have become successful businessmen and farmers, living in expensive houses and driving expensive cars.

Following the attack the gang hid the weapons in a hedge in a field in south Armagh. A number of weeks later and after the dust had well settled, the weapons were recovered by McClure and returned to the safekeeping of Mitchell's farmhouse. No one was ever charged with the murders, despite the fact that the RUC have known for twenty-six years exactly who was responsible. Three members of the gang, including McClure, are still alive and have long retired from terrorism.

Today McClure is a respectable member of the south Armagh community with an elegant wife and grown-up children. He lives in an expensive country house, drives an expensive car and works in a government-related job. He has long renounced violence and condemns those who still use it. During King Rat's campaign of the 1980s and 1990s - when the farmhouse was once again used as a safe-house for hiding guns - McClure condemned Mitchell ('an old fool') for allowing himself to be 'used' by 'these people'. However, he has yet to make amends for the twenty plus murders he himself carried out on both sides of the border during his own years in terrorism.

In the twenty-six years since the murders the Reavey family have suffered continuous harassment from the security forces. Their homes and cars have been regularly searched and some members of the family have been physically and verbally abused at vehicle checkpoints across south Armagh. Eugene Reavey, the third eldest son and the brains behind the business success, on one occasion had the wheels stripped from his car by British soldiers at a checkpoint. The vehicle was then rolled over a hedge into a valley and came to rest in a nearby river. On numerous occasions gates to farmlands have been opened by members of the security forces allowing livestock to stray onto public roads.

But the worst experience of harassment was, oddly enough, visited upon Mrs Reavey, mother to the murdered boys, and probably the most unlikely terrorist in all of south Armagh. For two weeks following the shooting she visited her injured son Anthony in Daisy Hill Hospital on a daily basis. On each journey to and from the hospital her car, driven by one of her daughters, was stopped by police and soldiers and searched, causing her at least thirty minutes delay each way. Both women then invariably had their clothes, hair and ears searched for guns and explosives. 'Any gelignite behind your ears there, Mrs Reavey?' soldiers would sneer. On numerous occasions during this sordid business, officers, aware of the tragedy and suffering visited upon the family, proffered Mrs Reavey their condolences: 'We envy you Mrs Reavey; you've never had a worry in your life.'

But the ultimate act of depravity occurred the day Mrs Reavey returned from hospital carrying the blood-soaked clothes of her dead sons, John and Brian, in the boot of her car. A policeman manning a checkpoint conducted a routine and now familiar search of the vehicle. On discovering the clothing in the boot he pulled them to the road and spat on them.

Policemen, too, it must be stressed, and their families have suffered greatly from terrorist violence over the course of the last thirty years. That is a fact that cannot be gainsaid. But the harassment of Mrs Reavey - a grieving mother of a large family who had just lost three sons also at the hands of terrorists - by police officers is proof, if proof were needed, of the urgent need for a new policing service in Northern Ireland, not just a watered-down version of the RUC.

No member of the Reavey family can explain exactly why harassment against them (which continues to the present day despite the peace process) by the security forces commenced after the murders but never occurred beforehand. One theory is that certain elements within the security forces will simply not accept that during the Troubles innocent people got shot. In their minds if they were attacked by loyalists then they must have been 'involved'.

For twenty-six years the Reavey family have campaigned to have the perpetrators (the three remaining suspects still living, that is) of the murders brought to justice, but without success. According to Eugene Reavey the authorities don't want to know.

> We have lobbied politicians, police, even journalists - anyone who is prepared to listen - but it's like beating your head off a stone wall. The RUC know who did the murders and they have given us the names, but yet nothing is done. My brothers were totally innocent of any crime. No member of our family has ever been involved with any organisation or political party. We have never been involved in politics in our lives, yet we are made to suffer this terrible tragedy for the remainder of our lives. It's dreadful.

In 1996 the Reavey family, along with a number of other victims' families from the Murder Triangle, set up a lobby group to pressurise the authorities into bringing those responsible for the killings in the Murder Triangle to justice. Its chairman was Eugene Reavey. The group lobbied the Northern Ireland Office, local politicians and wrote detailed memoranda about the killings to the RUC. The response in general was disappointing. Correspondence to the RUC was acknowledged but nothing was done.

In January 1999 the Rev. Ian Paisley, in a surprise and unprecedented move, read to a shocked House of Commons in London, a list of names of Catholic men in South Armagh whom - he alleged - had been involved in terrorism. Eugene Reavey was named as the person responsible for organising the Kingsmills Massacre, which occurred within twenty-four hours of the Reavey killings in which ten innocent Protestants were shot dead by republicans. It is now believed that vested interests within the Northern Ireland establishment who feared the outcome of the lobby group's campaign, prepared a bogus dossier, which was then passed to Mr Paisley with a request that he name names in parliament. The move was designed to silence Eugene Reavey and his lobby group. Mr Paisley was not aware that the information was balderdash and that he was being used to cover up mass killing in the Murder Triangle. Moreover, the last thing the Reavey family needed was the ranting black doctor, who never baulked at an opportunity to stir up mischief, poking his nose into their already shattered lives.

Six weeks after the Reavey massacre, McConnell's mother died. It was a devastating blow to his morale and sense of security and one that he never got over. He was thirty-two, single and did not have a relationship with a woman. His mother was the *bean* of his life and there was now no woman to turn to. His younger sister Rebecca was an invalid and his father was old and infirm. His personal life was in tatters. But it did not deter him from engaging in his favourite pastime - killing Catholics on both sides of the border.

Thirteen days after his mother's death, McConnell carried out what was to be his last terrorist attack. On Sunday, 7 March, McConnell and McClure planted a car bomb outside the Three Star Inn pub in main street, Castleblayney, in County Monaghan, killing a 53-year-old local married man, Patrick Mone, and injuring seventeen others. The bomb, which was planted five hours before it exploded, was placed in the boot of a Mark III Ford Cortina, which was stolen in the Shankill area of Belfast by UVF men the previous day and delivered to Mitchell's farmhouse, where it was fitted with false Monaghan registration plates. Like the previous two bombs, the Castleblayney bomb was made in Mitchell's yard by Irvine and Mitchell from gelignite stolen by Irvine, and driven to Castleblayney by McConnell with McClure driving a getaway car.

It has never been established why McConnell risked leaving the bomb-car parked for five hours in the centre of Castleblayney, running the risk of it being discovered before exploding. One theory is that the timing mechanism failed to function at the designated time but functioned, by chance, a number of hours later. Another is that the bombers wished to be out of Castleblayney - a militant republican stronghold - before nightfall but felt safe the car would not arouse suspicion because of its Southern number plates.

Like Dundalk, the Garda investigation into the Castleblayney bombing was led by Dan Murphy. And like Dundalk - and Dublin, and Monaghan, and Sallins - the culprits were never found. For Murphy, who as a detective was nothing short of a disaster, a pattern was building up.

Seven weeks after Castleblayney, loyalists from north Down - not connected to the Murder Triangle - murdered a Dundalk man, Seamus Ludlow, whom they picked up hitching a lift after a night out in the pub. It was a random sectarian killing by drunken loyalists who crossed the border in search of a victim. The gruesome murder, in which Ludlow was shot several times at close range as he sat in the back seat of the car, was carried out by a well-known hitman called Sam 'Mambo' Carroll, who was connected to the loyalist splinter group, the Red Hand Commando. From Bangor, north of Belfast, Carroll was accompanied by two UDR men whom we shall call James F. and Richard L. A fourth man, Paul Hoskings, who did not take part in the attack, later provided the RUC with the names of the killers but nothing was done to apprehend them.

In Dundalk the investigation was once again led by Murphy but - as usual - the RUC refused to cooperate and Murphy did nothing about it.

Yet a year later, when in Ravensdale forest near Dundalk - a half mile from where Ludlow was killed and two miles from Kay's Tavern - Captain Nairac was murdered by the IRA, Liam Townsen, a Dundalk-based republican, was charged with his murder and sentenced to a life-term in Portlaoise prison in the Republic. And, of course, that is as it should have been. In arresting and charging the suspected killer of Nairac, the Gardai in Dundalk were only doing their duty. However, the relatives of those killed in Dublin, Monaghan, Sallins, Dundalk and Castleblayney could be forgiven for asking what was going on. Were the Irish authorities leaning over backwards so far to help the British that they were virtually up their own arses?

Dan Murphy is now dead and cannot answer the charges being laid against him. However, justice demands that his blatant incompetence - and downright malice - be brought into the public domain. In the Ludlow murder - and in a carbon copy of the Sallins case - Murphy lied to the Ludlow family by telling them the IRA committed the crime. And, like the Phelan family in Sallins, the Ludlow family, for twenty years, believed him. And, before closing the file, Murphy, in a second carbon-copy of the Sallins case, and to confuse the situation even further, let it be known around Dundalk that the Gardai believed the dead man was killed by members of his own family who 'wanted him out of the house'. Ludlow was a single man who lived with his married sister and her large family. However, nothing could be further from the truth than Murphy's allegation. He was deeply loved and much cared for by his family who were devastated by his murder.

No one can explain why Murphy did this. Was it an attempt to discourage distraught relatives - particularly younger males - from joining paramilitary organisations, at some future date, and taking retaliatory action against loyalists, if he told them the truth? Or was it simply a ham-fisted attempt to cover his own incompetence in failing to bring the culprits to justice, coupled with the fear of being forced to reveal to relatives the fact that the RUC refused to cooperate.

Meanwhile back in Castleblaney the local newspaper *The Argus* carried an interview with Murphy during the bombing investigation. This is what it said.

> Supt. Dan Murphy, who is leading the special garda squad in the investigation of the bombing, has appealed to everybody who was in Blayney from 3 p.m. until 8.30 p.m. on Sunday to get in touch with them through a

special telephone line - Castleblayney 399 or through the ordinary garda station numbers, Blayney 32 or 2063 in the hope of piecing together information which might be beneficial in their probe. He said they were anxious to hear from anybody on either side of the Border who might have observed any suspicious vehicle movements on Sunday. The bomb-car, a metallic blue Ford Cortina Mark III, has been reported stolen in the Shankill area of Belfast on Saturday, he said, adding that it had been fitted with false Monaghan plates. Supt. Murphy said that the investigation would also involve a questionnaire to people in the area about what they had observed on Sunday. 'Any shred of information which may help us in any way is vital', said Supt. Murphy. 'We have the manpower available and the success of our investigation depends on the wholehearted support of the public'.

Twenty-six years later Anna Mone, the heart-broken 72-year-old widow of Patrick Mone, the man killed in the explosion, is still waiting to hear from the 'special Garda squad' with 'the manpower available' about the 'success' of their investigation.

Twenty-nine days after the Castleblayney bomb, McConnell was dead. Despite his bravado, his naivete and self-confidence led to his own ignominious downfall at the hands of the IRA at the young age of thirty-two. On Monday evening, 5 April, McConnell decided to skip UDR target practice, telling a UDR colleague who called to collect him that he wished to spend the evening 'carting cow-manure' to a field on his farm for 'top dressing' (to help make the grass grow) with his tractor. After dark, McConnell visited the home of his cousin (also called McConnell) a mere 200 yards from his home. Both houses were at the end of a long, isolated laneway on the top of a hillside in the townland of Tullyvallen. McConnell's cousin was in hospital being treated for cancer and his wife was alone. McConnell watched television until 11 p.m. when his cousin's wife reminded him that it was time to put his invalid sister to bed. As the pair crossed the street to McConnell's home, linking arms in the dark, a male voice called out: 'Separate. This is a hold-up.' McConnell immediately let go of his companion's arm, grabbed his gun (which he carried with him at all times) and fired in the direction from where the voice had come but hit a tree. However, an IRA hitman, one of a three-man squad hiding in the bushes in McConnell's garden, opened fire and hit McConnell twice in the head. He was dead on arrival at Daisy Hill Hospital, Newry. After hitting McConnell, one of the gunmen rushed forward and searched his pockets but found nothing of use to republicans. The unit, which then made its escape on foot across fields in the direction of the border, was led by Peter Cleary, a leading south Armagh Provo, accompanied by two brothers from a notorious republican family near Cullyhanna in south Armagh. The brothers were part of the deadly south Armagh Brigade of the Provisional IRA, which three months earlier had carried out the Kingsmill massacre. They had crossed the border from the South, where they were based, to shoot McConnell. Later a local man was convicted of McConnell's murder but, whilst he played a minor role in the operation, the shooting was carried out by Cleary with the brothers providing cover. A short time later and in retaliation for Kingsmills, Cleary was murdered by an SAS assassination squad which crossed the border into the South and kidnapped him in the middle of the night from the home of a friend after breaking down the front door. It is believed the SAS unit was led by Captain Robert Nairac.

Today McConnell's relatives say Robert's murder was set up by British army intelligence officers, who 'wanted him out of the way'. They say the authorities have repeatedly refused to hold an inquest into his death and 'this is suspicious'. They say other strange things happened around his farm after his death which never happened before. Milk churns and other items were stolen. His personal protection weapon was confiscated by the RUC and never returned. Friends of McConnell have even claimed that Nairac passed details about his activities - and his movements - to republicans. However, there is no evidence to substantiate such a claim.

So great was the secrecy surrounding McConnell's unit that neither the public in south Armagh - nor the media - had the slightest idea that it existed or that McConnell was involved in terrorism. Three days after his murder one of the local newspapers in Armagh, *The Ulster Gazette*, carried the following report on its front page.

> Mr. McConnell's murder was in the countryside which the Army was supposed to be particularly guarding and into which it was supposed to have sent its S.A.S. men, said to be renowned for their efficiency. He was ambushed as he walked between the residences of his cousin and his own. His mother, Mrs. Sarah McConnell, formerly Miss McBurney, died only six weeks ago. Three gunmen opened fire with rapid fire Armalite guns, hitting him in the face and head. Mr. McConnell was rushed to Daisy Hill Hospital, but was dead on arrival. After the shooting three men were seen making off through fields in the direction of the Border, less than two miles away. Inside the house was Mr. McConnell's invalid sister Miss Rebecca, and his 76 year old father. Murdered Mr. McConnell worked at the White, Tomkins & Courage factory at Tandragee and was a member of the Orange Order being attached to Cladybeg Lodge. Neighbours have spoken of how wonderfully kind and considerate he was to his sister, who was so dependent on him, and to his father. What will happen to them now? Eye-witness to the murder was the wife of Mr. McConnell's cousin. She was returning to the farmhouse with her husband (sic) when they came upon the gunmen, who were lying in wait. She pleaded with the gunmen not to shoot Mr. McConnell, then ran off in fright. Seconds later she heard shots and when she returned found the victim. No attempt was made to injure her, but she was in a shocked state when she told Mr. McConnell's father and sister in the house what had happened. He [McConnell] was a constant attender at St. John's Parish Church,

Newtown [Newtownhamilton] and was a willing church worker. Every Sunday he brought his sister, affectionately, to worship. A Corporal in the UDR since its inception, he was attached to the 8 Platoon in Newtown.

At McConnell's funeral the then Church of Ireland Archbishop Dr George Simms described McConnell as a man who 'had worked ceaselessly to keep the peace in a community under constant threat. Mr McConnell gave his life that others might have security.'

The Bishop's description of McConnell - a psychopathic killer - illustrates the level of ignorance that existed in Northern Ireland (particularly amongst people who should have been better informed) throughout the course of the conflict. To describe a mass murderer as 'a man who worked ceaselessly to keep the peace' demonstrates how oblivious the bishop was to what was actually going on around him.

McConnell's funeral was also attended by an official of the Northern Ireland Office who represented the then Secretary of State, Merlyn Rees. The Colonel Commandant of the UDR at the time, General Sir John Anderson, and the regiment's Commander, Brigadier Mervyn McCord, also attended. The same day the *Belfast Telegraph* interviewed a local woman who knew McConnell. She told the paper: 'What happened would make any decent thinking person sick. He was a very likeable man. The people here were always saying it would be terrible if anything happened to him because his sister Rebecca was so dependant on him. He was very, very good to her.'

I'm sure he was.

CHAPTER 14

'THIS IS A HOLD-UP'

Within ten minutes of McConnell's attack on the Reavey family on 4 January - and as part of a coordinated operation - the second half of the Triangle killing machine was going into action less than twenty miles away in the north of County Armagh. Earlier in the evening Robin Jackson assembled his squad in the Mourneview Estate in Lurgan for a hit that would synchronise with McConnell's and would match it in both wickedness and savagery.

It was four days into the new year and Barney O'Dowd, his wife Kathleen, three of his sons and two daughters, along with his brother Joe and two of his daughters, were about to sit down to a meal as part of a post-Christmas get-together at Barney's home in the townland of Ballyduggan, four miles south of Lurgan. Both families lived within two miles of each other and each year in early January Joe O'Dowd with members of his family visited Barney's home as part of the New Year celebrations.

The O'Dowd clan had lived and farmed in north Armagh for generations. Barney, who was in his early fifties, had left the family home as a young man, got married and bought his own farm. In later years with the help of his sons - he and his wife Kathleen had eight children, six boys and two girls - he established a thriving coal and milk-round business in the area. He and his sons became well-known businessmen in north Armagh where they delivered coal and milk to both communities.

As Kathleen O'Dowd and her two daughters Mary and Eleanor prepared the meal in the kitchen to the back of the house, Barney, his 24-year-old son Barry, Joe and his daughters Deirdre and Bernadette were sitting down to drinks in the sitting room to the front of the house. Barney's second-eldest son, Declan, who was nineteen, was in the bathroom and the youngest member of the family, eleven-year old Cathal, was floating between the kitchen and the sitting room. The remainder of Barney's family were visiting friends in the locality.

As Kathleen O'Dowd prepared to serve the meal, she heard a knock on the back door of the kitchen which led into the farmyard. As she opened it a man with a mask poked a gun in her face and shouted 'This is a hold-up, we're here for your money'. She attempted to slam the door in the man's face but using a well-known terrorist tactic the man had already jammed his foot in the door - preventing it from closing. The intruder then abruptly brushed past her and headed for the hallway followed by two more masked gunmen.

From the bathroom Declan O'Dowd heard the commotion and rushed towards the kitchen to investigate. As he ran through the hallway he was confronted by the first gunman who shot him dead on the spot with a weapon fitted with a silencer.

The hallway led via a doorway to a corridor which in turn led, also via a doorway, to the sitting room. By a stroke of cruel luck both doors were closed, preventing the family members in the sitting room from hearing the commotion, or the shooting.

After shooting Declan, the gunman dashed towards the sitting room - from where he could hear the sound of voices - and burst through the door. Joe O'Dowd - immediately sensing what was happening - sprung from his seat and dived at the intruder. The gunman calmly levelled the weapon at Joe's stomach, pulled the trigger and Joe fell dead to the floor. Barney, who by this time had also risen to his feet and was attempting to grapple with the gunman, was shot five times in the stomach and kidney and fell to the floor on his mouth and nose.

By this time Barry, Deirdre and Bernadette, realising that the only exit door from the sitting room was commanded by the gunman, attempted to take cover behind a couch. The gunman stepped forward, ignored the two females and shot Barry dead as he crouched on the floor. The gunman, and his two accomplices, who had remained on guard in the hallway throughout but did not fire their weapons, then made their getaway back out through the kitchen to the farmyard.

On his way out the lead gunman ran into eleven-year-old Cathal O'Dowd in the hallway. As if puzzled about whether to shoot him or not the gunman, momentarily, stared into the boy's face and then ran off.

The gang then made their escape across fields to a waiting car parked down a side road which was also a cul-de-sac. The side road led to farmlands which were owned separately by O'Dowds and a neighbouring family but did not lead directly to the O'Dowd home. It was not a public road and was used only by both families. In the days and weeks following the murders it became self-evident that the gunmen had been provided with intimate knowledge of the area by someone local. The O'Dowd home was an isolated farmhouse positioned at the end of a long narrow lane. The lane was used only by the O'Dowd family and people visiting their home. If the terrorists had used this lane they ran the risk of being hemmed in by other vehicles - and unable to make their escape except by foot - driven by members of the O'Dowd family or visitors to their house, as the narrow laneway would not allow two vehicles to pass each other at the same spot. The side road which the gang used was unlikely to have other vehicles on it at 6 p.m. on a Sunday evening during the Christmas season. The gunmen were almost certainly aware of this.

The attack was a well-researched operation, with a finical attention to detail, beholden of experienced terrorists who knew what it took to murder people and escape without detection. The initial announcement by the terrorists that the attack was a 'hold up' was a carefully planned ploy to avert panic and chaos amongst the O'Dowd household - which could have resulted in the escape of the male members from the house. It allowed the gunmen time to get inside.

Back in the blood-soaked O'Dowd home Barney, despite the horrific attack, had somehow cheated death and survived the slaughter. When shot he spun around and fell to the floor on his face but none of the wounds were fatal - primarily because the bullets struck his stomach and kidney area but did not pierce his heart. Before his wife or daughters could reach him he raised himself up by grasping the handle of the door and staggered into the hallway where he collapsed again beside the body of his dead son Declan. He was then rushed to nearby Craigavon Area Hospital where doctors performed surgery on his stomach and removed a kidney. Fourteen days later he returned home to convalesce - his wounds having practically healed - and three weeks later was back on his feet again.

The O'Dowd murders were carried out by Robin Jackson's flying squad with Jackson himself doing all the shooting. With him in the house were Sammy McCoo and 'Shilly' Silcock, with a fourth member of the squad - whom I have failed so far to identify - driving the getaway car. The attack was designed to synchronise to the minute with McConnell's attack on the Reaveys but in the end fell ten minutes short.

The original master-plan, which was hatched at Mitchell's farmhouse by Jackson and McConnell, was to wipe out all adult male members of both families whom the terrorists believed (from intelligence provided to them) would be home around 6 p.m. on a Sunday evening just after Christmas.

The final details of the O'Dowd plan were worked out by Jackson and his squad in Harry's pub in Banbridge (a favourite haunt of Jackson's when operating on his home turf) the previous Friday evening. A local loyalist who was part of the discussion, but was not party to the attack, later provided members of the O'Dowd family with details of the discussion.

Like the Reaveys the O'Dowd family were innocent victims of a sectarian terrorist attack. Bogus information was provided to Jackson by corrupt RUC officers who told him the male members of the family were involved in the Provisionals' campaign. William McCaughey, the convicted RUC murderer, claimed during an interview for this book, that a bomb which killed a member of the security forces in Lurgan a short time earlier was made on the O'Dowd farm. However, an experienced member of the RUC's Serious Crime Squad told me later that McCaughey's information was 'bullshit' and that the bomb in question was assembled elsewhere. 'The O'Dowd family had nothing whatever to do with it,' he said.

Not only were the O'Dowds not involved with paramilitaries but both Barney and his wife Kathleen were active members of the Social Democratic and Labour Party (SDLP) and both worked as presiding officers for the party at polling stations during election time. Joe O'Dowd was also a member of the party.

The RUC investigation into the murders was once again led by the inimitable Frank Murray and a detective, long since retired. A colleague of Murray's, who, with Murray, arrived on the scene shortly after the shootings told me that when they arrived on the scene Murray expressed horror at what he saw: 'Jesus, this is fucking terrible, I could have prevented this,' he said. The crime squad detective did not press the issue but the conclusion to be drawn is, he believes, that Murray either received prior warning of the planned attack from an informer and did nothing to stop it or, worse still, he actively colluded in the murders.

Murray was one of the few Catholic policemen who rose through the ranks, and ended his career as Chief Super-intendent in charge of the Special Branch in Gough Barracks, Armagh. For a time he was tipped as a future Chief Constable. In June 1994 - three months before the first IRA ceasefire - Murray was due to travel on the ill-fated Chinook helicopter which crashed on the Mull-of-Kintyre on its way to a security conference in Scotland, killing all twenty-eight security personnel on board. He changed his mind at the last moment, however, and was due to travel by air the following morning. Some people now believe in the light of the conspiracy theory surrounding the crash that Murray smelt a rat and decided to travel privately instead.

During the early 1970s, while searching a field for guns and explosives with a colleague outside Lurgan, a bomb concealed under a wall exploded and blew off one of Murray's arms and legs, leaving him disabled for life. It was long believed by nationalists that as a result Murray bore a grudge against his own community and even went so far as to collude with loyalists in seeking revenge.

Shortly before the O'Dowd murders a number of incidents occurred which Barney now says should in hindsight have alerted the family to the danger. The first occurred when one of his 'local' customers drove into the yard to buy coal a short time before the attack. There were 'three or four youngish men', Barney did not recognise with him in the truck. This was unusual, Barney says. The customer had bought coal 'several times' previously but never with 'strangers' in his vehicle. Barney has no doubt now that the men were 'taking stock' - 'getting a feel for it'.

The second incident occurred eight days before the murders when sixteen-year-old Loughlin O'Dowd was making his way on foot from his home to the main road leading to Lurgan. Halfway up the laneway he noticed two men with masks 'hanging about' in a nearby field. The incident was later discussed at home but dismissed as 'un-important' and 'allowed to pass'. The men, Barney says, were undoubtedly reconnoitering the area: mapping out arrival and escape routes.

The final incident occurred on Saturday morning thirty-six hours before the attack. Noel O'Dowd was on his way to work when he noticed a unit of UDR soldiers 'combing' the fields adjoining the O'Dowd farmhouse - the same fields through which the killers made their escape. Barney O'Dowd is in no doubt the soldiers were 'checking' that a bomb or trip-wire wasn't placed in the fields, endangering the lives of the terrorists as they crossed. It was the only occasion in his lifetime that Barney O'Dowd saw the army searching his farmlands. The ground was being meticulously prepared for the deadly assault.

Needless to say, no one was ever charged with the O'Dowd murders. Barney is not surprised and says he never expected that anyone would. He has 'no doubt whatever' that security force personnel colluded in the attack: 'The security forces do not usually prosecute themselves,' he says.

He is not immune to the suffering of others and recognises the great pain endured by so many people - from both communities - throughout the last thirty years. But he says people who have not been affected by the Troubles could never begin to appreciate what it is like to have three members of one's family 'murdered in front of one's eyes'.

> To see the bodies of two of your children - that you brought into the world, that you worked hard for, loved and cared for - lying dead on the floor in front of you, is beyond comprehension: unbearable. To see your brother lying dead beside them is even worse.

Following the murders the O'Dowd business folded and a short time later Barney moved his family to the Republic - where they still live. But the memory of what happened 'on that terrible night' twenty-six years ago still lives on. 'A single day never passes but we think about it,' says Barney who is now in his mid-seventies. 'It is something you can never forget. The fact that the killers broke into our home and murdered our family within the sanctity of our own home makes it all the more difficult to accept.'

CONCLUSION

The catalogue of murders carried out in the killing fields of the Murder Triangle horrifyingly documented throughout the latter half of this book have largely been forgotten by both the public and the media. In June 1988 Robin Jackson, the chief instigator of the slaughter, died of cancer. He will now never - in this life at any rate - answer for his crimes.

As mentioned in chapter 10, Jackson was arrested and jailed for seven years in 1979 - and served three - on a firearms charge. In 1980 - while Jackson was still in prison - at the trial of two policemen William McCaughey and John Weir for the murder of Ballymena shopkeeper William Strathearn in 1977, Jackson was named in court as the killer. Despite this revelation he was still not charged with the murder.

When asked by the judge why 'this man' is not 'under arrest for the murder', a police witness, Cecil West, replied: 'For strategic reasons, Your Honour.' Many people believed then, and still do, that Jackson's imprisonment on a minor firearms charge was a convenient ploy by the state to get him off the streets for the duration of the Strathearn case.

The horrors of the Murder Triangle will undoubtedly fade - with time - into the annals of history, and the perpetrators (including Jackson) will no doubt be canonised by their supporters as the 'defenders of Ulster'. The Cúchulainns of the twentieth century.

Indeed, the plaudits have already begun: 'He was a great guy; he did a lot for us and he was well respected within the organization,' the former UVF activist Frankie Curry said of Jackson's role in the Dublin and Monaghan bombings.

Indeed the Dublin and Monaghan bombings - and Jackson's role in them -probably helped to change the course of Irish history, as no doubt they were intended to. Had the attacks not taken place, avoiding the appalling loss of life, the 1974 power-sharing executive between the constitutional parties from both communities might just have survived - despite the UWC strike - and the present day peace process might have started many years earlier.

As mentioned in chapter 1, the decision by loyalists, assisted by their undercover allies in the various branches of the security forces, to bomb the Republic was taken shortly after the signing of the Sunningdale Agreement in December 1973 - long before the start of the UWC strike. The objective of both the bombings and the strike was twofold: (a) to collapse the Agreement and undermine the British Prime Minister of the time, Harold Wilson, whom sections of the right-wing of the British establishment believed was a closet communist with links to the Soviet Union and who was soft on republicanism and (b) to force the Dublin government into cracking down hard on the activities of the IRA.

On a visit to Dublin in 1972, as leader of the Labour Opposition, Harold Wilson had said in a speech that he could envisage a united Ireland within fifteen years. The speech outraged those right wing elements, including a group of right wing officers within MI5, who Wilson himself believed later plotted against him.

In an interview with two British journalists, Barry Penrose and Roger Courtiour, in 1976, and shortly after his resignation, Wilson claimed that a right wing MI5 faction had been collaborating with American and South African intelligence to organise a smear campaign against him in the 1974/75 period. 'I'm not certain,' Wilson declared, 'that for the last eight months when I was Prime Minister I knew what was happening fully in Security.' He complained that the security services were incapable of distinguishing between socialism and communism and that a story had been put about of a 'pro-Soviet cell in No 10'. He alleged a level of interference by the security services that bordered on professional treachery and suggested a Royal Commission be set up to examine their accountability.

In his book *Spycatcher* the former assistant director of MI5, Peter Wright, talked about the attempts by a group of officers within the Service to smear Wilson and bring down his government.

... As events moved to their political climax in early 1974 with the election of the minority Labour Government, MI5 was sitting on information which, if leaked, would undoubtedly have caused a political scandal of incalculable consequences. The news that the Prime Minister himself was being investigated would at the least have led to his resignation. The point was not lost on some MI5 officers. One afternoon I was in my office when two colleagues came in. They were with three or four other officers. I closed the file I was working on and asked them how I could help.

'We understand you've re-opened the Wilson case,' said the senior one. 'You know I can't talk about that,' I told him.

'Wilson's a bloody menace,' said one of the younger officers, 'and it's about time the public knew the truth.'

It was not the first time I had heard that sentiment. Feelings had run high inside MI5 during 1968. There had been an effort to stir up trouble for Wilson then, largely because the *Daily Mirror* tycoon, Cecil King, who was a long-time agent of ours, made it clear he would publish anything MI5 might care to leak in his direction. It was all part of Cecil King's 'coup' which he was convinced would bring down the Labour Government and replace it with a coalition led by Lord Mountbatten. But the approach in 1974 was altogether more serious.

People in Ireland today who say allegations of dirty tricks - including murder - by the security services, and their colleagues in the army and RUC, is just Provo propaganda, would do well to examine Wright's allegations in the context of what was happening in Northern Ireland at that time.

Earlier in the book Wright talks about his brief involvement in the Irish conflict after been asked by his boss Michael Hanley, the then Director General of MI5, to develop 'one of your bright ideas' to counter the Provisionals.

The only major recommendation I made was that we should devise a system of tapping the telephone lines of the Irish Republic. Lines across the border were well covered, but vital Provisional IRA communications flowed back and forth from the west coast of the Republic to Dublin. I devised a scheme for intercepting the microwaves from the attic of the British Embassy in Dublin using a device no larger than a packing case, but although MI5 endorsed the plan, the Foreign Office vetoed it. This was in the period leading up to what became the Sunningdale Agreement, and the Foreign Office were terrified that news of the plan might leak. I pointed out to them that the basic lesson from Cyprus (where Wright had operated as an MI5 agent in the 1950s during a guerilla war against British colonial rule) had been the inherent instability of political solutions negotiated without a decisive security advantage, but they would not listen. It was no surprise to me when Sunningdale collapsed... I lost heart once the Dublin scheme fell through. It seemed to me a measure of how far the bureaucrats had taken control. Twenty years before we would have tackled it without any worries at all. I did suggest examining the possibilities of planting booby-trapped detonators on the Provisionals. It would have been a feasible operation in conjunction with MI6, along the same lines as the Cyprus plan to plant fake receivers on Grivas... [Colonel George Grivas, the Cypriot guerilla leader].

There is no doubt that MI5 - or at least senior officers from within its ranks - have been involved in illegal activity and possibly even murder, over the course of the last thirty years. Peter Wright's book is dripping with other details of such activity. Whether or not these officers were involved in the Dublin and Monaghan bombings is an open question, but the very strong possibility is that they were. Peter Wright is on record as having said that there are things he knew happened during the Irish conflict that he would 'never talk about'. We will probably never know what these 'things' were - as Wright is now dead - but we will no doubt have our suspicions.

In March 1987 Barrie Penrose, at this time Ireland correspondent for the *Sunday Times*, carried an interview with a former MI5 undercover agent, James Miller, who claimed he was part of an MI5 plot to help promote the Ulster Worker's Council strike in 1974 which led to the collapse of the executive. Miller, an Englishman married to a Northern Protestant, lived in Monkstown, north of Belfast, and worked as a lift engineer. In 1970 at the age of thirty-eight he was recruited by army intelligence and MI5 and asked to spy on prominent loyalist politicians and members of paramilitary organisations. He was later asked to infiltrate the UDA, which he did, and for five years was one of its senior military commanders. In 1974 he was asked by his MI5 handlers to use his position within the UDA to push for a strike. *The Sunday Times* interview continued:

> I did a dangerous job over there for nearly five years and many UDA and IRA men went to prison as a result', Miller said last night. 'But I could never understand why my case officers, Lt. Col. Brian X and George X, wanted the UDA to start a strike in the first place. But they specifically said I should get UDA men at grass-roots level to 'start pushing' for a strike. So I did. Yesterday, Home Office officials working with MI5's legal adviser confirmed that Miller had worked for the security forces in Northern Ireland. Later, Admiral William Higgins, secretary to the D-Notice Committee at the Ministry of Defence, requested *The Sunday Times* for security reasons not to identify Miller's present whereabouts or his case officers. Miller says his work for MI5 backs up claims by other former intelligence agents that the security service used the Northern Ireland problem to discredit the Labour government. Last night Miller said he planned to give his evidence to Merlyn Rees, the former home secretary,

and other former Labour cabinet ministers, who are pressing the government for an inquiry into 'unlawful' M15 activities in the mid-1970s.

As we now know only too well, the strike Miller talks about was the cover used by loyalists and their security forces allies - such as Brian X and George X to mention just two - to bomb Dublin and Monaghan and bring down the executive.

So what have successive Irish governments done about people like Miller and his dirty tricks handlers such as Brian X and George X? Have they taken up such matters with the British government? The answer is we simply don't know because we will not be told. But what we do know is that for the best part of thirty years the authorities in Dublin have known about British army and RUC dirty tricks in the North - and indeed sometimes in the South. We also know that for twenty-eight years the Garda Síochána have known who carried out the Dublin and Monaghan bombings. They also know that members of the British security forces - including the RUC - were involved. In 1992 the then Fianna Fáil government press secretary, P.J. Mara, an intelligent man with a sharp brain, told me during an interview that 'no one was in any doubt that the British army were involved in the bombings'.

In an interview on the ITV documentary on the bombings, the former Garda commissioner, Eamonn Doherty, told the programme: 'I didn't believe at the time that the loyalists acted alone and I don't believe it now.'

After sixteen years of research I have now absolutely no hesitation in stating the following: the 1972/73 Dublin bombings were organised and executed by the UVF led by Jim Hanna and Billy Mitchell (both of whom travelled to Dublin to plant the bombs) with help from four British army intelligence officers based at army headquarters in Lisburn, Co. Antrim. The names and ranks of these four officers are known to me but cannot be named here for legal reasons.

The 1974 Dublin and Monaghan bombings were also organised and executed by the UVF led by County Armagh man Billy Hanna with help from six British army officers, four of whom were based at army headquarters in Lisburn and two of whom were based at battalion headquarters in Kitchen Hill in Lurgan. The names and ranks of all six officers are also known to me but they, too, cannot be named for legal reasons. The name, address and rank of a middle-ranking RUC officer (now retired) who colluded in the 1974 bombings is also known to me but for the same reasons he, too, cannot be named. During research for this book I visited this man's home and interviewed him twice and found him extremely pleasant. On both occasions his wife served tea and sandwiches.

Following the ITV documentary on the bombings - which criticised the Coalition government of the time for its failure to have the bombings properly investigated - a number of former members of that government, including the inimitable Conor Cruise O'Brien, commented publicly on the criticism. Those comments have already been dealt with in chapter 5 of this book.

However, Dr O'Brien made a number of statements about the programme in a back page article in the *Sunday Independent* entitled 'A Slur That Adds Insult to Injury', five days after the broadcast, which I have not yet commented on, but am delighted to do so now.

In a rambling and intemperate diatribe against the programme makers - which inevitably included me, as I was the chief researcher on it - Dr O'Brien says:

> the programme did contain certain matter that was startlingly new and sensational in its implications concerning the then government of the Republic and the Gardai. Concerning the Gardai, First Tuesday said... 'The Gardai knew how the bombings were carried out, and the identities of the perpetrators, but they were powerless to act'. Why were they powerless to act? First Tuesday provided the answer a little later in the programme. The Gardai, said a voice 'could only report back to their political masters'. I listened to these words with a kind of sick horror. The clear implication is that

the Coalition Government of 1974 knew from the gardai who the perpetrators of these bombings were but failed to take action to bring them to justice, thereby acquiescing in the murder of some of those citizens whose protection is the first duty of the government. As a member of that government I was outraged by that monstrous and utterly unfounded innuendo. But my resentment of it was greatly aggravated by a personal factor. My daughter Kate was within a minute of being a victim of the South Leinster Street bomb. She was coming out the back gate of Trinity College at the time. If she had come out a minute earlier, she would now be dead or maimed...Neither the government nor the committee [government security committee] was ever presented with Garda evidence of 'the identity of the perpetrators'. The reason for that is that evidence which would stand up in court was not available and that therefore there was nothing on which to base a recommendation to the government... As far as concerns its [the programme's] novelty and excitement, First Tuesday is a disgrace to all who had a share in its making...

Dealing with the aspects of the programme which accused the government of failing in its duty to pursue the bombers Dr O'Brien says:

We are speaking of 15 ordinary human beings, with at least the normal share of faults and failings... If we had behaved as First Tuesday suggests, then we were, as Government Ministers, grossly and culpably delinquent in our duty. Even worse than that, we were, as human beings, unspeakably depraved, real moral monsters.

Of course there is no suggestion whatever that Dr O'Brien attempted to stifle the investigation. But it is his attitude towards the victims and their relatives that gets up my nose.

Nowhere in the article does Dr O'Brien once express regret for the thirty-three victims who were killed. Or their relatives, or the 300 others who were injured, most of whom are still suffering the physical and mental scars - much of it as a result of the abject failure of Dr O'Brien's government, and its security forces, to track down and punish the perpetrators of the bombings.

With chilling insouciance Dr O'Brien ignores the plight of the bereaved families and throughout the article appears preoccupied with preserving the image of what was after all little more than a rag-bag government (which, during its four-year tenure of office, plunged the country into chaos with rampant inflation, unemployment and soaring interest rates) and to hell with the victims. They're not very important people anyway. Most of them were humble working-class folk. None were professors of history, or veterinary medicine. Not a single economist or lawyer amongst them. But then lawyers and professors don't usually get killed by indiscriminate bombs, for some strange reason. Perhaps it's because they seldom go shopping in crowded little streets on Friday afternoons.

Perhaps if Dr O'Brien's daughter Kate had been scraped into a body bag from the South Leinster Street pavement - and thank God she wasn't - then her father might be more concerned with catching those who planted the bombs than with pouring scorn on those journalists who for the fist time in nineteen years attempted to uncover one of the biggest scandals in the history of the State.

For the guts of thirty years this ranting Anglophile has been a purveyor of unionist/British propaganda in this country. Irish nationalism is a dirty word. Those who speak the Irish language and pursue Irish culture are seen as fellow travellers of the Provisionals. It appears to be some sort of crime - a form of delinquency - to want to be Irish and embrace Irishness.

Since his rejection by the voters of Dublin north-east in the 1977 general election - following years of anti-Irish rhetoric as a TD for that area - Dr O'Brien appears to believe that the Irish electorate have no right to do wrong (where did we hear that one before?). In other words they had no right to reject him and for that they are now getting it in the neck. In more recent times we find him making mischief, coat-tailing with the lunatic fringe of Unionist rejectionism in Belfast. Not a pretty sight. But then I suppose no one else would have him.

But despite the abysmal failure of Dr O'Brien's government and the Gardai to track down the bombers it is still not too late to act. Following the conclusion of the Barron Enquiry (and there may yet be a full judicial one where witnesses will be compelled to attend), the Garda Siochána, in consultation with the Director of Public Prosecutions, must evaluate the evidence and decide if there are grounds for prosecutions against those loyalist suspects still alive. If there are, then extradition warrants must be issued to the RUC forthwith followed by criminal trials in Dublin. This matter must not be allowed to fester for another twenty years - which it inevitably will if justice is not at least seen to be done. Not only that, but Barron's terms of reference must immediately be widened to include the entire gamut of fatal attacks by loyalists in the Republic throughout the course of the Troubles. In all, forty-six people were killed and almost 400 others injured - not to mention the tens of millions of pounds worth of damage caused to property - and yet not a single individual has been convicted for as much as one of these murders. This is a monstrous indictment of our Gardai and our justice system in general and cannot be left unchallenged. Craven excuses such as 'we could not find evidence that would stand up in court' by Garda spokespersons will simply not wash any longer. Consider the number of people convicted - both in the wrong and in the right - for similar murders on the British mainland by Republicans during the same period. It tells us much about the difference between the two justice systems.

On the political front - and in keeping with the very welcome changing situation taking place in this country under the terms of the Good Friday Agreement - the Taoiseach, Bertie Ahern, must speak to the British Prime Minsiter, Tony Blair, about these army officers (still alive) and suspected of involvement in the bombings. Mr Blair must be persuaded to order an investigation within the Ministry of Defence to flush

273

them out. They must not be allowed to hide from justice any longer. For thirty years republicans (and indeed loyalists) have done their time for the crimes they committed during the conflict. It is now the turn of the soldiers. There cannot be a law for one side only.

Epilogue

In the Conclusion of this book I referred briefly to Dr Conor Cruise O'Brien's espousal of unionism and his denigration of Irishness in this country - particularly his insidious attacks on Irish nationalism and Irish culture over the last thirty odd years.

But this inimical behaviour is by no means confined to one old and infirm revisionist academic. 'Ireland bashing' has been around for some time now and has become something of a fad in recent years, particularly amongst what could loosely be described as the chattering classes of the Dublin media: that so-called elite of Dublin society known as the Dublin Four Set.

Undoubtedly this pale practice - as one commentator described it - was begun by the inimitable Dr O'Brien as far back as the early 1970s. But in recent years Mr O'Brien has been joined by such renowned luminaries as Eamonn Dunphy, Fintan O'Toole, Kevin Myers, John A. Murphy, Hugh Leonard, Bruce Arnold - to mention but a few - and last but by no means least that redoubtable spin-doctor of the so-called liberal left, Mr Eoghan Harris. (Politicians such as John Bruton and Micheal McDowell - amongst others - have played a peripheral role in this but by no means to the same extent as the aforementioned.)

Most if not all of these people - who appear to fall over each other in their endeavours to malign their own country and culture - will be familiar to the majority of the Irish public through the columns of our national newspapers, for which most of them write. Mr Murphy, an eminent professor of modern Irish history, will be familiar to many as a prolific and proficient speaker of the Irish language. Indeed - and to add further to the confusion - Professor Murphy would probably consider himself something of a 'Gaeilgeoir' and even an admirer of that much lauded Irish revolutionary and fellow Corkman, Michael Collins. But let nobody be fooled: Professor Murphy is no admirer of Irish nationalism. Through the pages of the *Sunday Independent* - that high pulpit of anti-Irish invective - Professor Murphy has continuously and consistently propagated an anti-Irish/pro-unionist bias in his writings and utterances.

Mr Dunphy, that splenetic little polecat of the Roy Keane fame, who, during his term as columnist with the *Sunday Independent* also spewed out a continuous diatribe of venemous and malicious harangue against just about everything Irish - nowadays professes (or pretends to profess) an admiration for (of all people) that delectable former IRA Chief-of-Staff and now government Minister, Martin McGuinness. Is Mr Dunphy on his way to Damascus? Methinks not.

But the *Sunday Independent* (and its sister the *Irish Independent*) has not been alone in this infernal business either. *The Irish Times* (once a beacon of fairness and middle-of-the-roadness) has, under its current editor Conor Brady (now retiring), moved decidedly to the right and degenerated into little more than a cabal for anti-Irish boil and vitriol through a number of its columnists and so-called security correspondents.

Take one of its best-known columnists, a certain Mr Fintan O'Toole (mentioned above), who, like Mr Harris, would probably (and mistakenly) be considered an icon of the intellectual liberal left (whatever that is). Mr O'Toole writes a column for the paper each Tuesday in which he discusses everything from the future of the Abbey Theatre to violence against women to the current scandals unfolding at the various tribunals. Fair enough - very laudable subjects. But Mr O'Toole has a darker and much more vituperative side. But before we get into that let's look at where Mr O'Toole - and indeed his ilk - is coming from, as they say in today's parlance.

Mr O'Toole is - as they say - a child of the 1960s. Grew up on Dublin's southside (where else?) into a comfortable middle-class family. Studied arts at UCD, excelled in his exams and graduated at twenty.

In the late 1970s he began his writing career - like many of his fellow hacks today - with a little known and at times mildly pornographic magazine called *In Dublin*, in which he wrote about everything from cinema to theatre to the destruction of Georgian Dublin. In the 1980s he moved to what was at the time Ireland's answer to *Newsweek*: the now famous current affairs magazine called *Magill*, and started writing about politics. *Magill* at this time was owned and edited by that other icon of the Dublin media, the one-time radical and champion of the left, Vincent Browne. So when in Rome do as the Romans do. During his term with *Magill* - part of which he spent as editor - O'Toole espoused a radical and at times even nationalist bias.

Take this extract from an editorial about the behaviour of the Gardai during the now infamous release by the courts and re-arrest by the Gardai of the wanted republican activist, Evelyn Glenholmes, in March 1986. (We do not know if O'Toole wrote the article but it was published under his editorship).

> Of far greater import (than the firing of a gun by a detective) were the unlawful acts committed by Gardai prior to this incident. It is worrying ... that sections of the Garda force believe that the laws of the land do not apply to them as they apply to the rest of us.

Strong stuff indeed. Shortly after this O'Toole moved to the *Sunday Tribune* and from there to *The Irish Times*, where he now appears to have found a permanent home. By 1996 - and ten years after his departure from *Magill* - O'Toole (the radical) had squirmed a full 180 degrees in his views on law and order and republican violence.

Take this extract not from *The Irish Times* but from the London *Observer* (Mr O'Toole writes and broadcasts occasionally for the British media) in April 1996 - the day before the eightieth anniversary commemorations of the 1916 Rising - in which Mr O'Toole disparagingly muses about the rebellion and its place in Irish history today. But first his childhood memories of the fiftieth anniversary celebrations thirty years earlier.

> In 1966 my friends and I stopped playing cowboys and Indians and started playing Irish and English instead. It was the fiftieth anniversary of the Easter Rising, when two small Irish nationalist splinter groups occupied

some buildings in Dublin ... For an eight year old the Rising was a wonderful discovery... it was we were told, the point of origin for an independent Ireland...

But was there no independent discussion on the merits of the Rising Fintan - the whys and wherefores?

There was no historical debate, no teasing out of the relationship between violence and democracy...

My God!
And how is the Rising viewed in Ireland today in the context of the last thirty years of the Troubles, Fintan?

The Rising is still the most potent argument for the legitimacy of political violence in Ireland. It was an armed coup undertaken without a democratic mandate...

Wow! The Brits must have loved that.
So we should never have had a Rising: never have had a War of Independence, never have had a Treaty, and the Irish State should still be part of the UK. Nationhood is a load of codswollop. Is that how you see it, Fintan?
Well, let's get serious here for a moment.
What is Mr O'Toole getting at and what audience is he endeavouring to impress? It is interesting to note that he has never - as far as I am aware - written this kind of stuff about the Rising in an Irish newspaper.
OK, Mr Pearse and his comrades may not have had a democratic mandate but then come to think of it how many people in Ireland at the time voted for Asquith's government - which put down the Rising with overwhelming force? How many Irish votes did Lord Wimborme, the Lord Lieutenant of Ireland in 1916, or the head of the British executive in Dubin Castle at the time, Augustine Birrell, receive? How many Irish people voted for conscription in Ireland - for Irish men to fight in Europe's dirty war - by the British government in 1918? How

many Irish people voted for the deployment of the notorious Black and Tans in Ireland in the 1918-19 period, or how much of a 'democratic mandate' did these Black and Tans have when they opened fire on unarmed civilians in Croke Park on Bloody Sunday in 1920? One could go on. But let's work this one out.

Patrick Pearse - as Mr O'Toole insists on calling him - and his comrades did not have a mandate from the Irish people to attack the GPO. Of that we are all agreed. Or are we? Michael Collins and his comrades, on the other hand, probably did have a mandate to wage war against British forces during the War of Independence. The Sinn Féin party, which was linked to the IRA and the IRB, won an overwhelming majority of the Westminster seats in the 1918 election and Collins himself won a seat in Cork both at that time and again in 1921. Could it be that the 1916 leaders had some sort of retrospective mandate - considering that many of the rebels (including Collins himself) who fought in Easter Week also fought in the War of Independence - or was it simply an act of terrorism, as O'Toole suggests?

One thing *is* certain however: the British government did not have a mandate, firstly to occupy the country and secondly to carry out the outrageous acts of savagery, which its armed forces did.

Despite the protests of some historians today that, because the Home Rule Party, which opposed armed force, commanded the majority of Westminister seats up to 1918 and supported the Liberal government in parliament - because it promised Home Rule - the British government was seen by a majority of Irish people as the legitimate government of Ireland, I - and probably the majority of Irish people today - profoundly disagree, for the reasons outlined above. So who has legitimacy here in this equation? Mr O'Toole appears to have his democratic mandates in a twist.

Is he suggesting for instance that the Hungarian Uprising of 1956 (against imposed Soviet Communism) or the armed uprisings of the Marsh Arabs and the Iraqui Kurds against Sadam Hussein's fascism in 1991 (to mention but a few notable events in world history) - were armed coups? Of course not.

The reality is that in instances such as the invasion of Afghanistan in 1979 - to take another example of recent world history - the Russians (or the Soviets as they then were) and their puppets in Kabul would probably be regarded - by commentators such as O'Toole - as the legitimate government of the country were they still there 700 years from now.

For Mr O'Toole to describe the Easter Rising as an armed coup (perhaps he means an attempted armed coup) - and by clear implication the position of the British government and its armed forces as legitimate - is a monstrous and grotesque misrepresentation of history. The reality is that British rule was 'tolerated' by a majority of Irish people because it was the only alternative to war - 700 years of it.

But this is not the only time Mr O'Toole gets his arse in his mouth when it comes to recent Irish history. Only last year he was at it again, this time on the occasion of the re-burial in Glasnevin cemetery of the remains of Kevin Barry and his comrades who were hanged in 1920 and 1921. Commenting on Barry's role in the War of Independence and his part in the killing of British soldiers, O'Toole writes:

> It should be remembered that the September 1920 attack on British soldiers for which Kevin Barry was hanged was one in which civilians were recklessly endangered. The ambush was staged in a bakery off a busy city street. A bullet went through the window of the dairy next door, missing a baby in a pram by pure luck. Of the three soldiers who were killed, one, Matthew Whitehead, was, at 17, even younger than his killer, Kevin Barry.

That - as O'Toole points out - was September 1920. Fifty-three years and eight months later a bomb in Parnell Street - three streets away from Barry's attack - planted by a loyalist (which was given to him by British soldiers) didn't miss 'a baby in a pram by pure luck', it blasted two of them out of their pram and catapulted their tiny bodies through the cellar grating of the Welcome Inn pub. And for good measure it killed both their parents as well (see chapter 1). When in 1916 the British army was ordered to crush the rebellion, the lives of civilians on the streets of Dublin weren't 'recklessly endangered'; they were slaughtered in their hundreds by the advancing forces.

Condemning the 'elaborate State funeral', 'staged' - as he puts it - by Bertie Ahern's government on the day of the re-burials in the aftermath of September 11, O'Toole writes:

> Yet even before the events of September 11th, an elaborate State funeral was a very bad idea. It was likely to achieve two things: sickening many citizens by its ghoulish cynicism and offering a great boost to those who want us to feel that the only difference between a terrorist and a patriot is the passage of time.

How does the editor of *The Irish Times* justify employing this fucking asshole? He should pluck him up and boot him out. As for the myth that surrounds his so-called intellect and public persona, Mr O'Toole is nothing short of a disgrace and a traitor to his country.

But of course this kind of self-abasement could only happen in Ireland. Imagine a British journalist (writing in an Irish newspaper) describing Brigadier Lowe, who led the assault against the rebels in the GPO, as a terrorist? Imagine an American journalist (writing in the London *Times*) describing George Washington or Thomas Jefferson as terrorists? Not in a million years.

I've no problem with Mr O'Toole condemning violence. He has every right to do so. We live in a democracy now where the rule of law is paramount and private armies are not tolerated. But it's Mr O'Toole's selectiveness. On the question of decommissioning Mr O'Toole asks: 'How long more can we hold our noses?' Fine, I've no problem with that either.

However, I've not heard of Mr O'Toole holding his nose while we await the arrest and prosecution of those British soldiers who planned the Dublin bombings in 1974. Nor have I heard of him hold his nose while we await the arrest and prosecution of the soldiers and policemen who planned the murders of solicitors Pat Finnucane and Rosemary Nelson. But then maybe those murders are different. Not all murders are the same. Or are they? Not all murders are as murderous as other murders, particularly when they're carried out on behalf of the State. Tell that to Geraldine Finnucane or Paul Nelson.

Mr O'Toole and his tiny clique of arrogant, middle-class, Dublin-based hacks - who practically dominate the national print media in Ireland - do not, by any stretch of the imagination, represent the views and values of the majority of Irish people. Most Irish people are not anti-Irish language, are not anti-Irish culture, are not anti-TG4, are not anti-1916, are not anti-Fianna Fáil, are not anti-Catholic church and - above all else - do not believe that a centuries-old nationalist tradition should be ashamed of its past and apologise for it and should now give way to a West-Brit/unionist dominated one. And if the truth were known the majority of right-thinking unionists do not think so either.

Over two-thirds of the population of the 26 counties live outside Dublin. The overwhelming majority of these - as well as a substantial number of people living in Dublin - do not speak with West Brit accents and do not believe that the sun rises and sets in Conor Cruise O'Brien's arse. Few people in west Mayo or west Kerry or north-west Donegal or south Waterford or Mullingar - or wherever - believe that a tiny elitist clique of newspaper propagandists based in the comfortable, leafy middle-class suburbs of north and south Dublin, speak for them.

I am not a particular supporter of conservative Ireland. I have never voted for Fianna Fáil and I am certainly not an admirer of the Catholic church. However, I believe that both Mr O'Toole's and Dr O'Brien's continuous bashing of both organisations has a lot more to do with getting at nationalist Ireland - which they particularly despise - than it has to do with getting at Bertie Ahern or Desmond Connell.

ADDENDUM

The following is a list of names of 25 Northern Ireland loyalists suspected of involvement in the Dublin and Monaghan bombings. 20 of these have been on a Garda "wanted list" since 1975. However, as seven of the 20 are now dead the wanted list is reduced to 13 and these now form part of the file being compiled by retired Supreme Court Judge, Henry Barron and his staff as part of the Commission of Inquiry set up by the government to investigate the bombings.

British soldiers and RUC personnel suspected of involvement do not form part of the Garda wanted list as the Gardai at official level have never openly accepted that they were involved. However, many individual members of the Gardai privately have, on numerous occasions, expressed a different view.

Those members of the security forces suspected of involvement by this reporter are listed according to letters of the alphabet for legal reasons.

Northern Ireland Loyalists

1. Derek S. (B.Fast)
2. Ewan B. (B.Fast)
3. William Mitchell (C.Fergus)
4. David Mulholland (P.Down)
5. Billy Hanna (Lurgan)
6. Robin Jackson (Lurgan)
7. Harris Boyle (P.Down)
8. Wesley Sommerville (D.Gannon)
9. Ed. P. (Armagh)
10. Red R. (Armagh)

11. John M. (Armagh)
12. Mr. Fy. (Armagh)
13. James Mitchell (Glenanne)
14. Billy Fulton (P.Down)
15. Stewart Young (P.Down)
16. Nicko Jackson (P.Down)
17. J.G. (Lurgan)
18. George A. (Antrim)
19. William Marchant (B.Fast)
20. John Bingham (B.Fast)
21. Charles Gilmore (P.Down)
22. Sammy Whitten (P.Down)
23. Ross Hearst (Armagh)
24. Nelson Young (P.Down)
25. John "Jack" Irvine (Armagh)

Members of the Security Forces

1. Mr. A (army) Lisburn
2. Mr. B (army)   "
3. Mr. C (army)   "
4. Mr. D (army)   "
5. Mr. E (army) (Lurgan)
6. Mr. F (army) (Lurgan)
7. Mr. G (RUC) Co. Armagh